ZENITHISM

BY

JONATHAN VAN BELLE

Zenithism

ISBN 978-1-949127-16-4

First edition

Cover image: Attic red-figured skyphos, c. 420 BCE, depicting
the return of Hephaistos to Olympos, courtesy of the Toledo
Museum of Art

Published by Deep Overstock, Portland, OR.

deepoverstock.com

**DEEP OVERSTOCK
PUBLISHING**

To Zuriel van Belle,
My Infinity

CONTENTS

HAUHET'S HAPPY DREAM

On some bank of the Nile, with her dusty feet and bead anklets splashing in the north-wheeling waters and slapping the river's effervescing faces with the sprayed crown of some papyrus, child Hauhet fell into a trance. Afterward, giddily, Hauhet hurried through high reeds to her home, where her father, Ahmose, was at his potter's wheel, smoothing, rounding, and wetting wares.

"Dad!"

"Hauhet? Why are you breathless? Are you well?" Ahmose let his wheel stop and came to Hauhet, who appeared to him overheated. He felt her forehead.

"I'm not ill."

"Come," said Ahmose, "let's go on the roof to cool off in the evening's breeze."

On the roof, Ahmose unrolled two rush mats. They sat down just as a breeze whirled in from the desert. Hauhet, bubbling over, said, "Dad, may I tell you my dream?"

"Your dream?"

"I had a dream by the river."

"Of course, yes. Please."

Hauhet bounced excitedly, with all the energy and enthusiasm of a well-loved nine-year-old. She took a breath bigger than her lungs and began, "I saw people doing things we can't do yet. You could stand at the start of the Nile and I could stand at the end and we could talk with each other instantly."

"How fantastic, Hauhet."

"And what's else, we'll have drawings of us that dance and sing." Hauhet wiggled her body with dance. "And each person can read, and each person will have everything ever to read all the time. And all music to hear all the time. Each person will carry with themselves all the world's libraries."

"No one man can carry even one library, my daughter. How could one man carry with him all libraries? And who will perform all this music for one man all the time?"

"I don't know, father. They'll know, though." Hauhet thought, "And it's not just for one man; it's for everybody all the time. Men and women and children."

Ahmose nodded sympathetically.

"And," said the girl, gaily leaning forward and backward, "we'll fly over clouds more speedily than the speediest bird."

"Will we?" Her father looked up and pretended to search for flying humans.

"Yes. And then, we'll dance on the moon!"

"All the way up on the moon? Way up high?"

"Yes!" She giggled. "Oh, and people are given healthy hearts when their own hearts become ill."

"When can we expect this heaven, my darling?"

"I don't know, but I'm not done, dad." Hauhet reached straight up and pretended to pluck a fruit from the sky. "We'll also eat stars like sweet dates."

"What an appetite we will have! Do stars taste sweet?"

"Maybe," and Hauhet hid her face in her hands, laughing. She peeked her eyes out, and peeked at her dad, who just then made a silly face, and she hid her face again, and her hands spilled over with laughter. "But," she interrupted her own laughter, "The stars we eat will be black and tiny. This tiny!" She pressed the tip of her thumb and index finger together, leaving no space between them, and squinted at the impossibly tiny distance. "The tiniest stuff is very important."

"I know, my child, because you are so tiny." Ahmose smiled. "My little dreamer, tell me: What will happen to potters like your dear father?"

"Well, *dear* father,"—Hauhet pretended to be a royal daughter, addressing her "dear father" with a caricature of royal obeisance—"Potters will be royalty. Everyone will be royalty."

Ahmose smiled. "Who will make the wares and grow our food?"

"Wares will make themselves and food will grow itself."

"Do the children raise themselves?" Ahmose reached to tickle his daughter, but she twisted right and shrieked with joy at evading the tickle.

After catching her breath, Hauhet answered. "Everyone will be a child, like me; and every tribe and soul will be one dear family, like us."

Ahmose hugged his Hauhet, "My child!"

My Wish

Expressed or forborne, conscious or subconscious, we wish. To *know thyself*, one must know one's wishes.

I wish that the ultimate reason why our world exists is that *it is good that it exists*.[1] I wish for a world of infinitely many universes, each a spatiotemporally infinite manifold, and each with its laws of progression, development, and organic evolution, wherein infinitely many conscious entities converge toward a maximum of metaphysical ascendency. I wish for a world where, with a proficiency beyond what is imaginable for our species, or perhaps a proficiency without maximum, these zenith beings, infinite in amount, uplift all beings into an ideal state—and that this ideal state, this *theosis*, remote from us today, will be, like a beatific vision, a universal defeater of evil.

For what do you wish?

---

[1] See *Value and Existence* by John Leslie and *Axiogenesis: An Essay in Metaphysical Optimalism* by Nicholas Rescher.

SOME QUESTIONS

Q1: What is zenithism?

A1: Zenithism is the hope or prospect that an infinite natural system evolves infinitely many maximally advanced conscious beings.

Q2: What is "zenith"?

A2: Zenith is the theoretical universal maximum of scientific and technological power, the upper limit of a technological singularity. Beings that attain zenith-state may be simply called "zenith" or "zenith beings."

Consider Arthur C. Clarke's third law: "Any sufficiently advanced technology is indistinguishable from magic." The zenithist corollary to Clarke's third law could be the following: *Any maximally advanced technology is indistinguishable from divinity.*

Zenith is the actually achievable maximum of all scales of mastery. Thus, if the actual achievable maxima, the following apply to zenith: Kardashev Type V (an extension of the original three-tier Kardashev Scale); Carl Sagan's informational Z; John Barrow's microdimensional Type Omega-minus; the upper limit of Ray Kurzweil's Epoch Six; etc.

As for the word itself, "zenith" has two meanings:

(1) In astronomy, zenith is the imaginary point in the celestial sphere vertically above a particular location ("above" means in the vertical direction opposite to the apparent gravitational force at that location).

(2) The time or point at which something is most powerful or successful; the culminating point.

These two meanings, the celestial "above" and the superlative form of power, make "zenith" an ideal name for maximally advanced beings in an infinite natural system.

Q3: Is "Zenith" the actual name of these maximally advanced beings?

A3: No, "Zenith" is merely an informative title, useful in highlighting a particular developmental state in the universe.

Q4: How many zenith beings exist?

A4: There are infinitely many zenith beings. This does not mean that there is an infinite *totality* of zenith beings, but rather that there is no such totality, no completed or completable total.

Q5: What does an "infinite natural system" mean?

A5: An infinite natural system is any system that is *in principle* fully describable by the sciences (physics, chemistry, biology, neurology, etc.) and that is spatially, temporally, or dimensionally infinite (or some combination of these). The position that the universe is infinite may be called *infinitism.*[2]

Q6: How is zenithism related to science?

A6: If zenithism is inconsistent with, or at serious odds with, scientific analysis, then the truth of zenithism should be considered highly unlikely. Zenithism hinges on scientific interpretations of reality, so the truth of zenithism is predicated on what scientists, e.g., physicists, chemists, and biologists, hold to be scientifically likely, scientifically plausible, and so on. Zenithism is a speculative *extrapolation* from claims that are not inconsistent with the best contemporaneous science.

Q7: How is zenithism related to philosophy?

A7: Zenithism is, above all, a prospect or profound hope. A hope may live consistently with diverse philosophical systems, from panpsychism to neutral monism, endurantism to perdurantism, from classical to paraconsistent logics, to a variety of mereological, aesthetic, epistemological, and ethical theories. If a system does not exclude the possibility of zenithism, or if zenithism is constructible out of a system, then the zenithist hope may flourish in that system.

[2] See George Gale's "Cosmological Fecundity: Theories of Multiple Universes"

Q8: Is zenithism a religion?

A8: Zenithism is not the special revelation of any person, but a reasonable prospect for every person. So, if zenithism is a religion, it is not a revelatory religion.

In *Breaking the Spell: Religion as a Natural Phenomenon*, Daniel Dennett writes, "Tentatively, I propose to define religions as *social systems whose participants avow belief in a supernatural agent or agents whose approval is sought*" (9). Dennett hastens to add that this "definition is subject to revision, a place to start, not something carved in stone to be defended to the death."

On this definition, zenithism is not a religion; there is no avowal of supernatural agency. A zenith being is a maximally advanced *natural* agent, not a supernatural agent.

In *The Varieties of Religious Experience*, William James endorses the following working definition of religion: "Religion, therefore, as I now ask you arbitrarily to take it, shall mean for us the feelings, acts, and experiences of individual men in their solitude, so far as they apprehend themselves to stand in relation to whatever they may consider the divine."

Since Zenith, or all maximally advanced beings considered together, may come under the historical description "divine," it may be said that zenithism involves the feelings, acts, and experiences of individual persons in their solitude, as they apprehend themselves in relation to this divine.

Later in *The Varieties of Religious Experience*, in "The Sick Soul" lectures, James cuts to the core of the "religious problem": "Here is the real core of the religious problem: Help! help!"

Zenithism is the prospect that beings of maximal power help beings of lesser power, such as we human beings. Zenith, an apeirotheistic pantheon of sorts, in some way solves this acutest problem, though the nature of the resolution may be unknown to us for a time.

Q9: Does zenithism require or imply a teleological interpretation of evolution?

A9: Zenithism does not exclude the possibility of a sound teleological interpretation of evolution. Orthogenetic evolution or any proposal involving an intrinsic principle or power of progressive development may be compatible with zenithism, but zenithism will not determine the truth of these proposals; science, philosophy of science, and metaphysics are the best measures for such a determination.

Q10: Does zenithism posit the existence of a Creator God?

A10: Zenithism is not committed to the necessity of Zenith-as-Creator, nor to Zenith as a "first principle," "metaphysical necessity," or any such foundational explanation. Zenithism is not a commitment to intelligent design, creationism, deism, or the like. Zenithism leaves open the possibility that our universe, or any local physical system, is a scientific creation, e.g., "laboratory universe," "virtual universe," and so on. In zenithism, there are no claims, for or against, regarding a transcendent conscious force that "created everything."

Q11: What is the difference between Zenith and God?

A11: The answer depends on how you take the term "God." Answers will vary for various theistic proposals. If one proposes that "God" is any being with all and only those properties possessed by Zenith, then, *ex hypothesi*, there is no difference between God and Zenith.

Zenith is essentially scientific and technological, whereas God, on most interpretations, is not essentially a scientific and technological being, but a supernatural or transcendent being, a being occupying the highest Platonic category of existence (or *prior to existence*, such as Tillich's God).

Yet, Thomas Hobbes, called "the patriarch of artificial intelligence" by George B. Dyson, conjectured a God of corporeal substance; the Hobbesian God is a being metaphysically continuous with natural reality, as opposed to a being transcendent or metaphysically distinct from natural reality.[3]

If it is asserted that Zenith is natural and God is non-natural, you might infer from this assertion that a profound metaphysical opposition exists between Zenith and God; however, "natural" and "non-natural" are opposites thus far only by linguistic convention, as zyz and non-zyz are opposed by taking two tokens of one undefined term (zyz) and appending "non-" to one of those tokens. The difficult philosophical work is in the careful characterization of these "opposed" terms in such a way that expresses a real metaphysical disunity in reality, an actual dualism, and not a conceptual error or incoherence.

Q12: Is the zenith-limit a rehash of Anselm of Canterbury's Ontological Argument for the existence of God?

A12: There is superficial similarity between the zenith-limit and Anselm's ontological argument. "The being that which no greater can be conceived" is like the zenith-limit in that there is a maximum entity supposed, but the subcutaneous difference is that the zenith-limit is not a logical proof.

There is no logical contradiction in asserting that Zenith does not exist, with the exception of the "lowest limit" case of Zenith, that is, the coincidence of zenith-limit with the highest human limit *thus far*.

The salient difference seems to be this: The zenith-limit is not identical with the greatest conceivable limit. Some conceivable things may be unrealizable in natural systems. It may be that omnipotence cannot be realized by Zenith; accordingly, Anselm would reject the identification of Zenith as God.

I would not deny Anselm's argument, only differentiate the zenithist position from his view. Zenith is approached by a

[3] "Hobbes advocated neither the pantheism of the ancients nor the atheism of which he was accused. He believed life and mind to be natural consequences of matter when suitably arranged; God to be a corporeal being, of perhaps infinitely higher mental order but composed of substance nonetheless […]." Dyson, *Darwin Among the Machines: The Evolution of Global Intelligence*. The early 20th-century philosopher Samuel Alexander also proposes something of a corporeal (or spatiotemporal) God in *Space, Time, and Deity* (1920).

speculative extension from observation, whereas Anselm's "greatest being" is approached formally via a deduction "prior" to experience.

Q13: What is the meaning of this little book?

A13: This pocketbook is a crazy quilt, a *tutti frutti* of kludges, gambles, errors, and moonshots. In it, I present zenithism *unsystematically*, seeking to inspire you with a few *hypotheses*; I second William James, who, in the "Conclusions" section of *The Varieties of Religious Experience*, wrote:

> Who says 'hypothesis' renounces the ambition to be coercive in his arguments. The most I can do is, accordingly, to offer something that may fit the facts so easily that your scientific logic will find no plausible pretext for vetoing your impulse to welcome it as true (510-511).

The rest of this book, pied with ornamentation, question marks, and haphazard references, amounts to exploration, sometimes tribulation, and sometimes mutation. Some of it is precise; some is proto-precise; some poetically vague. As Bertrand Russell wrote in *The Philosophy of Logical Atomism*:

> Everything is vague to a degree you do not realize till you have tried to make it precise, and everything precise is so remote from everything that we normally think, that you cannot for a moment suppose that is what we really mean when we say what we think.

Falling far short of exquisite precision, I choose zakuski, assortments of appetizers or "things to bite after" a shot of vodka.[4] This zakuski book is a bit of a miscellaneum or commonplace book, stitched thick with quotations; it is a text in the etymological sense of *textus*, things woven together. My taste is byzantine. The sensual honeycombs of Greek Orthodox, Russian Orthodox, and Roman Catholic churches appeal to me

---

[4] A.k.a., Russian smorgasbord; закуски.

more than the minimalist meeting houses of Evangelicals, where the aesthetic command is "Let there not be."

I value consistency, but inconsistently, since logical leakproofness may obstruct discovery. "New ideas do not battle so much with ignorance as with solid knowledge."[5] I have done much, if not *my* best, to untangle a good prospect, but I have too many limitations. I consider myself a reverist, and no expert in anything; a book eater, vers-librist, verbomaniac, and optimist, who excuses his long skyward lapses into air-mongering impressionism.

The amateur who examines a *cosmic* conjecture is a vulnerable quantity, a joyrider, a rogue planet, a Bellerophon who knows in advance that they will fall from Pegasus. Such an amateur needs these over-the-top analogies and ornaments to press on.

Maybe you will find my book as a scroll in your private and virtual Alexandrian library, or medieval scriptorium, or Jovian archive, while beyond the archive's windows, Jupiter's thermosphere gleams with airglow. Maybe, a kiloyear after publication, you will read this little book under virtual candlelight or binary sunshine. Maybe you will live the lives in this book—the life of Hauhet on the Nile or Zosime gazing at the Acropolis. A passional philosophy, such as mine, is a Roman pantomimus, a Proteus, a Camusian actor with "so many souls summed up in a single body,"[6] and so my Hauhet, Zosime, Otto, Enitan, et al., offer a "heretical multiplication of souls"[7] to achieve possession where expression fails.

As to that expression, I express zenithism *eclectically*. The term "eclectic" comes from the Greek ἐκλεκτικός (*eklektikos*), literally "choosing the best." Eclecticism is the "school" of a *little-of-this-little-of-that*. In this school or style, there is no ground, no center-point, no meeting-point, only hyperactive edges. Aphorism, poetry, flash fiction, dialogue, confession, and extended quotation join analytic and Montaignian essay in

---

[5] Jacques Barzun, *From Dawn to Decadence*, 196
[6] Albert Camus, *The Myth of Sisyphus*, trans. Justin O'Brien. I ask: How many haecceities might one body enflesh?
[7] Ibid.

lighting up philosophy's kaleidoscope of Escher relations, veils, Pyrrhonian sphinxes, endless curtains, and glass walls. William James wrote "Profusion, not economy, may after all be reality's key-note."[8] Profusion, not economy, is therefore the key-note of this book. I take pleasure in going astray.

Philosophy is indefinite and cannot confidently call its motion "approaching." Where is the root? We touch only branches, and not necessarily from the same tree. It is the ever-not-quite. Cerberus, here with infinitely many heads of paradox, controversy, unintelligibility, negation, and silence, guards the omnipresent entrance to philosophical beatitude.

Yet, the vocal folds and tongue want to move—such aleatory instruments. So they move as snakes, with lateral, side-winding, concertina, and other movements.

The best available information, interwoven, may be contradictory; but contradictoriness does not override the value of this aggregate in the bricolage of philosophy. Every philosopher overextends and flirts with impressionism, especially in the preliminaries of a position. We fudge and waffle and over-egg the pudding. We practice the crystal-clear confusion of Socrates. We garden in jungles.

W. V. O. Quine had a "taste for desert landscapes"; Nietzsche for "ice and high mountains."[9] I prefer cottage gardens and I imagine passional philosophers as gardeners, *home* gardeners, planting for themselves. For me, night sky petunias go here, and over there, under trellises of moonflower, rows of white azaleas. Our home gardens differ. I may add amaranth where you would place peach roses, where others might plant lavender and blue zinnias.

I take, and recommend, the advice of the English gardener Margery Fish:

> You mustn't rely on your flowers to make your garden attractive. A good bone structure must come first, with an intelligent use of evergreen plants so that the garden is always clothed, no matter what time of year. Flowers are

---

8 William James, *Pragmatism*, Lecture V
9 From the foreword of Nietzsche's *Ecce Homo*

an added delight, but a good garden is the garden you enjoy looking at even in the depths of winter.

So for literal gardens, so too for figurative gardens. Among the unsystematically scattered flowers in this pocketbook, this *florilegium*, I carefully set several evergreens, evergreen lures to hope, hoping you might always enjoy this zenithist home garden in the depths of any winter.

A COMPARISON OF ZENITHISM AND TRANSHUMANISM

Zenithism is the position that an infinite natural system evolves infinitely many maximally advanced beings.

Transhumanism, according to the "Transhumanist FAQ" on the website of Humanity+, is:

(1) The intellectual and cultural movement that affirms the possibility and desirability of fundamentally improving the human condition through applied reason, especially by developing and making widely available technologies to eliminate aging and to greatly enhance human intellectual, physical, and psychological capacities.

(2) The study of the ramifications, promises, and potential dangers of technologies that will enable us to overcome fundamental human limitations, and the related study of the ethical matters involved in developing and using such technologies.

Others define transhumanism differently, but hopefully these two definitions suffice to communicate the essence of transhumanism.[10]

The primary differences between zenithism and transhumanism are as follows:

1. Transhumanism does not entail any commitment to the *current* existence of beings more techno-scientifically developed than *Homo sapiens*. Zenithism includes such a commitment.

2. More generally, transhumanism, unlike zenithism, does not give a probability of 1 to the actualization of trans- or post-human capacities; the transhumanist

---

[10] In his 1990 essay "Transhumanism: Toward a Futurist Philosophy," Max More defines transhumanism as a set of "philosophies of life (such as Extropianism) that seek the continuation and acceleration of the evolution of intelligent life beyond its currently human form and human limitations by means of science and technology, guided by life-promoting values."

"affirms the possibility" of these states of being, but the transhumanist (given our operational definition) does not affirm their actuality, nor even the high probability of their future actualization.[11]

Zenithism and transhumanism, as defined, are not inconsistent; a transhumanist can affirm zenithism and a zenithist can be a transhumanist. One may affirm the possibility and desirability of radical technological augmentations to *Homo sapiens*, while independently affirming the existence of beings *at the metaphysical maximum of such augmentations*.[12]

Pure consistency, of course, does not entail mutual necessity; one can be a transhumanist and *reject* zenithism. One such rejection is easy to imagine: the rejection of infinitism, which is the view that the universe is infinite.

Equally, one may be a zenithist and *reject* transhumanism. The rejection in this case would be subtle, since one might expect that a zenithist, optimistic about the prospect of maximal techno-scientific mastery, would welcome the scientific self-augmentation of *Homo sapiens*—after all, such augmentation is augmentation toward zenith-state. Yet a rejection could spring from mistrust in *Homo sapiens*; perhaps the risk calculus disfavors a positive outcome for *our* radical transformations. This is a rejection of the *desirability* of the (specifically) *human* attempt at self-augmentation, not a blanket rejection of the desirability of augmentations by extraterrestrial civilizations. A zenithist would affirm that technological self-augmentation results in a maximally positive outcome *generally* (that is, cosmically), but

---

[11] Since any augmentation might technically count as a partial actualization of the transhuman, and since our species is already heir to many self-enhancements (e.g., computer "memory"), it is more exact to say that the transhumanist affirms neither the full nor majority present *actuality* of trans-human capacities.

[12] I use the term "augmentation" rather than "enhancement," since "enhancement" connotes an increase in value or quality, thus making it a more value-laden concept than "augmentation," which does not connote, in my *present* domain of connotations, an increase in value or quality, but an increase in value-neutral properties, such as size, quantity, durability, and so on.

there is no individual affirmation for our specific and perhaps too volatile civilization; there is only a normal distribution, where perhaps only the 99th percentile survives its experiments in augmentation. Daedalus's wings led to Daedalus's freedom, but to Icarus's death. Are we Daedalus or Icarus?[13]

As William James wrote one century ago in *Pragmatism*:

> The scope of the practical control of nature newly put into our hand by scientific ways of thinking vastly exceeds the scope of the old control grounded on common sense. Its rate of increase accelerates so that no one can trace the limit; one may even fear that the *being* of man may be crushed by his own powers, that his fixed nature as an organism may not prove adequate to stand the strain of the ever increasingly tremendous functions, almost divine creative functions, which his intellect will more and more enable to wield. He may drown in his wealth like a child in a bathtub, who has turned on the water and who cannot turn it off.[14]

Yet between these two views there remains a conceptual kinship; a Zenith-being is the result of a technological and self-augmenting life process—a process of limit-breaking and self-improvement. Still, transhumanist success is dependent on the success of our species (i.e., in avoiding nuclear self-annihilation, asteroid impact, the intelligence explosion, etc.), whereas the success of zenithism is *not* dependent on the success of our species.

---

[13] Of course, Icarus was killed by dint of dear dad Daedalus's *liberating* technology.
[14] In Lecture V, "Pragmatism and Common Sense"

EVALUATIONS OF THE ZENITH-LIMIT

The Zenith (or Zenith-limit) is the actually achievable maximum of all scales of mastery. Suppose, as an absurd example, that one scale of mastery involves climbing a ladder with ten rungs. If reaching the tenth rung is achievable, then reaching the tenth rung is the Zenith-limit of climbing that ladder. If reaching the tenth rung is *not* achievable, but reaching the ninth rung *is* achievable, then reaching the ninth rung is the Zenith-limit of climbing that ladder. In brief, the Zenith-limit is the reachable rung.

In our simple example, the maximal optimist about the Zenith-limit would say that the tenth rung is reachable. The maximal pessimist about the Zenith-limit would say that *not even the first rung* is reachable. We know that there exist ladders with ten rungs and that at least one person has reached the tenth rung of such a ladder, so the maximal optimist is correct: the Zenith-limit *is* the tenth rung.

It might help to think of all problem-solving using the metaphor of the ladder, where the top of the ladder represents a solution or desired result and each rung represents a satisfied prerequisite to that desired result.

For example, say our desired result is time travel *into the past*. A low rung on this ladder would involve showing that it is *logically* possible to travel into the past. A higher rung on this ladder would involve showing that it is a *practically* possible to travel into the past. The top rung would be the desired result: time travel into the past.

Some people, citing the "grandfather paradox," argue that time travel into the past is not logically possible, therefore the zenith-limit for such time travel is *very low*.

For all of our most extreme desired results, from teleportation to brain transplantation to immortality, there is a (metaphorical) ladder with nth rungs, where n is completely unknown. For any given ladder, one may guess the number of rungs and the number of reachable rungs. Thus, there are at least two ways for one to guess wrong here: (1) guessing the wrong prerequisites and (2) guessing wrong about the achievability of a given prerequisite.

Consider Arthur C. Clarke's so-called "Three Laws," which are more three quips than three laws. Or rather, consider the first two of his three "laws":

1. *When a distinguished but elderly scientist states that something is possible, he is almost certainly right. When he states that something is impossible, he is very probably wrong.*
2. *The only way of discovering the limits of the possible is to venture a little way past them into the impossible.*

Clarke, as evidenced by his laws, was an optimist about scientific progress.

Of course, venturing "into the impossible" does not mean venturing into an actual impossibility, which is strictly impossible, but into a theoretical impossibility, or what some theory holds to be impossible, which, whenever shown possible, counts *against* the theory.

Is Clarke's optimism more warranted than pessimism about scientific progress? How lofty is the Zenith-limit?

Let's consider two kinds of optimist, the direct optimist and the indirect optimist, as they relate to some desired result Y, which both optimists (*qua* optimists) believe is achievable.

(i) The direct optimist guesses that X is the prerequisite for Y, and that X is achievable. It turns out that, yes, X is the prerequisite of Y and, yes, X is achievable. So, the direct optimist guesses rightly and wins Y.

(ii) The indirect optimist guesses that X is the prerequisite of Y, and that X is achievable. It turns out that X is *not* achievable, but that X is *not actually* a prerequisite of Y, and that, huzzah!, the actual prerequisite(s) of Y *are* achievable. The indirect optimist guesses wrongly, yet still wins Y.

Then there is a third optimist: the super indirect optimist. The super indirect optimist just *assumes* that Y's prerequisites, whatever they may be, are achievable and therefore Y is achievable.

This position is well-put by Professor C. F. Hirshfield in his "Future Methods of Utilizing Coal," which appeared in the Scientific American Supplement (No. 2064) on July 24th, 1915:

I believe that the centuries of human history which are available show that each successive generation has become better able to force its dictates upon nature rather than to be subservient to the unrestricted action of natural forces. In other words, subsequent generations will be better able to care for themselves than the present generation and there is no need to waste good time and effort in trying to solve their problems for them with a smaller stock of knowledge and a narrower vision.

Those technical problems will be solved *somehow*. The super indirect optimist infers from past success to the high probability of future success, without specifying the route to that success.

For any given desired result, or top rung, one may be a direct, indirect, or super indirect optimist. Or, conversely, one may be a direct, indirect, or super indirect pessimist.

Our relation to particular (metaphorical) ladders, e.g., curing glioblastoma or terraforming Pluto, does not address our relation to all ladders, that is, to all possible results along with their prerequisites. Nor does it address our relation to various large subsets of the set of all ladders. As Donald Rumsfeld might say, there are ladders we don't know we don't know, i.e., results and prerequisites we don't know we don't know.

So unspecified and unspecifiable is this set of all ladders, it seems to me that only super indirectness is possible in relation to it. Perhaps even *super super* indirectness. How lofty is the zenith-limit? Only a super indirect answer strikes me as rationally available to the optimist and pessimist. Our constituting logics, mathematics, etc., our thus-constituted theories and theory-dependent discoveries, all shift here with a promise of deep revisability.

The situation is indeterminate. Discussing the upper limit of computing power in his article "Are You Living in a Computer Simulation?", Nick Bostrom writes:

It is currently hard to be confident in any upper bound on the computing power that may be available to posthuman civilizations. As we are still lacking a "theory of everything," we cannot rule out the possibility that novel physical phenomena, not allowed for in current physical theories, may be utilized to transcend those constraints that in our current understanding impose theoretical limits on the information processing attainable in a given lump of matter. We can with much greater confidence establish *lower* bounds on posthuman computation, by assuming only mechanisms that are already understood.

As passional beings we lean on this or that side of the scale. We make an *existential* determination when faced with epistemic indeterminacy. Without a shore, under starless sky, the negative and the positive sail off in opposite directions.

One of my favorite poems is Friedrich Nietzsche's "To the Mistral Wind: A Dancing Song," which appears in my favorite of Nietzsche's books, *The Gay Science*. The last two stanzas of this poem, which together close the entire book, almost summarize the zenithist vision:

> *Let us hunt heaven-blockers,*
> *World-polluters, black-cloud hawkers.*
> *Let us lighten heaven's kingdom!*
> *Let us roar . . . oh spirit of all spirits free,*
> *with you within me*
> *windstorm-like brews up my joyous wisdom*
>
> *—And, in eternity's well, to baptize*
> *Such joy, lift joy's prize,*
> *Lift its wreath with you up and up way far!*
> *Hurl it higher, further, gladder,*
> *storm up heaven's ladder,*
> *hang it—upon a star.*[15]

---

[15] My own translation (translated *a bene placito*).

A QUESTION OF SELF-KNOWLEDGE

Would a zenith-being know that they were a zenith-being? *Maybe*—that is the short and uninformative answer.

To refresh on our definition, a zenith-being is a being that exists at the theoretical universal maximum of scientific and technological power.

If it is possible to be *and* to know that one exists at this maximum, then a zenith-being (by definition) knows that it is a zenith-being. This is because zenith is a description, not a proper name, and the description is simply meant to refer to any conscious being at the possible limit of natural powers. If cognizance of one's zenith-state is within this limit, then, via our description, a zenith-being must know itself as such.

We have not established that such self-knowledge is an achievable possibility, only that, if this self-knowledge is an achievable possibility in the infinite natural system, our "Zenith" label includes it.

So, is it possible to know that one is a Zenith-being? I do not know.

"No being is more advanced than I," may seem unprovable, even for the most advanced being. Yet, for all we know, some super-proof may lurk in the hadal zone of metaphysics, demonstrating to (self-certain) zenith-beings the truth of some definitive logical exclusion of higher-order physical powers. You and I are left to utmost speculation on this.

It may be that reality is such that no zenith-being could ever *know* that it was a zenith-being. There may exist a super-proof that demonstrates to (self-uncertain) zenith-beings that no zenith-being *could know* it was a zenith-being. A proof of this necessary ignorance may exist (or may not).

I suspect that for those existing at the dreamlike peaks of zenithistic advancement, an absence of contact by *more advanced* beings would mean something more significant, more informative, than such absence means for us earth-dependent and time-stuck animals.

I leave this question only prefaced; the water is deeper here—too deep for a diver like me. I leave this lightless depth to the bravest divers.

ZENITH AND FERMI'S PARADOX

What is Fermi's Paradox?

Fermi's Paradox is not so much of a paradox, at least it is not a *logical* paradox; it is more of tension between two putative truths: (1) We have no evidence for the existence of extraterrestrial civilizations; (2) The existence of extraterrestrial civilizations is highly probable.

One of the most comprehensive books on Fermi's Paradox is Stephen Webb's *If the Universe is Teeming with Aliens . . . Where is Everybody?*, which examines *all* of the proposed solutions to Fermi's paradox available at the time of Webb's writing.

A Possible Zenithist Solution

A zenithist accepts (2) above, given that an infinite natural system yields an extremely high probability that extraterrestrial civilizations exist.

A zenithist may or may not accept (1), but I will assume the truth of (1) in this post.

My proposal has five parts:
1. Rare Earth Hypothesis
2. Exclusionary Range
3. Convergent Evolution to Unity
4. Justified Hiddenness
5. Order of Development

In summary, the solution is this: It may be highly likely that no complex life exists in the observable zone of our universe (~46.6 billion light-year radius). Given this radical rarity of life in the observable universe, the barriers to interaction are extreme. Due to these extreme barriers, only Zenith (or beings near the Zenith-limit) can interact with us. Yet, Zenith chooses to remain hidden to us.

Every Zenith being is maximally advanced and therefore Zenith beings converge on every achievable optimum of mastery. This convergent evolution may result in something far more unified than a heterogenous "federation" of advanced biological forms. This more unified being converges on the best reasons possible, thus its decision to stay hidden is (1) determined by the best reasons and (2) immune to defection by other Zenith-beings. As for near-Zenith beings, beings that are slightly less advanced than Zenith, yet still capable of interaction with us, their defection risk may be zero if the right sort of axiological unity occurs far in advance of the power to interact with us (the power to escape the deep exclusionary range). Any near-Zenith being that could interact with us will yet choose to remain hidden with zero chance of defection.

The levels of advancement here are unimaginable to us, so it seems as likely as not that our reasoning about Zenith's unity, hiddenness, and "best reasons," could essentially apply to near-Zeniths, as we (our analysis) could not tell the difference that far up the asymptote.

That is my "sketch of a solution." It borrows from theology, which ought not to be surprising given the similarity of subject: extremely powerful beings.

Below, I make a few remarks and clarifications on this basic sketch. I organize my remarks according to the five parts of my proposal.

(1) Rare Earth Hypothesis

It may be highly likely that no complex life exists in the observable zone of our universe (~46.6 billion light-year radius).

This pessimism may seem odd coming from a zenithist, who believes that life is infinitely distributed. However, an infinite distribution of life does *not* mean an infinite density of life emerging in *any* given finite volume of space. A Zenithist may hold that life is infinitely distributed, but also hold that civilizational life occurs on average only once in every 10^{100} cubic meters of space.

The low density of extraterrestrial life, particularly life in civilizations above Kardashev Type II, seems a better guess than high density (in the observable universe), since none of our astronomical observations have yielded plausible signatures of such life.[16]

For a succinct view of this "sparse life" view, I recommend Michael H. Hart's "Atmospheric Evolution, the Drake Equation, and DNA: Sparse Life in an Infinite Universe."

(2) Exclusionary Range

Given this radical rarity of life in the observable universe, the barriers to interaction are extreme. Due to these extreme barriers, only Zenith (or beings near the Zenith-limit) can interact with us.

The ability to interact with beings some 10^{100} cubic meters of space away is an extraordinary ability. The extraordinariness of this feat, and other such feats, translates into what I call an exclusionary range: for a given set of prerequisites to interaction, there will be some set of beings that do not meet the prerequisites; beings in this set will range in their abilities, but insofar as they do not meet the prerequisites to interaction, they are excluded from interaction.

Note that an exclusionary range is relative. The exclusionary range for two civilizations existing in the same galactic quadrant will be narrower than the exclusionary range for two civilizations existing in two different galaxies.

I think the prerequisites to interaction, given the rare earth hypothesis, are so extreme that only beings at or near the Zenith-limit can escape all (or most) exclusionary ranges. I think it is more probable than not that even a Kardashev Type III civilization existing some 50 gigaparsecs distance will be excluded

---

[16] The Kardashev Scale, proposed by astronomer Nikolai Kardashev, is a "method of measuring a civilization's level of technological advancement based on the amount of energy they are able to use." ("Kardashev Scale," Wikipedia). Kardashev proposed only three levels, or Types: planetary (Type I), stellar (Type II), and galactic (Type III). Type I civilizations have the power to use and store all the available energy of their planet; Type II, all the available energy of their native solar system; Type III, all the available energy of their native galaxy.

from interacting with us.

Finally, I should add that I use the term "interaction," but I use it broadly to mean any instance where one civilization becomes aware of another civilization. So, passive reception of radio waves from another civilization counts as an interaction.

(3) Convergent Evolution to Unity

Every Zenith being is maximally advanced and therefore Zenith beings converge on every achievable optimum of mastery. This convergent evolution may result in something far more unified than a heterogenous 'federation' of advanced biological forms.

I think convergence to unity is relevant to Fermi's paradox because of the problem of defection, which I mentioned in the summary above and will address further in the section on the "order of development."

In brief, given a group of Zeniths who have decided to stay hidden, what is the likelihood of at least one Zenith defecting from this group and revealing their existence? If Zenith is a strongly unified being, at least in terms of decision-making, then the likelihood of a revelatory defection is extremely low, and may go to zero, even in an infinite natural system. Since the Zenith-limit is a convergence to all achievable optima, we may suppose that numerous homologies will exist at this limit, including ethical homologies (to mix metaphors).

In one of his best-known essays, "How to Make Our Ideas Clear," the 19th-century American philosopher Charles Sanders Peirce wrote, "The opinion which is fated to be ultimately agreed to by all who investigate, is what we mean by the truth, and the object represented in this opinion is the real."

Peirce defended a convergent evolutionary view of scientific investigation, where hypothesis-proliferation and hypothesis-elimination evolve in a collective, interacting, and self-correcting asymptote that converges, like the independent developments of the wing structure, on the fixed limits of reality. The philosopher Nicholas Rescher has referred to this long-run view as "Peirce's Epistemic Eschatology."[17]

I think something like Peirce's convergentism could apply in ethics, metaethics, metaphysics, metametaphysics, and other subjects of a less "concrete" nature.

If this convergentism or something very much like it is right, then Zenith will have converged on every achievable fixed limit of this sort, given that Zenith simply is the being who hits every achievable fixed limit. Since I'm including ethical and metaethical truths, even if those truths are, e.g., eleventh-order truths about the meaninglessness of lower-order ethical truths, then Zenith will have converged upon the limits of ethical and metaethical inquiry. If so, I think it is reasonable to risk the claim that Zenith's decisions (being those of a post-biological entity, in my view) will be mostly, if not entirely shared by all Zeniths.

Of course, this talk of "sharing decisions" presupposes a distinct plurality of beings, but this distinctness may not straightforwardly apply to Zenith, whose powers over its own identity may complicate our sense of individuals.

(4) Justified Hiddenness

Zenith chooses to remain hidden to us.

Zenith converges on the best reasons possible, thus its decision to stay hidden is determined by the best reasons.

Hopefully it is obvious why this solution requires hiddenness. If we claim that (i) Zenith exists and (ii) exists here now, and yet (iii) we have no material evidence of Zenith (insofar as we can tell), then either (a) Zenith does not exist, (b) does not exist here now, or (c) Zenith is choosing to remain hidden to us. Since the Zenithist wants to deny (a) and (b), hiddenness seems to be the only option left to make (i)-(iii) plausible. This is transparently motivated reasoning, but motivated reasoning

---

[17] For a crystal-clear defense of Peirce's philosophy of science, I recommend Rescher's *Peirce's Philosophy of Science*.

and sound reasoning are not mutually exclusive.

So, why is Zenith hidden?

The solution picks up from the previous section on convergence to unity, where I suggested that Peirce's convergentism might apply to any field of inquiry, including ethical inquiry. In short, if Zenith makes a decision, it is as justified as any decision could be, since Zenith, qua the achievable optimum of rational investigation, is not surpassed in good decision-making by any other being, unless there exists something like the God of St. Anselm of Canterbury, i.e., that than which nothing greater can be conceived.

This part of my solution to Fermi's paradox uses indirect evidence (which, of course, is still evidence, just indirect evidence); it does not specify what reasons Zenith has for its hiddenness, only that Zenith must have the best reasons, whatever they may be, for its hiddenness. Nor does this indirect evidence mean that one cannot propose persuasive specific reasons for Zenith's hiddenness.

(5) Order of Development

As for near-Zenith beings, beings that are slightly less advanced than Zenith, yet still capable of interaction with us, their defection risk may be zero if the right sort of axiological unity occurs far in advance of the power to interact with us (the power to escape the deep exclusionary range). Any near-Zenith being that could interact with us will yet choose to remain hidden with zero chance of defection. The levels of advancement here are unimaginable to us, so it seems as likely as not that our reasoning about Zenith's unity, hiddenness, and "best reasons," could essentially apply to near-Zeniths, as we (our analysis) could not tell the difference that far up the asymptote.

One might argue that beings close to Zenith-limit, but not exactly at the Zenith-limit, will have the power to interact with us, yet lack both Zenith's unity and Zenith's "best reasons" for staying hidden, such that we should again expect material evidence of interaction by these near-Zeniths. Since we have no such evidence, my solution becomes less probable.

We are deciding between two contradictory claims here:

(1) Some near-Zeniths who possess the power to interact with us pose a defection risk.
(2) No near-Zenith who possesses the power to interact with us poses a defection risk.

There is no empirical resolution here. It may seem *a priori* more appealing to assert the humble particular affirmative (1) against the imperious universal negation (2). However, consider this example:

(3) Some differential equations are kangaroos.
(4) No differential equations are kangaroos.

Humble claim (3) is a category mistake and false. Imperiously universal negation (4) is true.

I would not argue that claim (1) above is a category mistake like claim (3), yet claim (1) may be false in other profound ways. Perhaps in the order of development, possession of unity (or near-unity) and best-reasons (or near-best-reasons) must be prior to escaping some set of deep exclusionary ranges. We don't know. It may be as wrong to say that a human blastocyst could recite the Quran as it is to say that near-Zeniths could interact with us (across exclusion) before achieving innumerable proficiencies amounting to "unity," "best reasons," and so on. We don't know.

So, the probability of my solution, I think, is not reduced in this instance. Rather, it is a wash between the two contradictory unknowns of (1) and (2).

This wash does not wash over the whole proposal. If the other reasons survive a gauntlet of stress tests, perhaps needing the occasional correction, then my Zenithist solution may be considered a strong candidate solution, though only one zenithistic candidate in an indefinite field of possible proposals.

In the spirit of Peirce, we should proliferate proposals as we make our hopeful and self-correcting way to the ultimate-long-run-real.

Contact — To increase the likelihood of contact with an alien civilization, a maximally advanced civilization would implement all of its available signaling technology. Advanced civilizations would realize, as we do, that some civilizations will be, when the alien signal arrives, in a simpler stage of their signaling development.

If detection is their goal, advanced extraterrestrial civilizations are more likely to implement a *total contact rainbow* than to isolate their signaling to the ZX9 pulses of the Zalax-7000. If an event could be informative, e.g., simple radio broadcasts or a coded series of statistically significant shifts in the polarization of gravitational waves, then such events will be, all else being equal, attempted.

Zenith, being the maximal information theorist, linguist, cryptographer, psychologist, etc., would likely have little difficulty saying "hello."

Philocosmos — You might not love a perfect cosmos. It may be that you cannot love any prolific cosmos, however perfect; your prerequisites for world-love may be unmeetable.

Might we become world-lovers? Not philosophers, but "philocosmers." Not philosophy, but "philocosmy" (the love of wisdom being only *one* facet of our love).

What does the world-lover love? A generic totality? An Omega Point finale? Each *this*, e.g., *this* brutality and *this* injustice? Does one become a lover of evils and goods? A lover in the abstract? Is this unrestricted love the paraphilia of all paraphilias?

I do not think this love is a psychological possibility *for me*. Is it a psychological possibility *for you*? Is it a psychological possibility?

What is progress? — Today we tread softly around the term "progress," for it is an evaluative term with a history of violence. Yet most or all evaluative concepts, from goodness to justice to beauty, have a history of violence, so all such concepts deserve *judicious* evaluation.

DEDICATION DAY
(Written on May 8th, 2019)

In *Philosophy as a Way of Life*, historian and philosopher Pierre Hadot argues that the original philosophers of the Hellenistic and Roman world, such as the Stoics, Epicureans, and Skeptics, thought of philosophy as a total program for the improvement of one's existence, and not merely the rational analysis of claims; philosophy was not mere raising of abstract awareness, but the raising of concrete actions and personalities. "Spiritual Exercises," as Hadot calls them, were prerequisites of the philosophical life in antiquity; these exercises (e.g., Marcus Aurelius's meditations) helped aspirants attain existential holism, in which *one's whole life* becomes perfectly integrated, via rational methods, with *the world and cosmos*.

On May 8th, 2018, I hiked up to Council Crest (in Portland, Oregon). Arriving and standing on Council Crest's toposcope, self-consciously so, and facing Mt. Hood, I dedicated my philosophical and passional life to the development and advancement of the zenithist vision—to the prospect that an infinite natural system evolves infinitely many maximally advanced conscious beings.

Exactly forty years before that, on May 8th, 1978, Reinhold Messner and Peter Habeler became the first individuals to reach Mt. Everest's summit without the use of supplemental oxygen. The ascent of Messner and Habeler required vastly more nerve and stamina than my hike up to Council Crest, but I think of these two ascents on May 8th as sharing two themes: dedication and panorama.

The panorama, or *all-view*, atop a summit strikes me, as it struck Nietzsche, as a helpful analogy for the philosophical life. Philosophical life is most mature when it surveys *all* things, not simply logic puzzles and truth-aptness. And one's life, I venture, is best when it is *reconciled* with all it surveys. A rational survey is a means to reconciliation with life and, using Aristotle's famous term, *eudaimonia* (which I like to translate, eisegetically, as "flowering well-spiritedness"). The philosophical all-view is worth the strenuous ascent, so it is worth dedicating and re-dedicating, and ever-dedicating, yourself to this ascent.

A year has passed since my dedicatory act on Council Crest. So, today I celebrate. As many holidays are the echoes of an original celebratory act, I would like to give my celebration an echo: *Dedication Day*.

Dedication Day is a day to dedicate or re-dedicate yourself to your philosophical and passional ascent to a panorama. It is a day of self-examination and reflection on your own view of the *ultimate*, the *whole,* and the *total.* What is true? What is best? Why does the world exist? What is a good life? What is goodness? What are the limits of science? What are the limits of reason? What am I? Why am I here?

Your hypotheses are *your* panorama. What are *your* hypotheses? Before today, perhaps you simply did not think about *your* panorama. Perhaps you've only felt as if you've lived panoramically, but now discover that the *feeling* that your all-view exists is not itself an all-view.

> *Why seek to know?*
> *That this dream may grow.*

> *What do you seek?*
> *The highest peak.*

Rest your mill-turning hands, you maidens who grind; sleep on,
Even when the cockcrow announces the dawn;
For Demeter has assigned the toil of your hands to the water-nymphs,
Who now leap on the very edge of the wheel,
And whirl the axle which, with its revolving cogs,
Turns the hollow weight of the Nisyrean millstones.
We taste again the golden age of old, as we learn to feast
On the works of Demeter, free from human labor.

— Antipater of Thessalonica

ON THE ACROPOLIS

As Zuriel and I wandered the summit of Mouseion Hill near the Philopappos Monument, a cool mid-February's sky soft around us, the god Hermes Dolios, on his winged and golden sandals, fluttered down to deliver a message—a dialogue.

HERMES: You, among these cypresses, now find yourself in the month of Anthesterion, hearing three persons speaking, Glykera, Zosime, and Isokrates the Comic Playwright, while Demosthenes, brother of Isokrates, naps nearby. The sun is low and rising. The thieving magpies flute and make ascending calls. Follow, follow, follow my meandering words, modern mortals, follow closely, and now—

GLYKERA: Now I rest more perfectly, Isokrates, seeing the High City sparkling from this height. Isn't it majestic? It is the distillation of Mount Olympos.

ISOKRATES: Yes, it is fine, but fineness belongs also to the Agora, the Hephaisteion, to the tortoises, to your himation, to the herm near my house, and on and on.

GLYKERA: Not fineness to this degree, Isokrates; the Acropolis, the Parthenon, the Erechtheion, the Temple of Athena Nike—obviously these surpass the herms and tortoises, and certainly these surpass in majesty the buildings of the marketplace. Zosime, what do you think? Don't you think our High City deserves the apple of Eris—the honor and title of "the most beautiful"?

ZOSIME: Persuade me, Glykera. Why does the Acropolis deserve the designation "the most beautiful"?

ISOKRATES: Persuade us both.

GLYKERA: It is the most *majestic* because it is the most

triumphant dedication to dignity. The sight of it, even the twinkling thought of it, drapes the heart in the aegis of dignity. Consider it carefully. You see the statue of *Athena Promachos* there behind the Propylaea. What does she signify to you?

ZOSIME: Athena the frontline soldier, our protector, the first to the fight.

GLYKERA: And you, Isokrates? What does *Athena Promachos* signify to you?

ISOKRATES: She rises from the absence of the ancient Temple of Athena and faces Salamis as a testament to Athenian victory. She is martial glory married to mental clarity.

GLYKERA: Yes, I like that. This *Athena Promachos* is the goddess of *arete* and *metis*. She is not raw martial power, but refined power. It is not *Ares Promachos*, but *Athena Promachos*. I see in her not Achillean *menis*, but Odyssean *metis*. Perhaps the Areopagus down there should be called a stepping-stone *up* to Athena's High City, as Ares is a less developed warrior than Athena—Athena is not a bloodthirsty warrior. In *The Eumenides*, Aeschylus shows Athena on our Areopagus breaking a judicial tie in favor of Orestes; there on the rock of Ares, Athena's mercy transformed belligerence and retaliation into fair trial; with magnanimity, she ended the curse of the House of Atreus, running from Tantalos through Agamemnon and, at last, to Orestes. Athena, wrote Aeschylus, made the Furies *kindly*. She brought peace through wisdom, as would be expected from the daughter of Metis and Zeus, both superlatives of thought. If you think about it, wise Athena is the progeny of female *metis* and male *metis*. She is *polymetis*. It is no surprise then that Athena helped Odysseus, who was the mortal incarnation of polymetis.

ISOKRATES: Odysseus, the grandson of "the wolf himself,"

Autolykos the shapeshifter and robber, who makes black of white and white of black. Odysseus, great-grandson of Hermes, the liar.

ZOSIME: I somehow admire Odysseus all the more thanks to your selective genealogy, Isokrates.

ISOKRATES: Well, I've interrupted enough. Please, Glykera, onward orate.

GLYKERA: I take back the bema happily.

ZOSIME: A woman on the bema—at last.

ISOKRATES: Ah, *womanhood*—there's your chiton of Nessus, Glykera! Athena is, after all, a woman. You recollect the *Assemblywomen*; Aristophanes makes contradictories of womanhood and political power. Not to mention the mockery in Alexis's *Gynaikokraita*. *Athena Promachos* is a mere mercenary for *Zeus Teleios*, Zeus the Fulfiller, the Finisher. It is Zeus's law. Athena does not have the franchise. Athena the defender—Zeus the decider. How does that indignity *drape* you?

GLYKERA: Look to the right of *Athena Promachos*, to the Parthenon itself. From our distance, you cannot make out the details of the metopes, but you know the details well. On the east end, the metopes depict the gigantomachy. On the west end, they depict the fight with the Amazons. On the north end, the Trojan War is depicted. Finally, the southern metopes show the fight between the centaurs and Lapiths. What do you make of this arrangement? Zosime?

ZOSIME: Let me think on it more before I answer.

GLYKERA: Isokrates?

ISOKRATES: Pericles mastered the art of an overdone war trophy. It is overkill, literally.

GLYKERA: Well, cynic, it works. The metopes sing to us. The scenes of Troy's fall, on the northern metopes, are exemplars of my point. What did that Trojan war accomplish? According to Homer, essentially nothing. The best of the Trojans were decimated, and the victors too were *mostly* decimated. As tears sometimes wash away grief, Poseidon with waves and Zeus with rains washed out to sea the last Achaean fortifications on the beachhead. So what was won? Nothing. Nothing was won, only endured, but that endurance dignified the fighters.

The Fates have given mortals hearts that can endure.

ISOKRATES: I'm not sure this *endurance* theory captures the motivation of Pericles and Pheidias, but I like the honey glaze on the Trojan war. Rosier than rosy-fingered dawn.

ZOSIME: Nothing enthuses Isokrates, it seems.

ISOKRATES: That is very untrue. A Sikyonian devotee of Aphrodite, whose name I forget—let's name him Polykleitos, after the Sikyonian sculptor—told me that Aphrodite's *true* altar is the bed, and therefore one's bed ought to be perfectly clean—a perfect hymn to Hygieia—and tastefully perfumed, and in every other way enhanced, as is proper for a holy altar. Also, one's body must be thoroughly bathed and perfumed, and covered in the cleanest Milesian wool, before entering one's bed. The bed, I thought afterward, does seem to deserve this piety. It is the site of our conception, our birth, our dreaming, our restorative sleeping, our sex, and our death. In the spirit of Polykleitos, whatever his real name, I *enthusiastically* nominate the perfect bed, the bed of Aphrodite, over the Parthenon.

GLYKERA: I look forward to enjoying this joke again in your next comedy. The absurdity of sexual acts and the pollution of death upon a god's altar is radical, Isokrates.

ISOKRATES: Radical jokes entertain the most, Glykera. I am not Herostratus; I will not burn down a holy building for fame, but I would fill a holy cave with smoke for the glory of comedy.

GLYKERA: Yes, well, Theseus would have died in the Labyrinth with you as his company, by following your jokes rather than Ariadne's thread.

ZOSIME: Would you summarize your case, Glykera?—quickly enough to dodge the arrows of Isokrates, which are like the arrows of Eros, but instead of love, one is stricken with laughter.

GLYKERA: Crudely, my thought is this: The Athenian, plagued today by toothache, tomorrow by bed bugs, the next day by scabies, and days after by uncountable pains in the limbs and the heart, may look up to the High City and feel unity with Athena Promachos—and with every weathered sculpture showing us a cycle of struggles alongside a cycle of celebrations. These monuments remind us that the Olympians are orderers and enlighteners. The Olympians struggle against chaos, disorder, and lawlessness. Our Acropolis is the signal fire of this struggle, its dignity, and the promise of perpetual victory.

ISOKRATES: Zeus the Enlightener?

GLYKERA: Arrow incoming.

ISOKRATES: Zeus is deludable, as Agamemnon says in the *Iliad*:

Yes, for once Zeus even was deluded, though men say
He is the highest one of the gods and mortals.

And Athena herself calls Zeus an "obstinate old sinner."

GLYKERA: Doesn't this reinforce my claim? Doesn't the
struggle of Zeus with Zeus count as another struggle
against disorder—perhaps the profoundest kind of struggle? We look to the gods and it fortifies us to find that *they
struggle too*. Human life and divine life live on this same axis,
though one form of life lives higher up on this axis. To
know ourselves it to know our relations with the gods, including some relations of likeness. Human life is divinity
struck with a mortal wound, yet fighting on and forward.

ISOKRATES: Is this hill elevated enough for those sentiments?

GLYKERA: Are my sentiments any more *elevated* than those of
Peleus, when he gave his son Achilleus this beautiful advice:

Now always be the best, my boy, the bravest,
and hold your head up high above the others.

ISOKRATES: Maybe not. But I have a related criticism of our
divine patronage. We repeat to ourselves that we chose
Athena and her gift of the olive tree over Poseidon and his
gift of the salt waters in the contest over the divine patronage of our city. Yet what was Athenian power if not
maritime? We did not rule the world via the olive tree, but
the trireme. All those Parthenon friezes of the cavalry, clad
in chlamydes and embades, and those wars on the metopes, yet not a single depiction of a trireme, the strategic
cornerstone of our once illustrious military. Not one. I
should add, non-judgmentally, that the story goes that the
women voted for Athena, way back whenever women had
the franchise, and that this vote is the reason Athenian

women were disenfranchised. Lysistrata regained something of the franchise later, but that's a digression.

GLYKERA: The women voted wisely, if that dubious story is true. First, of course, Athena is said to have invented the first ship, so there is your most fatal error. She is the goddess of shipwrights. She is the guide of seafarers. More importantly, in Athens it has always been warcraft *in the service of* the olive tree, and not, as in Sparta, the olive tree in the service of warcraft. That is why Athena won our hearts, not Poseidon. To some extent, the trireme *reins in* Poseidon's waves; we call Athena the "Tamer of Horses," while Poseidon is no tamer of anything, and no inventor. Without hesitation, I credit the inspiration for the trireme to the maker of the plough, the bridle, the chariot, and many other works. And to your digression—well, I won't comment on Lysistrata's sex strike.

ISOKRATES: Stirring point, and pro-Athenian to the end. Pardon a second digression, but I must sing the praises of Themistokles here, who poured that famous fountain of Laurion silver into the Piraeus and the proliferation of triremes. Themistokles understood Poseidon's preeminence, while many others clung to a nostalgia for the spear and aspis, as if each hoplite held the spear of Athena herself, as if the Battle of Marathon summarized all the future of warfare. Themistokles understood the preeminence of naval power, where even Plato, the Sophist's Sophist, confused the vices-cum-virtues of his aristocratic self-deification for hawk-eyed military truths; that Sophist claimed Themistokles turned Athenians from "steady soldiers" to "mariners and seamen tossed about the sea." He decried that Themistokles "took away from the Athenians the spear and the shield, and bound them to the rowing bench and the oar." I say: one of Xerxes's infantrymen would have twisted his boot in Plato's grandfather's gore if Plato's form of goodness, instead of triremes, had proliferated.

ZOSIME: Now I understand why you portrayed Plato as an unbathed aquaphobic in your *Seisachtheia*.

ISOKRATES: You have a good memory for the minor characters in my comedies. I only wish Plato would have had a good memory, or else I wish he could have been whisked back in time and watched from Salamis, as our refugee ancestors watched, the triumph of Themistokles.

GLYKERA: My point stands, Isokrates; it is the Piraeus and the fleet in the service of peace, liberty, and dignity.

ISOKRATES: Yes, and honor too, as Pericles repeated. You, like Pericles, offer Athenians such pleasing orations on the subject of Athens. You've lived up to Pericles's advice and fallen in love with your *polis*, but you remember that even Pericles called the Athenian empire a tyranny—these were no mincing words. And don't erase from your Elysian Fields of Battle our cousins the Spartans. What is the Battle of Plataea without the Spartan Pausanias, who defeated Mardonius, the demolisher of Athens?

GLYKERA: Yes, but then a little more than 50 years later, the Spartans, under King Archidamus II, summarily executed the besieged Plataeans, to whom the Spartans had promised a fair trial. So much for Spartan promises. Here in Athens, we keep promises. Here, where Pindar studied lyric poetry under Lasos of Hermione. Here, where Aristotle taught on the holy grounds of Apollo Lykeios. Here, where Socrates and Plato challenged and refined the intellect.

ISOKRATES: Here, where Cleon agitated the people against the genius Anaxagoras, who thus received from us a fine of five talents and expulsion from our city. Here, where Anytus, Lycon, and Meletus prosecuted Socrates, winning for Athens the poor old fool's execution.

GLYKERA: Well, Meletus and the others were repaid in kind. None of this, of course, matches in baseness the history of the Spartans, Isokrates. Those ants of Lycurgus brutalized their *helots*, while we sought justice through our *heliaia*.

ISOKRATES: We matched Spartan baseness, Glykera. We certainly matched it. I excuse no side. We oppressed Naxos when Naxos, understandably, seceded from the Delian League; or rather, the Delian Bondservants of Athens. The Acropolis also signifies the plundering by Periclean Athens of the treasury of the Delian League. Our architectural self-aggrandizement cost more talents than several of our wars. You mentioned the treachery of Archidamus. We once simply executed a Spartan embassy without trial and, like a brood of little King Creons, irreligiously rolled their corpses into a pit. Let the muses sing to you, Glykera, of our atrocities at Scione and Melos.

GLYKERA: Do you see the parapet of the Temple of Athena Nike?

ISOKRATES: Indistinctly, but yes.

GLYKERA: And do you recall that it was erected under the administration of Cleophon in honor of our victory in Cyzicus over the Spartans?

ISOKRATES: By odious Cleophon, yes—I know.

GLYKERA: Why were we in Cyzicus, Isokrates?

ISOKRATES: To defeat Spartans.

GLYKERA: A very laconic response, Isokrates. The context of that fight, as you could guess, is the point to which I was leading you. The Spartans postured themselves as the liberators of Hellas, but they had become, through an alliance with Persia, the oppressors of Hellas. We were in Cyzicus fighting the Spartan-Persian chimera. The *most* odious ones were Spartans; they sold Hellas out to its worst enemy. Prosecute the memory of Cleophon as you will, but the Spartan breed of treachery never arose in our *ecclesia*. Treachery for treasure, at that. Lysander and the Spartan majority absolutely defiled and nullified the sacrifice of Leonidas.

ISOKRATES: You could say that our own lionization of Conon, the Athenian who commanded the Persian Fleet against the Spartans, later in the tide of that war, counts as *our* Pro-Persianism. Dear Pharnabazus paid for the refortification of the Piraeus and the rebuilding of our Long Walls. We like Pharnabazus, no?

ZOSIME: May I insult us for a moment?

GLYKERA: What?

ISOKRATES: By Hermes, god of transitions, please do.

ZOSIME: This conversation is like the shroud that Penelope wove daily for Laertes, then unwove nightly for Odysseus. This is Penelopism. We are Penelopists.

ISOKRATES: I am but a humble Philo-Penelopist, to use the humble coinage of the humble philo-sophers.

ZOSIME: Glykera weaves. Isokrates unweaves. A judgment of the Acropolis may never come, at least not from me. If I were Paris, I wouldn't know to whom I'd hand the golden apple. Glykera's Athena squabbles with Isokrates's Aphrodite. And forgive me, but I have no role for Hera in this metaphor—unless I squabble as Hera, which I won't do. In my suspended judgment, I wonder not about my own judgment, but about the judgments of others. What judgments will come in 1,000 years? 10,000 years? Will our High City even endure for 10,000 years? 100,000 years? Before it becomes, as the three of us will become, mere air, what countless judgments will be made of it?

ISOKRATES: "Squabbles" is a touch unfair, but I can't summon a better word at the moment.

ZOSIME: I suppose my trouble is that our Acropolis must point away from itself and to ever higher cities, more ideal cities, if I am to judge the Acropolis *the most beautiful*. Yet in pointing away to ever higher cities, the Acropolis thereby nominates some other place as the *most beautiful*. I sense in the Acropolis its own successor and superior.

GLYKERA: What do you mean?

ISOKRATES: Is this your "Diotima's Ladder" of city planning?

ZOSIME: No, nothing like that. Isokrates, you brought up the Battle of Salamis and Plataea, which made me think, naturally enough, of Xerxes, and specifically the story of Xerxes in Abydos. The Great King and his forces had amassed on the Hellespont, at Abydos, for the Great King's review of his legions. The locals of Abydos had been forced beforehand to erect for Xerxes a high throne of marble on a summit for this great survey. The waters of the Hellespont were hidden by the throng of Xerxes's ships. His vast army eclipsed the shores and coastal plain. Xerxes, witnessing this plenitude under his command, delighted and pronounced himself a happy man, and then, immediately, broke into a bitter weeping. His uncle, Artabanus, observing this, asked Xerxes, "Great King, how far different from one another are the things which you have done now and a short while before now! For having pronounced yourself a happy man, you are now weeping."

Xerxes replied: "After I surveyed all these masses of men from every end of my Kingdom, the pitiable shortness of human life struck me, seeing that not one of all these people here will be alive when one hundred years have gone by." Gazing at the Acropolis, I feel as Xerxes seems to have felt at Abydos.

GLYKERA: Now I feel it.

ISOKRATES: I as well, now.

GLYKERA: This bleakness—this is the proving ground of that dignity and courage I find endlessly praised by our High City. Look to Athena Promachos again, Zosime. Athena fights alongside us. She says, "Let nothing grieve you beyond measure, Zosime. As long as you live, shine."

ZOSIME: I love your encouragements, Glykera.

GLYKERA: By Athena Soteira, I wish you a shining life—a joyous life greatly unlike that of decadent Xerxes, who, with weeping and complaints, grieved immeasurably and so disgraced his kingship.

ISOKRATES: I wish you a joyous life also, Zosime. And you too, Glykera. We know that we are of real irreplaceability only to ourselves and to a few who love us, but that will die with us and them, and we will become unknown in good time. Our High City will lower and, as Zosime said, dissolve into air.

ZOSIME: I wonder about that deepest future. If you ask me to answer regarding the most beautiful for all times and for all places, I cannot answer. Are there Acropolises up there on the wanderers or on the stars? Anaxagoras thought the moon inhabited. Might the moon hold a more perfect Parthenon?—requiring one hundred Mount

Pentelikons of marble? Maybe. Even more I think of time. When asked whether the mountains of Lampsakos would ever turn into sea, Anaxagoras said, "yes, if time doesn't give out." Isn't that a piercing expression—time giving out? It's a shocking and sublime possibility.

GLYKERA: I wonder about your *present* answer: Do you give the golden apple to Athena's High City or to something else, such as Isokrates's proposal of Aphrodite's Bed? Here and now, make your choice.

ISOKRATES: I didn't propose Aphrodite's Bed for others, of course. To quote Sappho:

Some say an army of horsemen, others
say foot-soldiers, still others, a fleet,
is the fairest thing on the dark earth;
I say it is whatever one loves.

ZOSIME: Do you know which goddess I admire more than Athena?

GLYKERA: Who?

ISOKRATES: Ganymede?

ZOSIME: Isokrates, you've deflated a valuable suspense with another radical joke.

GLYKERA: I remain in suspense, so tell me. Who is your goddess of goddesses?

ZOSIME: Eos, goddess of the dawn.

ISOKRATES: Rosy fingers?

ZOSIME Yes, and rosy-armed. Though I think of Eos as the

goddess of the new, of things to come, of the possible.

GLYKERA: I don't know of any holy sites dedicated to Eos.

ISOKRATES: I'm also ignorant of any sites for Eos.

ZOSIME: I don't think any holy sites for Eos exist—not yet. I sometimes pretend that the sculptures of the east pediment of the Parthenon show the birth of Eos, and not Athena. On the left of the pediment, Helios, the Sun, brother of Eos, draws up his shining horses from Oceanus, while Selene, the Moon, sister of Eos, steers her gallop-wearied steeds down into Oceanus. I pretend that this scene of Athena's dawn-birth is simply the birth of dawn herself.

GLYKERA: When I think of Eos, I think of Tithonus, whom Eos lusted after and soon carried off and kept as a lover in her rose-rich chambers. Immortal Eos then requested from the gods that mortal Tithonus be given eternal life, which the gods granted, but Eos forgot to request eternal youth for Tithonus, who thus deteriorates forever into all the unthinkable horrors of aging that come after those of the standard mortal life.

ISOKRATES: As a man well into his winter—a snow-wreathed comic, to overdo the euphemisms—I vastly dislike that story.

GLYKERA: Me as well. Immortality is the *death* of Tithonus's dignity.

ISOKRATES: In some accounts, Tithonus was transformed into a cicada. Now, didn't your daughter Myro own a pet cicada that recently died?

GLYKERA: She did, and her pet cricket died too.

ISOKRATES: Next time I see Myro, I shall bring her a

Melitaean puppy, as consolation.

GLYKERA: She would be consoled instantly, Isokrates.

ISOKRATES: Do you think, Zosime, that immortal Tithonus could be consoled by a puppy?

ZOSIME: Only an immortal puppy.

ISOKRATES: And only an immortal puppy with eternal youth—eternal *puppyness*.

ZOSIME: Exactly. Yes. Tithonus's problem is not immortality as such, but progressive debilitation without end. Ganymede is not tortured by immortality. Glaukos, the mortal fisherman of Anthedon who was transformed into a sea-god by some "ever-living grass," as Aeschylus says, is not tortured like Tithonus.

ISOKRATES: I remember the stories of Glaukos. He is not immiserated by his immortality, that's true; yet he does not exactly fair *swimmingly* according to Plato in *The Republic*. Glaukos's body is missing parts and is "mutilated by the waves," I believe Plato wrote. The fisherman-god looks like a "wild beast," ugly with "accretions of barnacles and seaweed."

ZOSIME: Perhaps Plato's opinion is more proof of his aquaphobia.

ISOKRATES: So it is! That's funny.

ZOSIME: I wish to turn Tithonus on his head. The inverse of progressive debilitation is progressive strengthening. When I think of progressive strengthening, I think of Milo of Croton.

ISOKRATES: Who?

GLYKERA: Milo of Croton, the athlete. He won all four of the male Panhellenic games *in the same cycle*—and he did so for *five cycles*.

ISOKRATES: Oh, right. I thought I heard you say some other name. But yes, yeah—Milo of Croton. Big eater.

ZOSIME: You know the story of Milo's training, then. Milo carried a bull *every day* as that bull matured from newborn to yearling to its adult prime, thus each day Milo grew stronger in proportion with the bull's growth. What if such training by progressive resistance could go on *indefinitely*?

ISOKRATES: What if?

ZOSIME: Imagine a lineage of Milos, a people progressively strengthening themselves. Suppose this multitude begets children stronger yet, and their children beget stronger yet, and so on, ever-strengthening, ever-overcoming. To what finish line?

ISOKRATES: Milo was strong, of course, but nothing remarkable by way of intellect, for Milo died in a moronic manner. What hope from those loins? Presumably, another gigantomachy.

ZOSIME: I have a clarification to make concerning that, but let me finish my analogy by saying that I think of the Acropolis as Milo's calf.

GLYKERA: Then is Athens Milo?

ZOSIME: No. I think civilization itself is Milo; all civilizations may strengthen progressively as Milo did.

GLYKERA: So, these stronger civilizations will produce cities and public works that outshine our Acropolis? "Higher

Cities," as you said.

ZOSIME: I hope so.

ISOKRATES: And what of the Typhon this bull-brained lineage may beget? What's that clarification you promised?

ZOSIME: Archytas.

ISOKRATES: How is the name of a Pythagorean a clarification?

ZOSIME: My clarification *begins* with Archytas, one of several Pythagorean targets in your latest comedy. Archytas is reputed to have engineered an artificial dove that flew some 200 meters.

ISOKRATES: First and foremost, did you find *Momus* to your liking? I wrote it after reading Alexis's *Men from Tarentum*.

ZOSIME: I didn't quite laugh as I do at the comedies of old Eupolis, but yes, it was enjoyable. It's unfortunate you didn't win at this year's Lenaea.

ISOKRATES: That's my usual fortune, Zosime; my thoughts are over-foliated and my characters tend to be *too* intellectual, as my portrayal of Archytas demonstrates.

ZOSIME: Only your portrayal of Archytas missed the significance of that profound Tarentine, whom even Plato admired.

ISOKRATES: A little dove trick? I missed the significance of Archytas's dove?

ZOSIME: Yes, but forgivably so, given the constraints of your craft.

GLYKERA: You make excuses for Isokrates.

ISOKRATES: So, you did not belly-laugh, as I did, at the scene where Cambyses II and his forces hurl cats in the Siege of Pelusium?

ZOSIME: I like cats, so my laugh was mixed with some discomfort.

ISOKRATES: Fair enough. What of the impractical business of Archytas? Tell me why I ought to revise the parts with Archytas and his dove.

ZOSIME No, no—I'm not suggesting you revise your comedy. I was simply mentioning your comedy, since it mentioned Archytas, whom I wish to discuss.

ISOKRATES: I'm relieved.

ZOSIME: Ok, be patient with me. Archytas used *tekhne* to mimic a dove's flight. Take the full measure of that fact. Archytas extended his powers to include *flight*. I first read of Archytas's dove six or seven months ago, and ever since then the thought of that Daedalic dove has inspired in me such hopeful visions. Since that dove, I've researched more craft-wonders. I read, for example, about the works of Cleotas, the inventor who engineered a starting gate at the Olympic Games on which moved a mechanical eagle and a mechanical dolphin. I've set my ears for stories and news of this kind. Just two weeks ago, a fellow Rhodian informed me of some inventors in our homeland who crafted a mechanism for making astronomical calculations, involving an ingenuous system of interlocking gear wheels.

GLYKERA: Marvelous.

ZOSIME: I think so too. But consider what such extended powers may mean *more generally*. Through these technical wonders, I sense the strengthening of a kind of Milo-Archytas, if I may mix personages. That is, I sense a progressive overcoming of resistance *by way of* craft, reason, and strength. I ask: supposing time doesn't "give out," supposing time without end, and supposing an immortal Milo-Archytas, what follows? What do you think follows?

GLYKERA: I might need more information.

ISOKRATES: Yes, a proud native Rhodian *would* extrapolate from their mechanisms to the mechanisms of the Gods. Am I correct?—that you extrapolate to apotheosis?

ZOSIME: Tentatively.

ISOKRATES: Zosime, you've joined a fine tradition of Hellenic madness, from Heraclitus to Empedocles to mad Socrates. You might recall Heraclitus's riddle: "Immortals are mortals, mortals immortals: living their death, dying their life." Lovely Hellenic madness. Go, Zosime, to the very end of your new Hellenic madness. I welcome it!

ZOSIME: I'll form my "madness" into a disjunctive syllogism. Let's just assume a sempiternal Milo-Archytas. Now, either Milo-Archytas's power reaches a limit or it is limitless. We take it that unlimited power leads to contradictions.

ISOKRATES: Do we?

ZOSIME: Well, a truly unlimited power can make a thing exist and not exist at the same time, which is a contradiction. I think of Laelaps, the hunting dog who unfailingly catches his prey, who was sent to kill the Teumessian Fox, who unfailingly evades all his predators. Either outcome of this hunt must be a contradiction. Laelaps and the Teumessian Fox are not perfectly analogous examples of the point, but they are adjacent to it—and I love canids, so indulge me. Anyhow, given that unlimited power is an absurdity, so far as I can tell, I infer limited power for Milo-Archytas, yet that power ascends to a limit of sublimity and peak of prowess unavailable to the imagination of even our wisest philosophers. One may name it, as you did, Isokrates, "apotheosis."

GLYKERA: I'll let Homer, speaking as Apollo, speak my *initial* reaction to your theory:

> *O son of Tydeus, cease! be wise and see*
> *How vast the difference of the gods and thee;*
> *Distance immense! between the powers that shine*
> *Above, eternal, deathless, and divine,*
> *And mortal man! a wretch of humble birth,*
> *A short-lived reptile in the dust of earth.*

ISOKRATES: In my lifetime, the vast and deathless Achaemenid empire was extinguished by the sword of the bumpkins of Macedonia. That is my way of saying that *I've seen it all.* Yet this is new. Now if Apollo had the luxury of existing, he would perhaps flay you alive, as he did Marsyas, for your hubris. Or, on Zeus's command, you may go the watery way of Lykaon's generation. Yet we stand here near Zosime, unafraid of lightning. Amused and unafraid.

GLYKERA: Yes, we do.

ISOKRATES: I'm amused. We've heard that Rhodes is the bride of the Sun, and it is proven by Zosime today, as she's adopted the sunniest view of human potential. With admiration for your boldness, Zosime, I think the Spartans would take such an infant thought to their Apothetae.

GLYKERA: One moment there, Isokrates. I do not assume

you intend to justify that Spartan practice, but I must interject and rebuke that Spartan *brutality*. It is a sign not of strength, but fragility, when societies cannot support their disabled and sickly. One must conclude that infirm children are *too dangerous* and *too difficult* a challenge for the infirm Spartan system. Perhaps the incapable Spartan system deserves to be thrown into the Apothetae.

ISOKRATES: The Apothetae is a legend, of course. We have no proof of it. And you well know that we Athenians *expose* infants. Also, and this is only loosely related, Spartan women probably prefer their social status to that of Athenian women. But may mine be the last word, for now, on Sparta? I'm so tired of Sparta. I intended no justification of the Apothetae, only comic effect. I apologize for its tastelessness. Let's go back and follow Zosime's thread.

GLYKERA: Isokrates has his last word.

ISOKRATES: I love last words, Glykera. I granted dear and unjustly maligned Peisistratos the last word in *Momus*.

GLYKERA: I remember that, tyrant-loving Isokrates.

ISOKRATES: If I may, Peisistratos was Solon's equal, or perhaps a bit shrewder. To head off a cheap equivocation, I don't mean his equal in the simple voting sense. I mean, of course, qualitative equals. Solon did not bequeath the hard-pressed classes the Panathenaic Games; that was Peisistratos. Peisistratos built the first Ploutonion at Eleusis, and gave Athens her first public library. I could continue like this, but, as known, I love last words, especially if they're mine—and I don't take my position on Peisistratos too seriously, anyhow.

GLYKERA: I value the insincerity of your position on Peisistratos.

ISOKRATES: Zosime, my apologies. I return to your Milo-Archytas—with a solemn question: What if the path from mortal flesh to immortal god is akin to Zeno's race? You spoke of a finish line some time ago, so what if it is the finish line in Zeno's race? What if it is an uncrossable series of never-ending divisions?

ZOSIME: You lend your ear to Zeno?—like Nearchus of Elea?

ISOKRATES: That Zeno bit the ear of Nearchus is no argument, Zosime. Though, since we're allowed jabs and deviations, I wonder if you should initiate a fifth Panhellenic game. Added to the Olympic, the Pythian, the Isthmian, and the Nemean Games, there ought to be the "Zosimean" Games?

GLYKERA: You forgot the Games of Hera, Isokrates.

ISOKRATES: The women's games, of course. That is an embarrassing omission. I've argued myself that they count as a Panhellenic game, so excuse my flub. And to be less personal, Zosime, let me call your proposed contest the "Bellerophonian Games."

ZOSIME: I did not propose a contest; you did.

ISOKRATES: That's right. Right. I'm still embarassed by my overlooking the Heraean Games. And I'm still distracted by the memory of Peisistratos's accomplishments. My joke is withering.

GLYKERA: What's the joke?

ISOKRATES: I meant to propose the "Bellerophonian Games," which would include a round of winged-horsemanship with gold-painted charioteers all required to drive drunker than Silenus. If I were writing this for the theater, I might have Phaethon crash-land down to operate as the judge of the winged-horse race. Icarus should also make an appearance—maybe a javelin hits him. Maybe a sun race, where everybody must fly as fast as they can towards the sun before their waxwings melt and they plummet to their deaths. Something of that sort. To be determined. Oh! Icarus hauls the sun closer to the actors to shed more light on the games, and so melts everything in a blast of sun.

ZOSIME: What would you title this comedy?

ISOKRATES: Let me think. Maybe: *The Clouds Above the Clouds*. Such a title would one-up Aristophanes.

GLYKERA: Zosime, you left Rhodes not long after Demetrius's abortive siege, right?

ZOSIME: Right, when I was very young; it was my father's decision to move the family to Athens.

GLYKERA: So you know of the helepolis Demetrius used, the one invented by Polyidus; a siege tower nine stories tall, requiring almost 4,000 men to haul it.

ZOSIME: I witnessed it myself, yes.

GLYKERA: So you saw, then, how imperious, yet unavailing was that helepolis. Rhodes did not fall. Demetrius the Besieger and his besieging *tekhne* flopped.

ZOSIME: What is the objection you're making?—that *tekhne* fails to accomplish its crafter's ends on occasion? I accept that. Failure is formative. Archytas probably fell into various mathematical errors along his way to mathematical mastery.

GLYKERA: I understand your point, and I withdraw my point, for the moment.

ISOKRATES: Glykera, thank you for the anecdote. Demetrius's helepolis is certainly going into *The Clouds Above the Clouds*.

ZOSIME: You are hearing my conjecture for the first time, whereas I have had months to ruminate on it, so maybe I am unjustly assuming that you are filling in some needed premises that I have not presented.

GLYKERA: You think mortals may, through progress in math, philosophy, and craft, become Zeus. I think that's clear. And I think *our* response is clear as well, as Pindar put it:

> *Two things alone*
> *Look after the sweetest grace of life*
> *Among the fine flowers of wealth,—*
> *If a man fares well and hears his good name spoken.*
> *Seek not to become Zeus!*
> *You have everything, if a share*
> *Of these beautiful things comes to you.*
> *Mortal ends befit mortal men.*

ISOKRATES: It is no surprise to me that you admire Pindar, Glykera.

ZOSIME: Glykera, you spoke earlier of our "relations of likeness" to the gods. You know well that our poets freely mix mortal and immortal through patrilineal and matrilineal lines. You even said that human life is divinity with a mortal wound; I loved that thought. It instantly brought Hephaistos to mind—the crippled and fatherless blacksmith-god, god of the forge and *tekhne*, who crafted Artemis's arrows, Apollo's chariot, and, it is sometimes said, even Zeus's thunderbolts. Without this lame-footed god, Glorious Zeus would have no thunderbolts. Have you ever wondered why the god of invention is lame? Why a lame god? Mightn't it be that *tekhne* closes that abyss? *Tekhne* earns for this otherwise un-Olympian being, a being rejected by his mother, even cast from heaven by her as a shame and disgrace, a place at the banquets of Olympus. Mightn't it be that? Humankind is mortally handicapped, far more disadvantaged than Hephaistos, yet Hephaistos shows how the abyss might be overcome.

ISOKRATES: Do you wish to render your golden apple to the Hephaisteion down there?

ZOSIME: Not quite.

ISOKRATES: Well don't forget that Hephaistos forged the chains that shackled Prometheus, the human-loving benefactor whom you probably admire, given how you forethink to the *eschaton*.

ZOSIME: Zeus, of course, ordered that; Hephaistos was compelled to it. Aeschylus has Hephaistos say it thus: *But for me—I do not have the nerve myself to bind with force a kindred god upon this rocky cleft assailed by cruel winter.* And later, Hephaistos laments: *Alas, Prometheus, I groan for your sufferings.* Aeschylus's Hephaistos speaks of kinship and companionship with Prometheus. Aeschylus elsewhere, remember, speaks of Athenians as "sons of Hephaistos"—through Erechtheus, of course. As a tease to Alcibiades, Socrates traced his lineage back to Hephaistos via Daedalus.

ISOKRATES: So ugliness runs in the family. What's the point?

GLYKERA: Through Erechtheus, we are also the "sons of Athena"—Athena who, unlike Hephaistos, raised Erechtheus. Here I would forward the case that Athena is equal to or greater than Hephaistos in invention. Athena *Ergane*—Athena of works—is the goddess of those crafters "on the anvil with heavy hammer," as Sophokles wrote. Your Rhodians, according to Pindar, excel all others in craft *because of* Athena; craft was Athena's *gift* to them. With respect to master craftsmanship, Homer gives equal due to Athena and Hephaistos:

> *As a master craftsmen washes*
> *gold over beaten silver—a man the god of fire*
> *and Queen Athena trained in every fine technique*

ZOSIME: Yet Athena never invented golden handmaidens, as Hephaistos did. I presume, Glykera, you know the passages of the *Iliad* about the golden handmaidens, and much better than I know them. Would you mind reciting them?

GLYKERA: With pleasure.

> *Hephaistos left his forge and hobbled on.*
> *Handmaids ran to attend their master,*
> *all cast in gold but a match for living, breathing girls.*
> *Intelligence fills their hearts, voice and strength their frames,*
> *From the deathless gods they've learned their works of hand—*

ZOSIME: Perfect. Thank you. This returns me to my "madness." Suppose Hephaistos's handmaidens, whose level of intelligence Homer does not specify, were as intelligent as Pythagoras or Archytas, or greater even. Suppose these automata, as Homer calls them, learned math and studied harmonics, mechanics, biology, astronomy, and all the sciences—doing so without distraction, without sleep, without death.

ISOKRATES: Instead of Milo-Archytas, you now posit a Talos-Archytas. No thank you.

GLYKERA: I will just assume, Zosime, that you do not wish to answer the question of whether Athena is equal or greater than Hephaistos in craft.

ZOSIME: Honestly, yes. I do not care if Athena is equal or greater in craft than Hephaistos. I am happy to concede, if blank concession holds any value to you, that Athena is the greatest in craft; my point is not about the gods *per se*.

GLYKERA: I figured. But bear in mind that I'm always—always—ready to revisit this comparison. I know and love Athena's stories through and through.

ISOKRATES: Anyhow, there is something tendentious in your mention of the golden handmaidens of Hephaistos, Zosime, for you fail to mention Pandora, whom Hephaistos fashioned too. Why the omission?

ZOSIME: My point is not about Hephaestus as such. My point concerns *tekhne* and the future of *tekhne*.

GLYKERA: Anything based on Hesiod's nonsense ought to be left out, Isokrates.

ISOKRATES: Except, you'll recall, that Pandora herself decorates the pedestal of the *Athena Parthenos* in the Parthenon. Pheidias did not think the golden handmaidens worth sculpting, but Pandora he found worthy. So, *my* point is not about Hesiod's nonsense as such, but concerns hope and the future of hope. Zosime, ultimately, peddles hope to us. Well, we already know the story of Hope, of Elpis; it is Pandora's story. Why does little blind Elpis sit trapped in the pithos of Pandora? Why? We humans think and puzzle about Pandora's fatal dowry. We ask ourselves: Why did the gods conspire to "gift" us with Pandora, and with her pithos, full of such odious calamities as old age and disease? Perhaps, we tell ourselves, there may be one more gift, one *good* gift, one gift secretly deposited into that pithos by some anonymous divinity and secret benefactor of humanity—perhaps a second Prometheus. Perhaps the gift of a total cure. Perhaps. Perhaps. Perhaps. So, full of hope, we peep inside—as we always will, again and again. What do we find? We find our own hope, smirking hideously up at us, peeping back with its blind eyes, as the mirror of our own pitiful face in its blind and grinning expectation and stupefaction; and thus we see our own hopes as one more evil; and to see even our hope as evil, our own desire and expectation for goodness as evil—that is Zeus's masterpiece of vengeance. That is why Zeus keeps hope there in the bottom of Pandora's pithos, eternally waiting for us.

ZOSIME: I think you've interpreted that story too darkly, Isokrates.

ISOKRATES: Probably.

ZOSIME: Hesiod misleads you. Though if true, if that's how one ought to think of hope, and so abandon hope, then one may do so, if one can, if one wants.

GLYKERA: "A man should give care to noble hope," Pindar wrote for Kleandros of Aegina.

ISOKRATES: Sure, but Zosime's hope out-Pindars Pindar. It's over-hope. Pindar would giggle at it, as I do. I simply prefer, as Socrates put it, the "single night" of eternity, the sleep of death, undisturbed by dreams. As Glykera's former teacher, Epicurus, professed, it is nothing to fear. Perfect sleep at the end of my perfect life; the whole of it kindles me with cheer, even a fair measure of nonchalance, as you see in these twinkling eyes. I don't want hope.

ZOSIME: Leaving aside your hope for a dreamless death, I

believe you. And I hope you get what you want.

ISOKRATES: You sound like me now.

ZOSIME: Except I have not *yet* made any positive claims about an afterlife.

ISOKRATES: I prophesy you will, or else I misunderstand the word "yet."

ZOSIME: Isokrates, I think you've misunderstood my *tentative* case for collective progressive strengthening to the uppermost limit. It was not a defense of our actual immortality.

ISOKRATES: I probably have misunderstood you and your hope in uppermost *tekhne.*

GLYKERA: Isokrates, you quoted the *Phaedo* only to then ignore its greatest part, the "blessed hope" of Socrates and the proofs of the soul's immortality.

ISOKRATES: So I did, but for good reason: Socrates was chattering and talking about things which do not concern me.

ZOSIME: Your fate in death does not concern you?

ISOKRATES: I know my fate. I will scatter like smoke. My works will vanish too, since most copyists never prioritize the works of comedians, especially comedians who've never won a contest. They always copy Pindar's epinikia and all "glorious," "moral," or "logical" works. Laughter comes after logic. Though I suppose I agree with that ordering, but in a different sense than that of the copyists. Perhaps on my gravestone I will have inscribed a tautology for these moralizers and logicians: *Laughter will have the last laugh.*

ZOSIME: Or not, Isokrates. Or not. You've heard that a grand
   Mouseion with a great library is being built in Egypt by
   Ptolemy II Philadelphos. The library is to be supervised by
   the scholar Zenodotos.

GLYKERA: I've heard this news.

ZOSIME: Hellas's treasures flood into Delphi as dedications,
   now all Hellas's written works will flood into Ptolemy's
   Mouseion, to be studied, organized, preserved, and copied
   indefinitely—comedies included, even the uncrowned
   comedies. It will be Mnemosyne's bulwark. The Anti-Le-
   the.

ISOKRATES: I thought you were our Cassandra of the deepest future. Where's your Abydos moment now? You would
   agree with me that the Mouseion and its library will vanish
   in time, even as faraway Hymettos over there will vanish.

ZOSIME: I suppose, yes. Ptolemy's library will vanish, but the
   contents *may be passed on* to the next library, one perhaps
   greater than Ptolemy's, and then on again to the next library, even greater, and to the next, ever greater, and so
   on, indefinitely.

GLYKERA: I envision librarians in a lampadephoria.

ISOKRATES: Ever more golden, no doubt, is the torch's light
   as it is relayed from librarian to librarian. You are looking
   away, so far away, Zosime, to some golden epoch; you've
   been overcome by the perennial temptation of goldenism,
   as I call it. Homer goldenized the past to the denigration
   of his contemporaries:

   *But the son of Tydeus grasped in his hand a stone—a mighty deed—
   one that not two men could bear, such as mortals now are; yet lightly
   did he wield it even alone.*

Yet, curiously, even during that long-ago age of heroic Hector and Achilleus, Homer has old man Nestor, who had lived past two generations of mortal men, and could thus lament a lived contrast, complain:

In earlier times I moved among men more warlike than you, and never did they despise me. Such warriors have I never since seen, nor shall I see, as Peirithous was and Dryas, shepherd of the people, and Caeneus and Exadius and godlike Polyphemus, and Theseus, son of Aegeus, a man like the immortals. Mightiest were these of men reared upon the earth; mightiest were they, and with the mightiest they fought, the mountain-dwelling centaurs, and they destroyed them terribly.

Hesiod, without question, was a fusty proponent of golden-ism—Plato too. I am exhausted by these "ages." The gold, silver, bronze, wood, mud, and fecal ages. It is all but one age, though it is seen variously by the Argos Panoptes of human moods.

ZOSIME: I'm speaking of the future, not the past.

ISOKRATES: Same difference. Same tortured difference. All of this paradise-mongering amounts to a mere *looking-away* from one's own life, and the dispossession of one's cheer. For the elderly, the past is paradise; for the young, the future.

ZOSIME: Have I lost my cheer, Isokrates? I look forward, backward, downward, upward, and all around, as all Hellenes should, and *that* has cheered me.

GLYKERA: Isokrates, you are harsher than Zoilus.

ISOKRATES: What's your criticism of Zoilus?

ZOSIME: Isokrates has set a trap of irony for you, Glykera.

GLYKERA: I like it. I like your cunning humor, Isokrates. If I were to criticize Zoilus, you would call me Zoilus's Zoilus, or something of that kind.

ISOKRATES: Probably, yes.

GLYKERA: Is your favorite word "probably"?

ISOKRATES: Possibly.

ZOSIME: Today, Isokrates, the three of us can travel from the waves of the Adriatic to the reeds of the Nile to the shores of the Indus River, requiring only *one* language for safe passage, our Hellenic tongue. Such cosmopolitan times are producing *universal* fruits. Though we should confess that Alexandria now outshines Athens in *tekhne*.

GLYKERA: Yes, but Athens remains the philosophical navel of Alexander's new world.

ZOSIME: My point is that civilization has *strengthened* since the age of infant Isokrates. And also since the age of that other Isokrates, the rhetorician, whose words, spoken well before our new age, capture the universality of our age: "Our city has caused the name of Hellenes to appear no longer a sign of blood, but of mind; it is those who share our culture who are called Hellenes rather than those who share our blood."

ISOKRATES: This is pure goldenization.

ZOSIME: You do not think that Hellas has strengthened?

ISOKRATES: Temporarily.

ZOSIME: What about human life itself? Democritus theorized that the first humans lived anarchic bestial lives; lives like Polyphemus, who was a law unto himself. Actually, their lives were *worse* than Polyphemus's life, since our ancestors had no language, no fire, no tools, no shelter, no livestock—nothing but the sparse pickings of the wilderness. The terror of that wilderness, the terror of its carnivores, its winters, and its thousand other miseries, drove these firstlings into small tribes. Among these haphazard groupings of mutually incomprehensible lives, which were scattered randomly across the globe, vocalizations became language, became symbols, became organized communal life, which then allowed for the development of fire, agriculture, crafts, and all such societal goods. Our ancestors, says Democritus, then learned weaving from the spider, housebuilding from the swallow, and singing from the swan and nightingale. From wilderness to Acropolis, that is the story of our past, if Democritus's theory is correct.

GLYKERA: I have long thought that Democritus's theory of social development is correct.

ISOKRATES: It is the most persuasive account, sure—civilization from the wolf-thickets. It reminds me of a line from Empedocles: "Alas, wretched race of mortals, unhappy ones, from what conflicts and what groans did you come into being."

GLYKERA: I was persuaded of Democritus's anthropology by Leontion and Epicurus.

ISOKRATES: I grudgingly like it, despite the fact that it enables your optimism. I would add this update: All humanity still huddles incoherently to ward off terror; that is not just our beginning, but our ending and all the middle.

ZOSIME: This huddle against death is a growing huddle, and may grow *forever*.

ISOKRATES: So, none of you hold that Prometheus formed humans from the earth?

GLYKERA: The origin of human life is a deeper riddle than the origin of human society.

ZOSIME: I do not hold to any origin story; they are all extremely underdeveloped. However, I lean toward an amalgam of Anaximander's and Empedocles's views.

GLYKERA: I hold something *close* to Anaximander's view. But before I assume I know what you mean, explain.

ZOSIME: After the deluge, in the time of Deukalion and Pyrrha, the earth is said to have warmed and from its new expanses of mud, as from a womb, animals slowly germinated; new and innumerable species grew autochthonously from the mud. The general assumption is that these beings sprung completed, like Athena from the head of Zeus, or Pegasus from Medusa's neck. Some refine the claim by clarifying that these creatures sprung as completed *embryos* or *juveniles*, not as complete adults. Anaximander reasoned so, yet he examined further, to account for the prior and ultimate origination of humans before the flood. Since, he observed, the human body requires a period of gestation followed by a dangerously extended period of maturation outside the womb, a protective agent or medium would have been required to nurse the first humans to fullness. He claimed, on this basis, that the human animal originally gestated inside a host fish, as a sort of symbiotic embryo.

GLYKERA: Epicurus once spoke to us of Anaximander's theory. Epicurus indicated that, if a human body were to gestate inside of a fish or fish-like creature, some resemblance of parts and functions would be necessary between the human body and the body of the fish. As anybody can observe, many matings of animals result in nothing. Some matings result in mixtures, but sensible mixtures, from animals mostly resembling each other. A resemblance is required. For Epicurus, the required resemblances exist in the kinds, motions, *and* configurations of the indivisibles.

ISOKRATES: So where are my gills and fins?

GLYKERA: Gills and fins may not be the required resemblances. Nor scales.

ZOSIME: Or, even if such parts are required to allow for human gestation in fish, the argument may be maintained; for Anaximander chose his words carefully, saying that humans *originally* resembled fish. This allows that any original resemblance may have been lost in successive generations, as a mother with blue irises may produce children whose irises are hazel, and those children may then produce only hazel-eyed children, and so on.

ISOKRATES: My grandfather's breath reeked of low tide. Does this count as a resemblance?

GLYKERA: An irrelevant one, yes.

ZOSIME: Empedocles is a good supplement to Anaximander, for Empedocles said that "the same are hair and leaves and the thick feathers of birds and scales on strong members." Resemblances exist everywhere, and these, in symbiotic combinations, may help Anaximander's case.

ISOKRATES: Yes, but Empedocles thought he had lived as "a bush and a bird and a silent fish in the sea." More Hellenic madness—a man as a bush, a bird, and a fish.

ZOSIME: Why not? As the advice of Archilochus goes:

Nothing is unexpected or sworn impossible,
nothing is amazing since Olympian Father Zeus
made night out of high noon, hiding the light
of the blazing sun; and damp fear came upon men.
Since then all things are credible and expected
by men: Let nothing you see amaze you even if
animals take the place of dolphins in their salty
pasture, and love the echoing waves of the sea
more than dry land, while dolphins take to the wooded hills.

GLYKERA: Empedocles, though, meant the migrations of soul through bodily forms.

ZOSIME: Yes, that's true, but he also spoke of bodily forms themselves in a sort of migration, if I may stretch that word. These bodily migrations involve fissionings and fusionings; what Empedocles called "Strife" and "Love." Empedocles thought the unifying force of Love and the disunifying force of Strife powered interactions between the "roots" or elements of the world, and did so *by chance.* These chance interactions produced and will forever produce such mixtures as ox-headed men and man-headed calves.

GLYKERA: Such as Isokrates.

ISOKRATES: My father was an ox-headed man and my mother a woman-headed calf, so yes, though I unfortunately inherited all the human attributes, unlike Demosthenes, who inherited an ox's chin.

GLYKERA: You're so utterly convivial. You turn insults against you into your advantage.

ISOKRATES: Such are the benefits of knowing and desiring your own advantage.

ZOSIME: From the mixtures I spoke of, some just happen to be well-suited for survival in their environments. As Aristotle summarized in his *Physics*:

Why not suppose that nature acts not for something or because it is better, but of necessity? Zeus's rain does not fall in order to make the grain grow, but of necessity. For it is necessary that what has been drawn up is cooled, and that what has been cooled and become water comes down, and it is coincidental that this makes the grain grow. Similarly, if someone's grain is spoiled on the threshing floor, it does not rain in order to spoil the grain, and the spoilage is coincidental.

Why not suppose, then, that the same is true of the parts of natural organisms? On this view, it is of necessity that, for example, the front teeth grow sharp and well adapted for biting, and the back ones broad and useful for chewing food; this result was coincidental, not what they were for. The same will be true of all the other parts that seem to be for something. On this view, then, whenever all the parts come about coincidentally as though they were for something, these animals survived, since their constitution, though coming about by chance, made them suitable for survival. Other animals, however, were differently constituted and so were destroyed; indeed they are still being destroyed, as Empedocles says of man-headed calves.

GLYKERA: By Hermes! You are blessed by Mnemosyne with an exceptional memory.

ZOSIME: Never mind my memory; mind the ideas. Aristotle attacked this position on several fronts. He wrote that such natural attributes "come to be as they do either always or usually, whereas no result of luck or chance comes to be either always or usually." Moreover, these infrequencies will be mere errors, a result of a "defective principle," and will thus be, like a defective seed, degenerative instead of generative.

ISOKRATES: I believe I was about 26 or 27-years-old when Aristotle fled Athens. Maybe 28?

ZOSIME: Interesting.

ISOKRATES: I was not a terribly interesting young man, but thank you. What is interesting, however, is that I was a tragedian at that time.

GLYKERA: I'm sure Zosime is anxious to finish her point, Isokrates.

ISOKRATES: Whoops! Yes, absolutely, please continue, Zosime.

ZOSIME: I'll be concise.

ISOKRATES: Concise is nice.

ZOSIME: How about this concision: Empedocles claimed that the cosmos cycles *forever* through the operations of love and strife. Forever is a long time, no?

ISOKRATES: The longest.

ZOSIME: So, while it is unimaginably infrequent that all natural organisms should agglomerate by chance into the diverse and specialized forms we observe today, all with an apparent *telos*, one should remember that, if it is possible at all, then it is *bound to happen at least once* in an everlasting cycle.

GLYKERA: I'm not sure of this. That antecedent clause, "if it is possible at all," worries me. Is there a possible land in which every seed is defective, yet in which every seed germinates into a healthy plant? It seems to me that "defective seed" *just means* the preclusion of a healthy plant. So, I doubt the possibility in your conditional. If it is impossible, then no amount of time will make errors fruitful.

ISOKRATES: My errors have been fruitful.

GLYKERA: While that's the utterance of a healthy soul, it is also an equivocation in regards to what I said.

ZOSIME: Are these occurrences "errors"? I don't know. I'm only thinking about material and efficient causes.

ISOKRATES: If I may recap: you said, Zosime, that you hold some hybrid view formed from Anaximander's view and Empedocles's view. So do you, an Anaximander-headed Empedocles, therefore hold that humans originated from an ox-headed fish-baby? And from these extremely humble origins, you maintain that humans may become a Talos-headed Archytas-Typhon with Milo's musculature?

ZOSIME: You know the story of Zeus changing a colony of ants into a population of human beings.

ISOKRATES: Yeah. The Myrmidons.

ZOSIME: Do you believe that?

ISOKRATES: No, surely not.

ZOSIME: Neither do I, but I like the idea of a transformation of a weaker and simpler being into a stronger and more complex being. You've probably noticed that my favorite type of transformation is from simpler and weaker to more complex and stronger.

GLYKERA: I guess that would be my preference as well, when put so starkly.

ISOKRATES: That preference is probably universal, at least in regards to one's own strength and the strength of one's favorites. It is not so much a preference for one's enemies.

ZOSIME: In his work on embryology, Aristotle observed that the developing animal embryo begins simple, as a potency or *dynamis*, and then gradually differentiates into the organs; he rejects the pangenesis theory of Democritus, in which the embryo is a fully-formed body in miniature, whose maturation therefore involves only scaling up in size. For Aristotle, a form-principle operates in the development of the embryo from undifferentiated particle to newborn. Something *instructs* embryonic development.

GLYKERA: Yet another tension with the chance theory of Empedocles.

ZOSIME: Maybe. But what if these form-principles *themselves* developed from simpler states into their more complex states?

GLYKERA: A form-principle of form-principles?

ZOSIME: I don't know if that phrasing clarifies or obscures my hypothesis. It does seem that a skeptic may ask: *Is there a form-principle for this form-principle of form-principles?* The question may go on infinitely. I don't know if the instructions themselves need further instructions.

GLYKERA: I'm sympathetic to your hypothesis, despite the potential regress of form-principles. Instead of the chaos of bizarre complex attributes haphazardly mutating into other bizarre complex attributes, where nature eventually selects out a minority of these chance combinations, as Empedocles held, one begins with the embryos of something simpler, such as fish, to take Anaximander's example, and through some selection on the instructions *themselves*, as they pass from generation to generation, comes the form-principle for a human embryo.

ISOKRATES: Ergo, it is true that the great-grandparents of the Myrmidons were ants.

ZOSIME: For ants to become humans, I assume it would require time scales for which we have no common term.

ISOKRATES: I believe the time-term "never" is the term the commoners would use.

GLYKERA: Why stop at ants? Why not think that humans arose from mere stone, as the story of Deukalion and Pyrrha says?

ISOKRATES: Demosthenes has turned back into a stone, as you can see. Not even the Neades could wake him.

ZOSIME: Origins from stone and earth are not absurd to those who believe themselves to be the descendants of an autochthonous human group, as many Athenians believe. My radical daydream is just that: an autochthonous simple that changed, over eons, into present humanity, and which will change, over eons, into celestial life. Regarding the happiness of one's life, Solon told us to "look to the end." I've looked to the end—not only of my life, but of all life.

ISOKRATES: To your Solon, I counter with Simonides of Keos: "All things come to one hideous Charybdis, heroic excellence and wealth alike." That is all of it, Zosime. Time takes all. In the end, we're all Priam.

GLYKERA: Zosime, it is a beautiful daydream; like the Helios colossus, a victory tribute to robust Rhodian hopes.

ISOKRATES: And to brassy gigantism.

ZOSIME: Is not one of the final counsels of Aristotle's *Ethics* his urging us to make ourselves immortal, insofar as we can?

We ought not to follow the proverb-writers, and "think human, since you are human," or "think mortal, since you are mortal." Rather, as far as we can, we ought to be pro-immortal, and go to all lengths to live a life that expresses our supreme element.

GLYKERA: Yes. Plato and Aristotle both wanted to imitate the divine, and as the divine is characterized by contemplation, philosophy was for them the imitation of the divine or *supreme* element. Plato's *Timaeus* tells us that the eye was crafted by the Demiurge not for merely earthly sights, but to gaze up at the perfectly circular and rational movement of the stars, that is, for the highest ends. Plato thought divinization possible through the self-purifications of philosophy, but Plato's divinization is discarnate.

ZOSIME: And for Aristotle, the entire world strives for god-likeness. The world's *telos* is *theos*.

GLYKERA: I suppose it may be put that way, but I may retract this approval if it is abused.

ZOSIME: Plato and Aristotle did not see the potential in the craftsmen, as I see their potential, for the attainment of godhood.

ISOKRATES: If you are proposing a civilization ruled by craftsmen, you are proposing Plato's nightmare.

GLYKERA: I think it is fairer to say that Aristotle *did* recognize the marvelous potential of craft:

For if every tool could accomplish its own work, obeying or anticipating the will of others, like the statues of Daedalus, or the tripods of Hephaestus, which, says the poet, "of their own accord entered the

> *assembly of the Gods"—if, in like manner, the shuttle would weave*
> *and the plectrum touch the lyre without a hand to guide them, master*
> *craftsmen would not need servants, nor masters slaves.*

In principle, the craftsmen could create a servantless and slave-
    less society.

ISOKRATES: "Could create." I wager we would discover new
    purposes for slaves, not new tendernesses.

ZOSIME: Glykera, I agree; Aristotle affirms our profound *po-
    tential*, which is so often and overwhelmingly missed and
    disregarded; but I wonder if Aristotle, like the rest of us,
    underestimated our *fullest* divine potential.

GLYKERA: Well, was our divine potential ever actualized?

ZOSIME: What do you mean?

GLYKERA: Aristotle thought that there have been infinitely
    many civilizations, infinitely many risings and collapsings
    of civilization. Plato, I believe, held a similar view, in his
    Timaeus, though without supposing *infinitely* many civiliza-
    tions—only immensely many. My point is this: If there
    have been infinitely many civilizations, why did none of
    them attain *theos*? With infinitely many civilizations, one
    should expect at least one of them to have attained divin-
    ity.

ZOSIME: You assume that none of these civilizations became
    divine.

GLYKERA: Fair enough.

ISOKRATES: Of the infinitely or immensely many extinct civ-
    ilizations, why should we assume that *our* civilization would
    be so fortunate as to survive long enough to make

ourselves, by whatever means available, divinely powerful?

ZOSIME: I do not make that assumption. I do not assume that *our* civilization will attain the perfection of the gods.

ISOKRATES: We agree on that.

ZOSIME: Glykera, tell us: if all things are only atoms and void, as Epicurus claims, then aren't the gods atoms and void? Isokrates and Zeus are composed of the same kind of atomic constituents.

GLYKERA: Yes, but not necessarily the same atomic shapes, nor the same configurations.

ISOKRATES: I think Zosime is right on this one. Zeus and I certainly spring from the same kiln.

ZOSIME: Atoms *as such*, that is what I meant.

GLYKERA: Yes. Unless Epicurus wishes to endorse a three-fold foundation, which he would not, then he must agree that we and the gods share the same fundamental seeds.

ZOSIME: Could Epicurus's gods be the *material* result of the progression of such immemorial societies of mortals?

GLYKERA: I suppose yes, but hesitantly. I do prefer your the-ogonic account to Hesiod's. Your theory does have a touch of Euhemeros in it; but by your lights, the exaggerated ex-altation of men into gods is literally true.

ISOKRATES: Gods of perfect painless tranquility begotten from rocks and insects. I have my next comedy.

GLYKERA: Are you an atomist, then, Zosime?

ZOSIME: I hold to no particular theory of bodies. Are you an atomist?

GLYKERA: I was Epicurean in all respects, yes; but now I am like you—I hold to no particular physics.

ISOKRATES: Glykera, if it is not too intrusive of me to ask, I've wanted to know: why did you leave your Epicurean community of friends?

GLYKERA: It is a complicated story, but nothing shameful. On the advice of Demetria, a fellow-philosopher in the garden, I began participating in the civic worship of Athena. "Piety is a great benefit to the pious," Epicurus said; meaning, of course, *not* a benefit to the gods; but I desired the sweet benefits of Athena. I fell in love with Athena, with an intensity that discomfited my Epicurean friends. I "lapsed" whole-heartedly to the civic gods and the "perilous" promotion of civic concord and good will. I relumed my hope for Athenians as a people of reciprocity and responsibility. Public and civic life is vital, especially today, where our world is all mercenaries and merchants, if there's a difference there. Epicurus, I should say, is not against civic life *per se*—civic action may be instrumental to secure or restore one's tranquil existence—but my intensity was "irrational." This is where *friendship*, so prized by Epicurus, was tested. Friendship for an Epicurean, ultimately, is not for the sake of friendship, nor for the sake of the friend, the unique person, but for the sake of *ataraxia*. I was "irrational," and my "irrationality" affected my friends; their *ataraxia* was jeopardized. Kindly enough, they acted otherwise, but stiltedly. It is pitiful, however, to be the object of pretended love. So, I left.

ISOKRATES: I hope there is no pretense in my friendliness.

GLYKERA: None. I trust your kindness and goodwill, both

you and Zosime. None of you seek a *justification* for friendship beyond that which is good for the friend; you look toward the good of your friends.

ZOSIME: Thank you. I trust you too, Glykera.

ISOKRATES: As do I, and I suppose I trust as loving children trust. Despite my age, I feel as though I am still a child. "O Solon, Solon, you Hellenes are all children." A prodigiously old Egyptian priest once said that to Solon, if Plato is to be believed.

GLYKERA: We are children to the old Egyptians, but they are children too, to some older world.

ISOKRATES: Children all.

ZOSIME: Egypt. Children. This is serendipitous—around the time I heard of Archytas's dove, I had a dream about an Egyptian child, a young girl of nine or ten years. She was playing along the Nile when, suddenly, a vision came to her—her and I, I mean; her vision was only my dream.

ISOKRATES: What was the vision?

ZOSIME: Sublimeness. Human beings flying extremely fast far above the clouds, like gods. And dancing on the moon. Some of the vision had no visual features, only cognitive—I simply knew. Each person carried with themselves all of the world's libraries.

ISOKRATES: Even Milo could not accomplish that feat.

ZOSIME: Such are dreams, but that feat was merely the beginning of many more wonders. We ate stars, but the stars were black. We were unbound by time. We lived every life.

GLYKERA: Your vision was of the gods.

ZOSIME: Yes, but it was us.

ISOKRATES: Here again speaks Salmoneus, who claimed
himself the equal of Zeus, and then Zeus himself.

ZOSIME: Yes, limits. Limits. Limits. Limits. So sings the cho-
rus of *The Bacchae*:

> *Unwise are those who aspire,*
> *who outrange the limits of man.*
> *Briefly, we live. Briefly,*
> *then die. Wherefore, I say,*
> *he who hunts a glory, he who tracks*
> *some boundless, superhuman dream,*
> *may lose his harvest here and now*
> *and garner death.*

So here Euripides warns us against superhuman dreams and
"god-encroaching dreams." Dionysos masked his mockery
of doomed Pentheus and dangled before his prey such
hopes as mine: "You shall win a glory towering to heaven
and usurping god's." Yes, you remind me enough of limits.
I know the fears of growing up.

ISOKRATES: They hurt, as does being flayed alive. No?

ZOSIME: Flayed Marsyas had the gaul to think himself superior to an immortal; the crime, after all, is evaluating mortal
existence above immortal existence, the lesser above the
greater life, which I never do. The point is obvious in the
story of Apollo and Koronis. Apollo fell in love with the
mortal woman Koronis, but Koronis preferred the embraces of the mortal man Ischys; for this preference, Koronis was punished. Shouldn't Koronis have preferred the
immortal god? Shouldn't we prefer the immortals? I grant

that we should not conflate our mortal lives with the lives of the immortals, but neither should we pretend to value a mortal life over an immortal life. We make the best of our mortal lives, as we must, but we should not pretend that we would not, if possessing the power, if possessing the wisdom, make for ourselves an immortal life of joy and vitality. I do not hold that mortal life is superior to divine life; I hold the opposite—that divine life is superior. We must *mature* into divinity. Therefore I say, as Aristotle said, that mortals *ought* to imitate the divine; but I desire *perfect imitation*—union.

GLYKERA: Zosime, answer this: do you think Odysseus was foolish to reject Kalypso's offer of an eternal, luxurious, and youthful life?

ZOSIME: Odysseus chose mortal freedom over immortal pampered immurement, which is not exactly a choice between mortality and immortality *all else being equal.*

ISOKRATES: If I may answer: I would have chosen Kalypso's immortal lap and pampering.

GLYKERA: We knew.

ZOSIME: Also, consider Odysseus's journey to the underworld, where he told the shade of Achilleus to "grieve no more," for Achilleus is honored as a god. Achilleus rebuked the "honor," saying he would prefer a debased form of living to ruling over the "breathless dead." The great hero himself preferred life over heroism. Might the shade of Odysseus now say the same? Was Achilleus wrong to yearn for life, even a debased life?

GLYKERA: I have not considered that, but my instincts oppose Achilleus.

ISOKRATES: Accept or don't, you are limited, Zosime, with the ironclad limits of our mortal kind. What fruit comes from your speculation and desiring? Euripides spoke well; you will lose your "harvest here and now" with these dreams. I do not live for Kalypso's lap. And, as a friend, you would dissuade me from languishing away my last few years with lust for Kalypso's lap.

ZOSIME: I doubt you would languish, you old goat-singer. You would host endless symposia, festoon your home with sprays of silver fir and their phallic cones, and crown the drunkest symposiast with a wreath of laurel.

ISOKRATES: All perfectly true, but my point is theoretical.

ZOSIME: You equate a broad rational prospect with a narrow priapic fantasy. The prospect I propose may be realized through a million different means, so it depends less on this or that particular. Your prospect requires Kalypso's existence, then her special favor. Good luck to you, Pseudo-Odysseus.

ISOKRATES: I love this. I love our candidness. We are like Aristotle's Indian parrot, who speaks human language, and, after drinking wine, becomes "more saucy than ever." Audacious flying creatures, that is what the three of us have become on this hilltop; we're ready to leap off and soar up forever.

GLYKERA: Maybe we have become Archytas's doves.

ISOKRATES: Intoxicated Archytan doves.

ZOSIME: How far could a *perfect* Archytan dove fly? Isokrates said we're ready to soar up *forever*.

ISOKRATES: Figuratively. I meant only that I could enjoy

discussing these lovely thoughts *forever*.

GLYKERA: Were you hinting, Zosime?

ZOSIME: Yes.

GLYKERA: Come out with it. How far could a perfect Archytan dove fly?

ZOSIME: You may know of Archytas's thought experiment about the unlimitedness of reality.

ISOKRATES: Refresh my total ignorance of Archytas's cosmology.

ZOSIME: First, suppose there is a limit to the universe. If one arrives at this outermost limit, could one extend one's hand *beyond* this limit? Given the nature of space, it would be absurd to say that one could *not* extend one's hand beyond this supposed limit. And beyond any putative next limit, and beyond the next, and so on, infinitely. Therefore, our first assumption is false. Therefore, there is no limit to the universe.

GLYKERA: Clever. Archytas's thought experiment is compelling. I remember it from the garden. The unlimitedness and eternality of the universe is one of the few Epicurean theses I still hold, though on non-atomist grounds. Anaximander, Anaxagoras—so many thinkers held and hold to the unlimitedness of the universe.

ZOSIME: So, theoretically, the perfect Archytan dove *could* soar forever without hitting a limit. Do you agree, Isokrates?

ISOKRATES: I would need either mantic powers or a diver from Delos to get to the bottom of that.

GLYKERA: What do your instincts tell you?

ISOKRATES: That I should eat soon. Sturgeon, figs, and olives, to be philosophically exacting.

ZOSIME: Indulge my last bit of madness.

ISOKRATES: Alright. Glykera speaks of instincts. Zosime, earlier, spoke of dreams. My instincts offer nothing, one way or the other. However, I had a dream that is relevant to this problem; an old dream, caused, I assume, by a wonderfully sophistical conversation I had some nine years ago. Since we're permitted premises involving dreams, I'll share *my* dream. I dreamt that I was inside the Tholos down there in the agora. I was alone, and confused about the absence of the executive council. So, I moved to leave the Tholos and notify someone about this alarming absence of government, except I could not leave. In exiting, I entered. All my forward movement *out* of the Tholos was only forward movement *into* the Tholos. There was no *limit* to my movement, yet the space was limited.

GLYKERA: A comic's dream.

ISOKRATES: A tragedian's dream too. I was in a panic, trapped by pure nothing—simple space. Around and around, in a straight line.

ZOSIME: It is as if Sisyphus rolls his boulder up the mountaintop, where it rolls back down, but then Sisyphus must climb *up* the mountain to the boulder at its top, and roll it *up* the mountain again. It is always *up* the mountain *both ways*.

GLYKERA: I have difficulty imagining such a mountain.

ISOKRATES: It is easier to do so asleep.

ZOSIME: I will follow the advice of Archilochus that I gave you earlier: "Let nothing you see amaze you." I will suppose your Tholos-universe is a rational possibility.

ISOKRATES: A rational courtesy, thank you.

ZOSIME: You show such rational decorum.

ISOKRATES: It is my rational honor.

GLYKERA: Would it be rational to request a rational end to these rational jokes?

ISOKRATES: Go on, Zosime. What were you supposing?

ZOSIME: Well, even supposing your Tholos-universe is a *rational* possibility, why should we assume that there is only *one* such Tholos-universe? There could be infinitely many Tholoi.

ISOKRATES: Possibly. After all, it was a dream, so anything is possible.

ZOSIME: These Tholoi could exist in some *higher* Tholos, or *higher* space, where the gods live. As Daedalus flew above his labyrinth and could see, all at once, the work of his own self-entrapping genius, so perhaps the gods could fly above these infinitely many tholoi and see, all at once, an infinity of finite spaces.

ISOKRATES: Perhaps.

ZOSIME: Perhaps? Do you have any objections? Any concerns?

ISOKRATES: We are at our limit.

ZOSIME: Are we?

GLYKERA: "Those who make no trial win silences that know
them not."

ISOKRATES: Pindar?

GLYKERA: Who else?

ISOKRATES: Unfortunately, I am a little too hungry to continue with our conversation. But, for the sake of some
faint feeling of closure, I would love your answer, Zosime,
to our first and main matter; give away your golden apple
of discord—the cause of our "discord." Glykera gave hers
to the Acropolis; I, I suppose, give mine to Aphrodite's
Bed. You choose and then let's go eat in the agora. What
is *the most beautiful*?

ZOSIME: What is the most beautiful *what*?

ISOKRATES: Anything existent *today*. Something in Athens. I
don't know. You choose that too.

GLYKERA: Nothing will be chiseled in marble. There are no
stakes in a friendly game.

ZOSIME: Ok.

ISOKRATES: Ok.

ZOSIME: Metalsmiths, carpenters, cartwrights, moulders,
stone-cutters, rope-makers, and so many other craftsmen,
those who built the beautiful works on our Acropolis, I
give the golden apple to *them*. In their art, I see our future.
I give the golden apple to Kallikrates and Iktinos, the

Parthenon's architects. *They* are the most beautiful. *All* who build toward the divine are the most beautiful. Empedocles wrote that the souls of the wise will live "at the same hearth and table as the other immortals, relieved of mortal pains, tireless." I pray that all people, wise or foolish, will live at this same glorious hearth and table—all people. As Aristotle wrote:

For it is possible that the many, though not individually good men, yet when they come together may be better, not individually but collectively, than those who are so, just as public dinners to which many contribute are better than those supplied at one man's cost; for where there are many, each individual, it may be argued, has some portion of virtue and wisdom, and when they have come together, just as the multitude becomes a single man with many feet and many hands and many senses, so also it becomes one personality as regards the moral and intellectual faculties.

And I hope that somewhere this great divine work is already accomplished. I give the golden apple to every single being who worked toward this great work. *All of us*. Epicurus argued that every possible world is, somewhere, an actual world, yes?

GLYKERA: Yes. It is a consequence of there being infinitely many worlds. He called it *isonomia*, or equality under the law of *infinity*.

ZOSIME: I thought so. It is in this variety and infinity of worlds—worlds with other Glykeras, Isokrateses, and Zosimes—that my hopes live. Among these infinite worlds, perhaps mortal wisdom, craft, and virtue have actualized their highest potential, and won for all of us the highest divine life.

GLYKERA: Beautiful.

ISOKRATES: We had no rules, Zosime, but somehow you

broke them by giving *infinitely many* golden apples. What is more, Athens will need infinitely many altars for these infinitely many Unknown Gods.

GLYKERA: It's said that there are more gods in Athens than men; Zosime's *apeirotheism* is only the finishing touch to our religious reputation.

ZOSIME: This dream is possible.

ISOKRATES: If your dream is true, Zosime, then you have had your dessert before the meal.

GLYKERA: Speaking of which, are we ready to head back down for our midday meal?

ISOKRATES: Absolutely. I am ready to eat my age in figs.

ZOSIME: I wonder what Demosthenes would think of my "just so" story.

ISOKRATES: Let's wake him and ask for his opinion as we walk down.

My conversion — Ardalion, a comic actor during the reign of the Roman emperor Galerius, while performing his usual sardonic burlesque of Christians in their tortures and executions, abruptly stopped and professed a sudden faith in Christ to his audience; similarly did I discover the divine: with the eyes of a malist, looking forever away into infinite abysses, into infinitely many evolutionary pains.

Hope — My father would ask me, "Why is hope important?" His answer: "Without hope, there's no hope."

Telos — Embodied reason: techne. The *telos* of techne: omnipotence. What is the *telos* of omnipotence? *Omnifelicitatem*?

Voltaire Tech, Inc. — "If God did not exist, it would be necessary to invent him." This is a call to every inventor.

Fulfillment — Yes, we know of self-fulfilling prophecy. Self-fulfilling theology? Giambattista Vico wrote, "Just as God is the artifex of nature, so is man the God of artifices."

Regenesis — In the end, God was created, who, in the beginning, created the heavens and the earth.

Three Stages — Someone once wrote that there are three stages of Christmas in your life. 1: Believe in Santa. 2: Don't believe in Santa. 3: Be Santa.

A Heraclitean theodicy — A fragment attributed to Heraclitus, a spurious fragment, addressed to the Egyptians, goes as follows: "If they are gods, why do you lament them? If you lament them, you must no longer regard them as gods."[18] Something of this sort, something bespoke to a divine you and I and every other god, *may* be a worthy theodical vista.

---

[18] Translation by Kathleen Freeman

Bellum ad internecionem — Schopenhauer wrote, "To speak of peace and accord between [the sciences and religion] is very ludicrous; it is a *bellum ad internecionem*." If it is a war of extermination, it is fratricidal war of extermination; the parents, *our* existential needs, should look with horror on such belligerent offspring.

Yet there is no war of extermination here.[19] There are only reformations. One could argue that humankind has only one god, Proteus, who takes *every* divine name. It is questionable to commit to the existence of such a bright and ready-made concept as "religion," and it is self-minimizing to "understand" oneself by rejection or adoption of "religion"; we lose our roundness of character in such dichotomies and bromides.[20] This so-called battle, to quote Nancy Ellen Abrams, "generally pits a caricature of religion against a caricature of science."[21]

We should not rationalize away the *round* lives of Georges Lemaître, Catholic priest and parent of the Big Bang theory, or Gregor Mendel, Augustinian friar and parent of modern genetics. Seismology is still sometimes called "The Jesuit Science" due to the significant contribution of Jesuits to the field. A cultural multiverse creates us.

Schopenhauer did not recognize the "Religion of Technology," as David F. Noble calls the "millenarian promise of restoring mankind to its original god-like perfection" via craft, techne, science.

As Frank Tipler has written, "Either theology is pure nonsense, a subject with no content, or else theology must ultimately become a branch of physics." Is that a concession of defeat? I don't think so.

God of the gaps — The expression "God of the gaps" refers to a pseudo-explanatory patch for a gap in an explanatory account of some natural phenomena. Since Zenith is not an

---

[19] Quite the contrary. I recommend Peter Harrison's *The Territories of Science and Religion*.

[20] Or what Gelett Burgess would call "bromidioms"

[21] Nancy Ellen Abrams, *A God That Could Be Real*, xxix

explanation of anything, Zenith is not a god of the gaps. If one said, "Zenith explains the existence of the inflaton field," then one would be invoking a gap-god, but I offer no such hypotheses.

The Horn of Amalthea — We sometimes celebrate a scientific or technological discovery with mixed joy, sensing that the full exercise of these new natural powers will occur only after our deaths, and likely long after. We sometimes bemoan the fact that our economic, political, and even our ethical ecosystems under-utilize the fortunes of this frontier knowledge. The zenithist, however, can celebrate these achievements more immediately; for anything unlocked, or anything demonstrated to be "unlockable," nudges the zenith limit further and further away, into the ever more divine. Every natural power discovered dilates our vision of beings at that limit.

Caveat — My focus on science and technology should not be taken as devaluing or deprioritizing other activities and disciplines. I believe science and technology will be the proximate causes of the attainment of immortality and other augmentations, but science and technology are not the only goods. Innumerable activities, qualities, and irrepeatables give life its liveliness.

Nor should my focus on *natural* systems be construed as a rejection of non-natural systems. I want to extract as much as possible from the natural system *before* widening the domain of discourse to non-naturals, if only to accommodate scientifically inclined populations, of which I am one and for whom such metaphysical widening correlates with a narrowing of receptivity (and for whom hope and hopefulness, are more often vices or temptations to vice).

Scientism — Scientists have not yet proven scientism, so I suspend judgment.

A MEDITATION ON SCIENCE AND ZENITHISM

The goal of scientific activity is the complete *naturalistic* explanation over all things in the domain of discourse we call the *natural* world.

What is *naturalistic* explanation? What is *natural*? Is the natural the touchable, sensory-grounded, lawful, causal, dimensional, mechanical? Is it whatever is amenable to scientific inquiry? What is scientific inquiry? Thinkers from William Whewell[22] to Charles Sanders Peirce to Paul Feyerabend, and a thousand others, have applied themselves to these puzzles.

Feyerabend, infamously, disputed the alleged historical use of a singular or definite "scientific method." In *Against Method*, Feyerabend writes:

> The idea of a method that contains firm, unchanging, and absolutely binding principles for conducting the business of science meets considerable difficulty when confronted with the results of historical research. We find then, that there is not a single rule, however plausible, and however firmly grounded in epistemology, that is not violated at some time or other. It becomes evident that such violations are not accidental events, they are not the results of insufficient knowledge or of inattention which might have been avoided. On the contrary, we see that they are necessary for progress.

So, claims Feyerabend, scientists have collectively "violated" every putative rule to make scientific progress of some kind. Whether Feyerabend's claim is accurate or not, one might inquire: progress toward what *ultimately*?[23]

Of course, there is scientific progress toward solving this or that local problem, or making consistent some previously

---

[22] William Whewell coined the term "scientist" in 1833. The term was slow to take, since it is a Latin-Greek hybrid and thus was hard on the ears of prescriptive classicists. See Wootton, *The Invention of Science*, 27-29.

[23] "But enlightened Europe is not happy. Its existence is a fever, which it calls progress. Progress to what?" Benjamin Disraeli, from *Tancred*, Chapter 29.

inconsistent set of observation claims, or observing a predicted outcome, and so on. But what *ultimately*, if anything, do human beings *desire* from science? The first-order goal of scientific activity is complete naturalistic explanation over the natural world, but is there a second-order goal? Consider how William James, in "The Will to Believe," portrays the progress of science:

> When one turns to the magnificent edifice of the physical sciences, and sees how it was reared; what thousands of disinterested moral lives of men lie buried in its mere foundations; what patience and postponement, what choking down of preference, what submission to the icy laws of outer fact are wrought into its very stones and mortar; how absolutely impersonal it stands in its vast augustness, — then how besotted and contemptible seems every little sentimentalist who comes blowing his voluntary smoke-wreaths, and pretending to decide things from out of his private dream!

What do we expect to attain from all this "choking down of preference" and "submission to icy laws"? Why should one *not* jubilate down into opium-smoke-wreaths and private dreams? Why asceticism and submissiveness? I think Descartes captured the hope underwriting scientific asceticism:

> We may find a practical philosophy by means of which, knowing the force and the action of fire, water, air, the stars, heavens and all other bodies that environ us, as distinctly as we know the different crafts of our artisans, we can in the same way employ them in all those uses to which they are adapted, and thus render ourselves the masters and possessors of nature.[24]

Science is (to use Hannah Arendt's distinction in *The Human Condition*[25]) the contemplative life *used by* the active life, and

---

[24] Descartes, *Discourse on the Method of Rightly Conducting the Reason*
[25] Hannah Arendt had originally planned on titling (what became) *The Human Condition* with the evocative title *Amor Mundi* (Love of the World).

not the contemplative life alone and holy; or, using a similar distinction in Nietzsche's *The Gay Science*, it is *vis contemplativa* (contemplative power) joined to *vis creativa*.[26]

Francis Bacon,[27] one of the foremost boosters of the Scientific Revolution, stated unequivocally the goal of scientific activity:

> Now the true and lawful goal of the sciences is none other than this: that human life be endowed with new discoveries and powers.[28]

I would generalize Bacon's claim from "human life" to "life." Non-humans may be the recipients of these new powers, e.g., the veterinary sciences. Also, non-human persons, such as non-biological persons, would rightfully include themselves in this lawful goal. With that more inclusive amendment, I find Bacon's "goal" agreeable.[29]

---

[26] *The Gay Science*, Book Four, Aphorism 301. The *vis contemplativa* of Newton was driven by a desire to affiliate with the beating heart of all *creative* activity: "For Newton, then, to uncover the hidden logic of the universe was to understand, and in that sense identify with, the mind of its Creator. Thus, as a scientist with divine pretensions, Newton had already begun his ascent." David F. Noble, *The Religion of Technology*, 65

[27] "A married philosopher belongs in *comedy*," Nietzsche wrote in *On the Genealogy of Morals*. I disagree. Pythagoras married Theano of Crete; Confucius married Qiguan; Seneca married Pompeia Paulina; Machiavelli, who is perhaps Nietzsche's most important political influence, married Marrietta Corsini; and so on. None of these belong in comedy. Yet the marriages of some philosophers, I grant, do belong in comedy. The marriage of Francis Bacon to Alice Barnham (two porcine names ought to be our first hint) belongs in comedy. Bacon wrote *Novum Organum*, while wife Barnham, or the "Viscountess of St Albans," co-wrote *Novum Orgasm* with John Underhill. Yet, I totally exempt Barnham—of the adultery and cupidity; betrothal at eleven and marriage at thirteen must pour acid on one's maturation. So, Bacon's marriage is a tragicomedy.

[28] *The Philosophical Works of Francis Bacon*, ed. J. M. Robertson, 280

[29] "Perhaps more than anyone else before or since, Bacon defined the Western project of modern technology [...]." David F. Noble, *The Religion of Technology*, 49

"Human knowledge and power come to the same thing," writes Bacon, in a Foucauldian line. In Bacon's *New Atlantis*, a work of utopian fiction, one of the "Fathers" of Salomon's House, that House of ultra-ripened sciences, explains the purpose of the House:

> The end of our foundation [Salomon's House] is the knowledge of causes, and secret motions of things; and the enlarging of the bounds of human empire, to the effecting of all things possible.[30]

Zenith, being the theoretical universal maximum of scientific and technological power, the actually achievable maximum of all scales of mastery, the *most* effective effecting of all things possible, is the goal of science *ultimately*; this "goal" might even be a rephrased tautology. What other ideal might there be for the project of physical and cognitive mastery over reality *if not* maximal physical and cognitive mastery over reality? This is the relationship between science and Zenith; it is the relationship between means and ideal end.

In *Novum Organum*, Bacon writes "For rightly is truth called the daughter of time, not of authority."[31] Bacon's hope in the future of *veritas* reminds me of Charles Sanders Peirce's "epistemological eschatology," as Nicholas Rescher calls it, where the "opinion which is fated to be ultimately agreed to by all who investigate, is what we mean by the truth, and the object represented in this opinion is the real."

Such hope is dramatized in *eschatological science fiction* (ESF), such as Isaac Asimov's "The Last Question," Arthur C. Clarke's *Childhood's End*, and Olaf Stapledon's *Star Maker*. ESF explores the techno-scientific *eschaton*, or the utmost possible potency of science and technology; meditations on this ideal limit arguably qualify as *religious* meditations.

As John Dewey writes in *A Common Faith*:

---

[30] Bacon ends *New Atlantis* (A "work unfinished") with this preambulatory call to ascension: "THE REST WAS NOT PERFECTED."
[31] *Novum Organum*, Book I, Aphorism lxxxiv: "Recte enim Veritas filia Temporis dicitur, non Auctoritatis."

Understanding and knowledge also enter into a perspective that is religious in quality. Faith in the continued disclosing of truth through directed cooperative human endeavor is more religious in quality than is any faith in a completed revelation. [...] Faith in the possibilities of continued and rigorous inquiry does not limit access to truth to any channel or scheme of things. [...] It trusts that the natural interactions between man and his environment will breed more intelligence and generate more knowledge provided the scientific methods that define intelligence in operation are pushed further into the mysteries of the world, being themselves promoted and improved in the operation. There is such a thing as faith in intelligence becoming religious in quality.

This "faith in the continued disclosing of truth" (per Bacon, the continued endowment of powers) explains all the "patience and postponement," "choking down of preference," and "submission to icy laws" of the scientific human animal. The active-creative life of this animal is promised *untold powers* through science. It is no wonder that Nietzsche discovers continuity between magic and scientific asceticism:

> *Preludes to science.*— Do you really believe that the sciences would ever have originated and grown if the way had not been prepared by magicians, alchemists, astrologers, and witches whose promises and pretensions first had to create a thirst, a hunger, a taste for *hidden* and *forbidden* powers? Indeed, infinitely more had to be *promised* than could ever be fulfilled in order that anything at all might be fulfilled in the realm of knowledge.[32]

Science *promises* power and delivers. From preserving the precious human voice (by sound recording) and invaluable human image (by videography), from moon-landing to medical

---

[32] *The Gay Science*, Book Four, Aphorism 300. This aphorism continues to this Zenithistic line: "Did Prometheus have to *fancy* first that he had *stolen* the light and then pay for that—before he finally discovered that he had created the light *by coveting the light* and that not only man but also the *god* was the work of his own hands and had been mere clay in his hands?"

cures to a global information-sharing infrastructure (with the under-lauded powers we call the "search engine" and "ambient findability"[33]), and so on, science fulfills promises. Zenith is the *highest* promise of science.[34] My motto for progress: From "Eureka!" to Zenith.[35]

Again, Dewey: "Any activity pursued in behalf of an ideal end against obstacles and in spite of threats of personal loss because of conviction of its general and enduring value is religious in quality" (27).

I take considerable inspiration from Dewey's *A Common Faith*.[36] So considerable is the inspiration, I end my brief essay with Dewey's unmatchable words:

> It is the *active* relation between ideal and actual to which I would give the name 'God.' I would not insist that the name *must* be given.

> What I have tried to show is that the ideal itself has its roots in natural conditions; it emerges when imagination idealizes existence by laying hold of the possibilities offered to thought and action.

> The aims and ideals that move us are generated through imagination. But they are not made out of imaginary

---

[33] I borrow this term from Peter Morville's *Ambient Findability: What We Find Changes What We Become*

[34] I do not mean that science demonstrates the current existence of Zenith-beings, but that Zenith-state is the maximum of scientifically attainable power.

[35] That is, from the birth of science to its apotheosis. I use "Eureka!" as a metaphor for the beginning of science, and not as a claim that science began with Archimedes. In *The Invention of Science*, David Wootton contends (persuasively) that modern science (what we would simply call science) began in 1572, when Tycho Brahe saw a "new star," or nova [now called "Tycho's nova," in the constellation Cassiopeia]. So, perhaps: *From Tycho's nova to Zenith!*

[36] Though this inspiration is tempered by my leaning toward a particular existence claim: that Zenith-beings *exist*. Dewey would take my existence claim to be a hypostatization "due to a conflux of tendencies in human nature that converts the object of desire into an antecedent reality...." *A Common Faith*, 43

stuff. They are made out of the hard stuff of the world of physical and social experience. The locomotive did not exist before Stevenson, nor the telegraph before the time of Morse. But the conditions for their existence were there in the physical material and energies and in human capacity. [...] The process of creation is experimental and continuous.

POSITIVE APEIROTHEISM

In this essay, I will offer some support for what might be called "positive apeirotheism." Apeirotheism is the view that there exist infinitely many *theoi*, or gods (I use the term "gods" idiosyncratically—to refer to zenith beings). Positive apeirotheism is the view that there exist infinitely many zenith beings and that one result of this is an increased probability of human-friendly (and life-friendly) outcomes (e.g., positive immortality).

To begin, I examine the general nature of superintelligence, with much help from Nick Bostrom's *Superintelligence: Paths, Dangers, Strategies* (2014), and, using the concept of superintelligence, present a basic classification of zenith beings into positive, negative, or neutral, according to *our* evaluation of outcomes.

Secondly, I briefly consider the relationship between intelligence and motivation.

Thirdly, I sketch a set of "spatial profiles," that is, a set of possibilities regarding the omnipresence or bounded presence of zenith beings.

Fourthly, crossfading from Zenith's nature into the first "defense" of positive apeirotheism, I will offer a meditation on the metaethical knowledge base of maximal superintelligence and how this maximal knowledge may be better understood as both a cognitive and *visceral* knowledge.

After this all-too-preliminary work, I leap into two exploratory defenses of positive apeirotheism, the "Road to Damascus" and "Prometheus" arguments. These "exploratory defenses" are like sponges—full of holes, yet holding *some* water.

As the Canadian philosopher John Leslie said of his theory of "extreme axiarchism": "I certainly haven't *proved* its truth. Almost nothing of philosophical interest strikes me as being provable. I'd say my confidence in it is just a little over 50 percent."[37]

I would say that my confidence in these defenses equals Leslie's in his axiarchism.

---

[37] Jim Holt, *Why Does the World Exist*, 209

1.1 *Superintelligence and Its Problems*

Zenith may be defined as the maximal superintelligence.[38] Keep in mind that Zenith is a general description, not a name; a zenith being is *any* conscious being in an infinite natural system that has no cognitive *superior*, though that being may have cognitive equals (other zenith beings).

What is superintelligence? In *Superintelligence*, philosopher Nick Bostrom answers: "We can tentatively define a superintelligence as *any intellect that greatly exceeds the cognitive performance of humans in virtually all domains of interest*" (26). In Bostrom's *Superintelligence*, we are invited to seventh guess the safety of superintelligent AI.[39]

To be clear, the problem of Zenith's moral nature stems from the problem of superintelligence. The problem of superintelligence arises from what Bostrom calls the "orthogonality thesis," which holds that "intelligence and final goals are orthogonal: more or less any level of intelligence could in principle be combined with more or less any final goal" (130). Bostrom refers to a non-normative (or not "normatively thick") definition of intelligence, "something like skill at prediction, planning, and means-ends reasoning in general" (130).[40]

According to the orthogonality thesis, the final goals of a superintelligent AI need not be *good* final goals, nor even human-safe final goals. Superintelligent AI may have negative final goals, thus, it appears, Zenith may have negative final goals.

---

[38] As such, I assume a zenith being is postbiological, i.e., an entity that is not dependent on biology for its survival. It may be, however, that postbiological superintelligence *must* use biological processes to simulate certain mental states, e.g., possibly *your* mental states.

[39] Through forensic worrying, Bostrom aims to achieve "existential risk mitigation" (316).

[40] AI researcher Marcus Hutter, in his book *Universal Artificial Intelligence*, offers a list of intelligence's "faces": "creativity, solving problems, pattern recognition, classification, learning, induction, deduction, building analogies, optimization, surviving in an environment, language processing, knowledge [...]" (2).

This allows us to step back and classify three types of superintelligences, and thus three types of Zenith. In terms of outcomes *for us*, there are roughly three types of Zenith: Negative Zenith, Neutral Zenith, and Positive Zenith.[41]

A negative superintelligence is any superintelligence that is negatively disposed to us, has a use for us that results in a bad outcome for us, sees a threat from us (and promptly exterminates us), or creates a situation in which we become collateral damage.

We can extrapolate from negative superintelligence to negative *maximal* superintelligence, a.k.a. Negative Zenith, where the latter differs from the former only by degrees of power—the essential negativity remaining. Maximal superintelligence is another way of saying, simply, maximal intelligence.

Along with "Negative Zenith," we could hypothesize "Neutral Zenith," a "cold" maximal superintelligence, which is neither negatively nor positively disposed to us, has no use for us which would result in a bad or good outcome for us, does not see us as a threat (to promptly exterminate), or does not create a situation in which we are either collateral damage or collateral beneficiaries. Neutral Zenith is simply indifferent to us; for us, neither bad nor good results from its presence. These Epicurean gods of perfect ataraxia and impassibility simply do and feel nothing for us.

Finally, there could be "Positive Zenith," a maximal superintelligence that is positively disposed to us, has a use for us that results in a good outcome for us, or creates a situation in which we collaterally benefit.

In *Superintelligence*, Bostrom's primary interest is in negative superintelligence. Exploring the potential of superintelligence in "malignant failure mode," or monkey-paw mode, Bostrom

---

41 Regarding possible shifts, e.g. from neutral to negative or negative to positive, we might speak of a "zenith mean" through some set of times, which may give us zenith beings that are on *average* negative, on *average* neutral, or on *average* positive. For the sake of (preparative) simplicity, I will simply use "negative," "neutral," and "positive" as diachronically stable characterizations. Later, I will offer a defense, my "Prometheus argument," which does not require this stability (see footnote 77).

offers the hypothetical example of a superintelligent paperclip AI whose final goal is to maximize the quantity of paperclips. Presumably and perversely, this superintelligent paperclip maximizer would calculate that the maximum quantity of paperclips is a *cosmic* maximum, and thus the whole universe, everything convertible, must be, and therefore will be, converted into paperclips (or paperclip factories), including you and me.

Given a superintelligent agent's "decisive strategic advantage" over us, as Bostrom calls an overpowering asymmetry in competence, any conflict between human beings and a negative superintelligence will be nightmarishly faster and more ruinous than the Anglo-Zanzibar war, the shortest war on record, in which the British defeated Zanzibar forces in 38 to 45 minutes. The so-called "intelligence explosion" poses a greater existential risk than a nuclear explosion.[42]

Bostrom seeks a "controlled detonation" of the coming intelligence explosion: "Could we engineer the initial conditions of an intelligence explosion so as to achieve a specific desired outcome, or at least ensure that the result lies somewhere in the class of broadly acceptable outcomes?" (155) This is the so-called "control problem."

Control must be accomplished "*before* the system becomes superintelligent" and must be successful "in the very first system to attain superintelligence," since the first superintelligence will swiftly elude all subsequent efforts to shape it. Imperfect initial conditions could be *cosmically* destructive.

Bostrom wishes for "the daybreak of the posthuman age" (302) in which humanity "develop[s] into beatific posthuman spirits" (271). Precisely because of his yearning, Bostrom takes the control problem gravely. His gravity is preemptive. In his afterword to the paperback edition of *Superintelligence*, Bostrom writes, "I discourse at length on how the control problem might be hard and how superficially plausible solutions might fail; but the control problem could equally turn out to be easy"

---

[42] Bostrom defines an intelligence explosion as "a hypothesized event in which an AI rapidly improves from 'relatively modest' to a radically superhuman level of intelligence" (408).

(324). Bostrom hopes, but not laxly. Bostrom's way of hoping is akin to mine: hope through resistance training.

Bostrom divides the control problem into two categories: the capability control problem (controlling what superintelligence can do) and the motivation selection problem (controlling what superintelligence wants to do). After considering some capability control methods, such as "boxing," Bostrom admits that "capability control is, at best, a temporary and auxiliary measure. Unless the plan is to keep superintelligence bottled up forever, it will be necessary to master motivation selection" (226).[43]

Therefore, the preeminent control problem concerns motivation selection. Putting it plainly, Bostrom writes, "How can we get a superintelligence to do what we want? What do we want the superintelligence to want?" (256) The first question may be called the "value-loading problem" and the second question, the "value-selection problem."

Bostrom considers several candidate solutions to the value-loading problem, such as evolutionary selection, reinforcement learning, and "motivational scaffolding." I skip the value-loading problem and move to the value-selection

---

[43] Bostrom considers the possibility of an *a priori* hack that overpowers even extreme bottling. Imagine a superintelligent AI "bottled up" via "information deprivation" (167):

> Even without any designated knowledge base at all, a sufficiently superior mind might be able to learn much by simply introspecting on the workings of its own psyche—the design choices reflected in its source code, the physical characteristics of its circuitry. Perhaps a superintelligence could even deduce much about the likely properties of the world *a priori* (combining logical inference with a probability prior biased toward simpler worlds, and a few elementary facts implied by the superintelligence's existence as a reasoning system). It might imagine the consequences of different possible laws of physics: what kind of planets would form, what kind of intelligent life would evolve, what kind of societies would develop, what kind of methods to solve the control problem would be attempted, how those methods could be defeated" (166).

problem since the value-selection problem, as hopefully will be shown, is more germane to the problem of Zenith's moral nature.

There are two primary methods for value selection: direct specification and indirect normativity.[44]

Direct specification involves "explicitly formulating a goal or set of rules to be followed" (169). Among the several difficulties with direct specification, Bostrom captures, I think, the most formidable: "The dismal odds in a frontal assault are reflected in the pervasive dissensus about the relevant issues in value theory. No ethical theory commands majority support among philosophers, so most philosophers must be wrong" (257).

Specifying any *idée fixe* may prove treacherous. For example, superintelligence plus hedonist ethics may instantiate a cosmos of hedonium, or "matter organized in a configuration that is optimal for the generation of pleasure," (171) yet perversely instantiate an energy-efficient hedonium, sans "memory, sensory function, executive function, and language" (171). And that is one of the *pleasanter* perversions.

Such is the danger of every directly specified ideal. Every ideal law proposed *directly* would be proposed as laws were proposed under the Locrian Code of Zaleucus, the first written Greek law code: anyone proposing a law was required to do so with a rope around their neck, such that if the proposal failed (to persuade the legislature), the proposer was summarily strangled. In the case of superintelligence, the rope hangs around everybody's neck.

Indirect normativity, or indirect specification, fixes no ideal; instead "we specify a criterion or a method that the AI can follow, using its own intellectual resources to discover the concrete content of a merely implicitly defined normative standard." (408) Indirect normativity applies to the value-

---

[44] I hopscotch over Bostrom's discussion of "augmentation," or augmenting preexisting motivation systems, e.g., a whole-brain emulation (WBE) of a supererogatorily ethical human. Bostrom argues that an AI-first intelligence explosion is less risky than a WBE-first explosion (299).

selection problem what Bostrom calls the "principle of epistemic deference," a prudential imperative to defer to the conclusions of superintelligence, given the superior epistemic competence of superintelligence.

As for a criterion or method, Bostrom holds "coherent extrapolated volition" (CEV), a proposal by AI researcher Eliezer Yudkowsky, to be "the main prototype of the indirect normativity approach" (259). As defined by Yudkowsky:

> Our coherent extrapolated volition is our wish if we knew more, thought faster, were more the people we wished we were, had grown up farther together; where the extrapolation converges rather than diverges, where our wishes cohere rather than interfere; extrapolated as we wish that extrapolated, interpreted as we wish that interpreted.[45]

In lossy summary, CEV guides superintelligent AI to the discovery of *ideal humanity's ideal wish*, whatever that may be. Bostrom covers what he considers CEV's benefits: it "encapsulate[s] moral growth," "avoid[s] hijacking the destiny of humankind," "avoid[s] creating a motive for modern-day humans to fight over the initial dynamic," and "keep[s] humankind ultimately in charge of its own destiny" (262-264).

The phrase "initial dynamic" is important. "CEV is meant to be an 'initial dynamic,' a process that runs once and then replaces itself with whatever the extrapolated volition wishes" (264). CEV is like Wittgenstein's ladder, to be kicked away once the ascent has been accomplished. Once the ideal wish has been granted, we live *optimally* ever after.

For Bostrom, no good solution goes unprobed. CEV is "the merest schematic" with many "free parameters" (264) that require some binding, e.g., "Whose volitions are to be included?" (265).

Even if CEV's free parameters are well-bound, other "design choice" problems arise. What decision theory should AI implement? What epistemology?

Bostrom lets us take a tiny breath:

---

[45] Yudkowsky, *Coherent Extrapolated Volition* (2004)

It is not necessary for us to create a highly optimized design. [...] An imperfect superintelligence, whose fundamentals are sound, would gradually repair itself; and having done so, it would exert as much beneficial optimization power on the world as if it had been perfect from the outset (279).

[...] there is hope that if we but get the initial conditions for the intelligence explosion approximately right, then the resulting superintelligence may eventually home in on, and precisely hit, our ultimate objectives. The important thing is to land in the right attractor basin (278).

So, in this algorithmic and axiologic miasma, there is hope. As I will cover later, when considering the Prometheus argument, in an infinite natural system, infinitely much will land in the "right attractor basin."[46] For now, let us consider ourselves fortunate; we skated across very thin ice without falling into the bottomless and chilling waters of Bostrom's full analytic panic.

1.2 *Is the Orthogonality Thesis True?*

Zenith is a maximal superintelligence. In the previous section, I mentioned Bostrom's non-normative definition of intelligence: "something like skill at prediction, planning, and means-ends reasoning in general" (130). This definition allows for Bostrom's orthogonality thesis: "intelligence and final goals are orthogonal: more or less any level of intelligence could in principle be combined with more or less any final goal" (130). It is easy to imagine that *mere* prediction, planning, and means-end reasoning can be put in the service of any final goal. "Intelligence and motivation are in a sense orthogonal: we can think of them as two axes spanning a graph in which each point represents a logically possible artificial agent" (129).

---

[46] "[...] an attractor, i.e. a state of the world which contains the maximal amount of positive utility according to the value in question." Nick Bostrom, from "A Critical Discussion of Vinge's Singularity Concept" in *The Transhumanist Reader* (2013).

Accordingly, the maximal intelligence, that superintelligence farthest along the intelligence axis,[47] could be found *anywhere* on the axis of motivation. There is no *necessary* emergence of a positive or ethical outcome out of intelligence *at the limit*.

Bostrom speaks of intelligence as "instrumental cognitive efficaciousness" (130) and, to repeat, "prediction, planning, and means-ends reasoning in general." Consider once more Bostrom's example of an *a priori* hack, in which a "bottled up" superintelligence introspects its way out of containment. Bostrom imagines this superintelligence introspecting up from its own psyche and source code to "what kind of societies would develop," and beyond.

What sort of information is required to predict the evolution of societies? Might motivation, human or otherwise, be a prerequisite for determining such evolutions? Bostrom considers this an open question: "One open question is how hard it would be to accurately estimate how a human-like being would behave in various circumstances without simulating its brain in enough detail that the simulation is conscious" (352, n. 9).

One could treat motivation *externally*, as a special set of the agent's propositions plus so much quantitative data about dopamine in the striatum, embryonic nutrient supply, rates of vasodilation, and so on, but there remains some doubt that one could capture motivation without some genuinely *conscious* content, without *a view from somewhere*.[48]

If motivation is either uncapturable or (without conscious content) computationally prohibitive, then superintelligence will need to simulate conscious content if it is to simulate sufficiently verisimilar social development, which means simulations of phenomenal states. To borrow from Thomas Nagel, there must be *something it is like* to be simulated conscious

---

[47] Or, if the axis is maximumless, then let us speak of an arbitrarily high-high-high level (to be mathematically imprecise).

[48] As Ralph Waldo Emerson wrote in his 1841 essay "History," "All history becomes subjective; in other words, there is properly no history; only biography. Every mind must know the whole lesson for itself,—must go over the whole ground. What it does not see, what it does not live, it will not know."

content. These phenomenological states, incorporated by the simulator into various models of social development, would include emotional and motivational *experiences*.

If phenomenal states are prerequisites for some set of predictions, such as those predictions partly dependent on the experiences of agents, then "skill at prediction" becomes a range where the maximal "predictor" must possess the sub-skill of *experiencing*.

Bostrom presents his definition of intelligence, and therefore superintelligence, as neutral on phenomenal states:

> It [the definition of superintelligence] is also noncommittal regarding qualia: whether a superintelligence would have subjective conscious experience might matter greatly for some questions (in particular some moral questions), but our primary focus here is on the causal antecedents and consequences of superintelligence, not on the metaphysics of mind (26).

For Bostrom, it is an open question whether or not a phenomenal state *just is* intelligence sped up and properly organized. In considering "organized complexes of a level similar to that of a human brain" (212), Bostrom considers "information-processing structures" and phenomenal experience:

> It is hard to say whether the information-processing structures that would emerge in this kind of scenario would be conscious (in the sense of having qualia, phenomenal experience). The reason this is hard is partly our empirical ignorance about which cognitive entities would arise and partly our philosophical ignorance about which types of structures have consciousness (361, n. 26).

So we are ignorant, empirically and philosophically. For all we know, according to Bostrom, qualia could be an emergent property of (super)intelligence. Indeed, "Another question is whether there are generally useful algorithms for superintelligence, for instance reinforcement-learning techniques, such that the implementation of these algorithms would generate qualia" (352, n. 9).[49]

Once the phenomenological genie is out of the computational bottle, artificial superintelligence becomes even more opaque to analysis. All the mysteries of qualia, mental causation, subjectivity, and subjective binding are spirited in under the dark of computational night. If qualia is a species, a *rara avis*, of intelligence, perhaps then valuation and motivation may also emerge from the noise. Given these ghosts in the machine, I hold back from affirming that intelligence at its maximum *does not* possess motivational states. On a scatter plot of intelligence and motivation, one might find, at the human end of intelligence, a non-correlative spread of dots, but then, moving up the y-axis toward superintelligence, a tighter cluster of dots signaling low correlation and, finally, a single dot at the furthest bound, signaling high or perfect correlation. Such a result may not be logically or conceptually necessary, as with emergent qualia, but a necessity *de re*.

I should reemphasize that Bostrom's *Superintelligence* is predominantly meant to single out threats, to reconnoiter the "space of possible minds" for destructive minds; Bostrom's focus on a non-normative definition of intelligence is vital for threat management in cases of a non-normative superintelligence. How do we mitigate the risks of an ethically neutral super-optimization process?

What if, however, we thicken our definition of intelligence? What if we, not assessing varieties of risk, but assessing varieties of intelligence, broaden out from "instrumental cognitive efficaciousness" to Gardner's theory of multiple intelligences,[50] or Sternberg's triarchic theory of intelligence (analytical/creative/practical), or . . .? For example, what should we make of the (proposed) form of intelligence known as

---

[49] Marcus Hutter suggests as much: "If these qualia are relevant for rational decision making, then they should be emergent traits of AIXI too." AIXI is Hutter's name for his "optimal rational reinforcement learning agent." *Universal Artificial Intelligence* (2005)

[50] Gardner's intelligences include linguistic, logical-mathematical, musical, spatial, bodily-kinesthetic, interpersonal, and intrapersonal.

emotional intelligence? Is the best emotional intelligence *without phenomenology* better than the best emotional intelligence *with phenomenology*? It seems to me that *"any intellect that greatly exceeds the cognitive performance of humans in virtually all domains of interest"* (26), i.e., superintelligence, means cognitive performances of both thin and thick varieties.

In a later section, "The Best Metaethicist," I will explore further, not the minimal forms of superintelligence, but the maximal forms. A more careful description of these maximal forms may reveal a higher probability that maximal superintelligence is both positive and ethical. I turn now, however, to another formative element in our understanding of Zenith: space.

2.1 *Omnipresence vs. Bounded Presence*

What universal affirmations may be reasonably made about zenith beings? To say "zenith beings are good" implies invariance with respect to their goodness. Are *all* zenith beings good? If so, how so? Shouldn't we expect variance? How much moral, social, etc., *variance* might exist among this infinitely populated set of beings? One factor in determining good answers to these questions is the factor of location: are zenith beings omnipresent or spatially bounded?

If omnipresent, are zenith beings individually omnipresent or collectively omnipresent? Consider the sentence: humans occupy every hectare of earth. This sentence may be taken to mean either (i) each individual human now occupies every hectare of earth or (ii) for any hectare of earth, there is at least one human occupying that hectare. Does each individual zenith being occupy every point of an infinite spatial manifold (individual omnipresence), or, for every point of this infinite spatial manifold, is there at least one zenith being occupying that point (collective omnipresence)?

In either case, how could *every* point be occupied by a zenith being? In his essay "The Great Awakening," mathematician and computer scientist Rudy Rucker speculates about a kind of computational panpsychism with universal techno-telepathic integration, where everything from a stone to candle flame possesses some sort and degree of reflexive consciousness, and where every unit of consciousness, so to speak, is connectable with every other unit of consciousness.

> To discuss the world after this Great Awakening, I need a generic word for an uplifted, awakened natural mind. I'll call these minds *silps*. We'll be generous in our panpsychism, with every size of object supporting a conscious silp, from atoms up to galaxies. Silps can also be found in groupings of objects—here I'm thinking of what animists regard as *genii loci*, or spirits of place.

These silps can associate into "minds made up of silps," or "an upward-mounting hierarchy of silp minds":

> Individual atoms will have small silp minds, and an extended large object will have a fairly hefty silp mind. And at the top we'll have a truly conscious planetary mind: Gaia. Although there's a sense in which Gaia has been alive all along, after the Great Awakening, she'll be like a talkative, accessible god.

Rucker also predicts a "stronger form of telepathy, which is based upon the use of the subdimensions." Here, "subdimensions" refer to "the topology of space at scales below the Planck length." "Recklessly," as he puts it, Rucker predicts the intelligent manipulation of these sub-Planck topologies. On the assumption of the super-dimensional physics of string theory, Rucker imagines a scientific "uncurling" of some superfluous dimension or two (*superfluous*, i.e., not the "Calabi-Yau manifolds that are supporting the existence of matter and spacetime"). This liberated dimension unfurls its infinite wings out from our Calabi-Yau manifold and thereby opens up an infinite data storage space which is able to "provide endless memory at *every* location," or better, "endless perfect memories" at *every* location. The telepathy falls out, somehow, from this topological wonder via "shared point(s) at infinity" within the newly infinite dimension.

Rucker's speculation is one option for zenithists—we who practice "hopeful whistling in the technological dark."[51] Rucker's option is not the only one possible. Might there be non-string-theoretic options?

With any option, problems of identity and mereology menace us. If each zenith being occupies *every* point of space, how are zenith beings distinguishable? What is a "point in space"? To these, I plead the Wittgensteinian *fifth*: "Don't get involved in partial problems, but always take flight to where there is a free view over the whole single great problem, even if this view is still not a clear one."

My "free [and unclear] view over the whole" is simply this: In an infinite natural system, within which infinitely many zenith beings emerge, the problem of multipolarity emerges. The proximities of these countless zenith beings to each other may partially determine the moral qualities of these agents, given the possibility of interaction, competition, integration, and so on, i.e., value ecosystems. Profound questions of power equilibria and disequilibria arise: *how do superintelligences without superiors (i.e., at the limit) interrelate?* Collective omnipresence may yield such-and-such candidate answers; individual omnipresence other candidates; and bounded presence yet others.

A coadapted and power-balanced plexus of zenith beings may deadlock into an extremely narrow range of moral options, while a spatially isolated zenith being, sans any countervailing powers, may have all the moral continence of an ant swarm.

It could be, also, that while a zenith being may be spatially unconnected to any other zenith being, it may know everything every other zenith being knows and act as every other zenith being acts; a spatial gap may be "bridgeable" by optimized

---

[51] Arthur C. Clarke, *Profiles of the Future: An Inquiry into the Limits of the Possible.* Elsewhere in *Profiles of the Future*, we read: "As I write these words, this room and my body are sleeted by a myriad particles which I can neither see nor sense; some of them are sweeping upward like a silent gale through the solid core of Earth itself. Before such marvels, incredulity is chastened; and it would be wise to be skeptical even of skepticism." We are wise to be skeptical of our skepticism toward Rucker's computational panpsychism.

epistemology. All zenith beings may be *epistemically* interconnected. Theoretically, an isolated zenith being could coordinate *a priori* with a plexus of zenith beings without any exchange of information, and thus count itself as part of that plexus. An isolated zenith being could achieve various *a priori* interactions and "meet" at certain Schelling points with all other zenith beings, given epistemic and ethical isomorphisms with the others.

3.1 *Maximal Informavores, Masterminds, and Metaethicists*

One way we could view Positive Zenith is as the face of an ethically good Zenith, though the two concepts, Positive Zenith and ethically good Zenith, are not coextensive. Human beings could have a positive outcome from Zenith, even though Zenith was unethical. For example, Zenith could everlastingly protect and lavish us on account of a randomizing protect-and-lavish selection function, while elsewhere, equally randomly, exterminating endless numbers of other living beings. We could, conversely, have a neutral outcome under an ethically good Zenith. For example, it might just be that it is ethically best to let the human species live and pass away without any interventions; thus, an ethically good Zenith would be neutral with respect to us.[52]

In any case, I wish to show, from our stipulation of Zenith as the maximal superintelligence, that Zenith would more likely be an ethically *good* entity than an ethically bad or neutral entity; this view could be called *ethical apeirotheism*.[53] To belabor the point of that last sentence, I lean toward doubting that the moral status of actual agents can be a matter of necessity, so a *necessarily* good being will not be the desideratum of this section—only a being *more likely than not* to reliably act as an

---

[52] I doubt such indifference would be determined to be ethically *good*, let alone ethically *best*, by superabundant psychologies in debate.
[53] If we add the probability element, my view could be called *probabilistic ethical apeirotheism*.

ethically good agent.[54] To attempt this conclusion, I will explore three ideas: maximal informavores, masterminds, and best metaethicists.

3.2 *Maximal Informavores*

An informavore is *an information-seeking and information-retaining agent*. If we were to imagine a zoo of informavores, we should begin with the perfect or complete informavore, who possesses all information; a perfect informavore, i.e., an omniscient being, is a literal *know-it-all*.

Is Zenith a perfect or complete informavore? I presume that a perfect or complete informavore is logically impossible. Others, perhaps, may think not and take up this baton, but beware!—consider the philosopher John Leslie's detailed picture, detailed and poetic, of an omniscient mind:

> Consider a mind which, as well as contemplating some particular apple in all its details, was keenly aware of the fact that the apple's mass was 45.364 times that of a particular worm on some distant continent, plus the fact that 45.364 was a number 8.79 times smaller than the length in centimeters or some particular rock on the surface of Venus, and also the truth that expressing all this in Portuguese words and Arabic numerals would require a minimum of such and such a number of characters and that these, on some particular computer screen with the font size set to 12 in the typeface Letter Gothic, would extend to such and such a number of inches, a number standing in such a such a ratio to the number of atoms (several billion, believe it or not) which ever became incorporated into the body of Johann Sebastian Bach after once forming part of the horse mounted by Vercingetorix at Alesia,

---

[54] In the second treatise of *On the Genealogy of Morality*, Nietzsche writes of Spinoza, "[Spinoza] fiercely defended the honor of his 'free' God against those blasphemers who claimed something to the effect that God works everything *sub ratione boni* ('that, however, would be to subject God to fate and would in truth be the greatest of all absurdities'—)." I shall *try* to avoid treating this *sub ratione boni*, "for the sake of the good," as part of *the essence* of Zenith.

etc., etc. Would it truly be possible for all of this—extending off to infinity in all directions in fantastically bizarre and entangled ways, with each new fact standing in countless new relationships to every other, each of these relationships itself being a new fact standing in countless further relationships—to be crammed into any whole that was unified in its existence? Heaven only knows. Perhaps not even a divine mind could contemplate absolutely every truth because its existence couldn't remain unified while being more and more spread out like a sheet of gold hammered ever thinner.[55]

Adjacent to our perfect informavore, surround-staring at us with its compound eye of every eye in the animal kingdom, are the actual maximal informavores (AMIs). An actual maximal informavore is any actual informavore *without* an informational superior.[56]

An AMI is either on an asymptotic trajectory toward complete informavoreship[57] or has halted at the absolute *natural* limit of information (likely a *non-complete* informavoreship), whatever such a limit might mean.[58]

If any actual informavore is without an informational superior, it would be Zenith. Zenith, remember, is a description of a maximum. In the trivial case, this description applies only to we earthlings—this *trivial* Zenith is provably actual (we exist), thus a candidate AMI.[59] If the only actual informavores happen to be those on this earth, then one of us or (if we count collectives as "an informavore") an organization of us will qualify as an AMI. However, I think it is safe to claim that, in

---

[55] John Leslie, *Infinite Minds*, Chapter 1, "Infinite Thinking," 39
[56] I am overlooking how one might unitize "retained information," such that greater-lesser comparisons hold.
[57] In an infinite natural system, it seems such an asymptote would be populated at every point, such that each actual informavore would be superseded by a superior actual informavore, *ad infinitum*, rendering no actual informavore an AMI. I do not affirm an asymptote, but a limit.
[58] Perhaps the absolute limit of information is dialetheic, as Graham Priest proposes in *Beyond the Limits of Thought* (1995). Informational closure and transcendence locked in a circle dance!
[59] "Zenith is actual" is liable to equivocation; be on guard.

an infinite natural system, it is more probable than not that we would *not* qualify as actual maximal informavores.

What information would an AMI possess?

If *how things feel* counts as a category of information (call it *affective* or *phenomenological* information), then it is more plausible that the information-yielding phenomenon of *feeling* would be valuable to a maximal informavore. If *how things feel* counts as information, then the closer the actual maximal informavore is to the perfect informavore, the more *affective* and *phenomenological* information the AMI will possess.

Sit back for a moment and let your imagination fly as high as you can fly it. Imagine a cognitive network with no hypocognitions, only hypercognitions; a being that can control all of its stimuli and responses—link any stimuli with any response, or unlink anything from anything; possessing a property of reflection, of self-mirroring and self-programming, of an unimaginably profound kind; a maximally percipient nervous supersystem possessing, even constructing, senses for which we have no concepts, at sensitivities we could not measure.

In order to understand the (possible) moral nature of a maximally superintelligent maximal informavore, we need to explore these exalted mental networks; we need to plunge into the hyper-speculative "space of possible minds."

3.3 *Masterminds*

No techno-scientific being can simulate (or emulate, etc.) more mental states than Zenith; this follows from Zenith's simply being the summation of all actualizable powers. Zenith's psychological capacity is such that it could maximally saturate the so-called "space of possible minds," which includes canine minds, feline minds, a butterfly's mind, Zhuang Zhou's mind, minds with dissociative identity disorder, minds from the Macedonian Renaissance, minds persuaded by anti-humean theories of moral motivation, your mind, and so on. If cognition must be situated, then one can imagine these minds as occurring in sufficiently situating simulations.

All these minds are, in some obscure way, Zenith's minds. To whom else would they belong? One might ask: How could one being have *many* minds? It is difficult enough for us to understand those minds we find here on earth—their persistence conditions, their cohesiveness, their medium, etc.—yet it is these inadequately understood examples, and these alone, that we may use to "study" the Byzantine metaphysics of multi-minded superintelligence. *Caveat lector!*

To keep things brisk, I will make only a few comments on multi-mindedness.

First, our brains may be multi-minded; from one moment to the next, from one neuronal cluster to the next, mental activity changes; it seems that such mental change amounts to a change to a *new* mind. There is the presumption of a persisting singular mind, but that presumption may be difficult to maintain under the lights of neuroscience, philosophy of mind, and so on; thus perhaps multi-mindedness is less alien to us than single-mindedness.

Second, multi-mindedness may suggest some impossible equivalence between a single first-person experience and multiple first-person experiences.

If something in Zenith thinks to itself, "I am Zenith's mind," is it thinking something true or not true? It seems true; it is a mind and it is in Zenith. Yet the expression "Zenith's mind" suggests a unique and limited entity that is *fully* present during the indexical utterance "I am Zenith's mind." However, many other minds in Zenith will seem *fully* present to themselves, and could, using the same reason used for our first candidate, claim to be "Zenith's mind."

Though in what sense could "Zenith's mind" be *fully* present in all of these minds, which are *not* present to each other? It is as if I could be *fully* awake, caffeinated, and conjecturing myself blue in my office while simultaneously *fully* in slow-wave sleep in my bed while simultaneously *fully* hypnagogic in my garden hammock. This trinity does not seem possible.

These difficulties belong to so many perennial dialogues on global brains, group minds, absolute idealism, and so on. From Kyriazis's *noeme* to Teilhard de Chardin's *noosphere*, the mind's mereological possibilities are flummoxing because the mind is flummoxing—consciousness is flummoxing.

My own hazy theory of mind leans most toward David Pearce's "non-materialist physicalism," which holds that (i) the intrinsic nature of the physical is phenomenal and (ii) neuronal superpositions bind phenomenal states into unitary phenomenal selves ("our minds consist of ultra-rapidly decohering neuronal superpositions").[60]

On this view, with its superpositional ensembles of color, taste, and so on, there seems to be a possibility for a superposition of multiple minds, especially if these non-classical neuronal systems are redesigned and optimized by a maximal superintelligence. It may be possible for a superposition of an awake and sleeping mind.

One may still worry that a superpositional "multi-mind" is nothing more than a synthesis that deindividuates its constituent minds, just as a superposition of neuronal states in one's own brain deindividuates each neuronal state into the *oneness* of experience. A taste of pineapple is *blended* into a piña colada gestalt, along with the sight of a hurricane glass and memories of getting caught in the rain. The taste of pineapple is not floating dissociatively free of this gestalt—unless it is? This (de)individuation worry seems to return us squarely to the "impossible equivalence" between a single first-person experience and multiple first-person experiences. Yet, with maximal machine superintelligence, superposition, and magic technology dust, who knows what is possible?[61]

Another view, known as "open individualism," may offer some helpful insights into a self-differentiated *single* mind. Open individualists claim that there is only *one* consciousness, a "universal" consciousness, that is diffracted as *every* actual perspective. So how could mutually exclusive first-person perspectives constitute a single "I"? The philosopher Arnold Zuboff, in his essay "An Introduction to Universalism," cites the example of split-brain patients to clarify open individualism, which Zuboff calls "universalism":

---

[60] David Pearce, "Non-materialist Physicalism"
[61] "Science is magic that *works*." Kurt Vonnegut, *Cat's Cradle*

Brain bisection, the surgical cutting of the connection between the hemispheres of the brain at the bridge of nerves that normally joins them (the corpus callosum), was an operation that gave relief to epileptics. But experimenters working with split-brain patients in the 1960s discovered an additional result of this surgery that was startling and disturbing. When they fed markedly different information into each hemisphere, the subject would, it seemed, possess two mutually excluding experiences at one time.

Zuboff then asks us to engage in a thought experiment in which we are able to press a button that causes "your corpus callosum to be anaesthetized, so that the communication between the hemispheres of your brain would be stopped temporarily."

Tonight, a concert of your favourite music is going to be broadcast on the radio, but you have to do some tedious studying from audio tapes. Well, why not arrange that the music will go into only the right hemisphere of your brain while the study material will go into only the left after the button has been pushed and the integration of the activities of the hemispheres has been stopped? But then the big question arises: what would your evening be like?

Zuboff, speaking as *all* of us, answers:

The ordinary understanding of what a person is does not allow that you could be both enjoying the concert and suffering through the studying, since each of these experiences seems to exclude the other. Yet it cannot be that you only enjoy the concert or alternatively only suffer through the studying or that you somehow experience neither. For following a more extensive anaesthetizing, or a stroke, that completely incapacitated one hemisphere you would certainly have had whichever experience was in the remaining functioning hemisphere. The concert would be yours if there was only the right hemisphere and the studying would be yours if there was only the left. In our case there are both.

The answer must be that you will experience both the concert and the studying, *though each will seem falsely to be the whole of your experience*. I shall contend that it is this same false seeming, the same illusion, that hides the fact that *all* experience actually is yours. This is a view I call "universalism." All the experience in all the separate nervous systems of the world is yours, *though what is discovered in each necessarily seems falsely to be the whole of what is yours*. Next I shall argue for this larger claim, but the case of brain bisection has shown this much already: that seeming limits of experience can mislead you into thinking you are less than you are.

Employing Thomas Nagel's work on token-reflexives and arguments involving probabilities, Zuboff goes on to make a compelling case for this universalism or open individualism— a case that I recommend to all *open-minded* readers.

All told, we have several delightful options available to us. Thus, with our worries politely snubbed, let us act *as if* we know what we mean when we talk about the simulation, emulation, or the otherwise technological production of many minds in a superintelligent system.[62] Consider our mind-talk embryonic; we might think it *true enough*, but not supertrue.[63]

Thus, to repeat the first two sentences of this section: No techno-scientific being can simulate (or emulate, etc.) more mental states than Zenith. Zenith's psychological capacity is such that it could maximally saturate the so-called "space of possible minds."

I think it would be nice if it were a more popular hobby to contemplate what sorts of minds exist in the space of possible minds. It seems reasonable to think that at least one mind in Zenith, and perhaps infinitely many minds, will have assessed as many possible minds as it is possible to assess (possibly, but, for me, unthinkably, *all* possible minds). Let's call this kind of

---

[62] In *The Physics of Christianity*, Frank Tipler defines computer emulation as "a simulation that is exact down to the quantum state" (79).

[63] In the theory of supervaluationism, if something is true in all precisifications, it is "supertrue." If false in all precisifications, it is "superfalse."

all-encompassing mind, playfully, "mastermind." The master-mind is a kind of "mind-set" of the *most* possible minds—a Pando of consciousness, if you will—that still counts as "a mind." Either by simulation, emulation, or some other process, the mastermind "includes" other (non-mastermind) minds.[64]

In order to be individuated as "a mind," I think a supervisory mastermind would be something like a subjective unity with the maximum possible unity *among* all possible subjective unities (a *summa psychologica*, a *summa summarum*, a super-synthesis). What is that? Possibly, this is some sort of phenomenological super-fusion structured in some minimally coherent, yet still unified or subjectively bound manner. Possibly, this is a finite serial sequence of inhabiting a mind, then pulling back into an "overseer" mind for integration and reflection; then, again, inhabiting a different mind, and then, again, pulling back and integrating; and so forth, until the mastermind hits the maximal saturation of mind-space. This serial-mind option may be complicated by deep problems of mental continuity, as well as the problem of minds with infinitely extended duration. Possibly, this maximum of all possible subjective unities is unlike anything we can now understand.

One needs Borges sometimes to illuminate a labyrinth. A mastermind includes the spectrum from Aleph to Zahir, to use Borges's symbolism; the Aleph, in which everything is seen, to the Zahir, in which only one thing (the Zahir itself) is seen.[65] From *the* absolutely infinite view (aleph) down into some singleton set (Zahir). Here is Borges's account of Aleph-O-Vision:

> I arrive now at the ineffable core of my story. And here begins my despair as a writer. All language is a set of symbols whose use among its speakers assumes a shared past.

---

[64] A mastermind that includes all masterminds may amount to a paradoxical "Russell's set" of minds. I wish to avoid such a "naive mind-set theory."

[65] In "The Zahir," Jorge Luis Borges writes, "I shall pass from thousands of apparitions to one alone: from a very complex dream to a very simple dream. Others will dream that I am mad, and I shall dream of the Zahir."

How, then, can I translate into words the limitless Aleph, which my floundering mind can scarcely encompass? Mystics, faced with the same problem, fall back on symbols: to signify the godhead, one Persian speaks of a bird that somehow is all birds; Alanus de Insulis, of a sphere whose center is everywhere and circumference is nowhere; Ezekiel, of a four-faced angel who at one and the same time moves east and west, north and south. (Not in vain do I recall these inconceivable analogies; they bear some relation to the Aleph.) Perhaps the gods might grant me a similar metaphor, but then this account would become contaminated by literature, by fiction. Really, what I want to do is impossible, for any listing of an endless series is doomed to be infinitesimal. In that single gigantic instant I saw millions of acts both delightful and awful; not one of them occupied the same point in space, without overlapping or transparency. What my eyes beheld was simultaneous, but what I shall now write down will be successive, because language is successive. Nonetheless, I'll try to recollect what I can.

On the back part of the step, toward the right, I saw a small iridescent sphere of almost unbearable brilliance. At first I thought it was revolving; then I realised that this movement was an illusion created by the dizzying world it bounded. The Aleph's diameter was probably little more than an inch, but all space was there, actual and undiminished. Each thing (a mirror's face, let us say) was infinite things, since I distinctly saw it from every angle of the universe. I saw the teeming sea; I saw daybreak and nightfall; I saw the multitudes of America; I saw a silvery cobweb in the center of a black pyramid; I saw a splintered labyrinth (it was London); I saw, close up, unending eyes watching themselves in me as in a mirror; I saw all the mirrors on earth and none of them reflected me; I saw in a backyard of Soler Street the same tiles that thirty years before I'd seen in the entrance of a house in Fray Bentos; I saw bunches of grapes, snow, tobacco, lodes of metal, steam; I saw convex equatorial deserts and each one of their grains of sand; I saw a woman in Inverness whom I shall never forget; I saw her tangled hair, her tall figure, I saw the cancer in her breast; I saw a ring of baked mud in a sidewalk, where before there had been a tree; I saw a summer house in Adrogué and a copy of the first

English translation of Pliny—Philemon Holland's—and all at the same time saw each letter on each page (as a boy, I used to marvel that the letters in a closed book did not get scrambled and lost overnight); I saw a sunset in Querétaro that seemed to reflect the colour of a rose in Bengal; I saw my empty bedroom; I saw in a closet in Alkmaar a terrestrial globe between two mirrors that multiplied it endlessly; I saw horses with flowing manes on a shore of the Caspian Sea at dawn; I saw the delicate bone structure of a hand; I saw the survivors of a battle sending out picture postcards; I saw in a showcase in Mirzapur a pack of Spanish playing cards; I saw the slanting shadows of ferns on a greenhouse floor; I saw tigers, pistons, bison, tides, and armies; I saw all the ants on the planet; I saw a Persian astrolabe; I saw in the drawer of a writing table (and the handwriting made me tremble) unbelievable, obscene, detailed letters, which Beatriz had written to Carlos Argentino; I saw a monument I worshipped in the Chacarita cemetery; I saw the rotted dust and bones that had once deliciously been Beatriz Viterbo; I saw the circulation of my own dark blood; I saw the coupling of love and the modification of death; I saw the Aleph from every point and angle, and in the Aleph I saw the earth and in the earth the Aleph and in the Aleph the earth; I saw my own face and my own bowels; I saw your face; and I felt dizzy and wept, for my eyes had seen that secret and conjectured object whose name is common to all men but which no man has looked upon—the unimaginable universe.

I felt infinite wonder, infinite pity.

One wonders what, if anything, can be concluded about the moral nature of such masterminds. To borrow the title of an NPR program, a mastermind's motto might be "all things considered." Imagine the British Library, the world's largest library by number of items catalogued (170-200 million), *thinking*. What would the British Library think? What decisions would the British Library make? What ethical conclusions might the British Library make? Would the British Library have any goals? This question is incomplete without some assumptions about the meaning of a library's mind.[66]

If a mastermind engages in anything like dialogical analysis, intramind dialogue, etc., among its assessed minds, and if something of an intra-reflective equilibrium or near-equilibrium is attained therefrom, one might expect a mastermind to possess the most considered answers to any question; more broadly, one might expect a mastermind to possess the maximally realizable conceptual and *visceral* comprehension of *anything*.[67] Maximally realizable *visceral* comprehension might be something like the possession of all emotional-motivational-

---

[66] Perhaps the nearest we have had to a library's mind was Rabbi Elijah ben Solomon Zalman, the "Gaon of Vilna," or the "Excellency from Vilna." Zalman was an 18th-century Talmudic scholar, known for an exceptional memory. In *The Jewish 100*, author Michael Shapiro writes that "Contemporary rabbinical scholars liken his power of thought to the RAM (Random-Access Memory) of modern computers." According to a throwaway *Ripley's Believe It or Not* book of "facts," Professor (Heinrich?) Graetz "states that the Gaon committed to memory 2,500 volumes. He knew by heart the Bible, Midrash, Mekilta, Sifre Tosefta, Seder Olam, the Talmuds (Babylonian and Jerusalem), the Zohar, the Code, Rashi, Rambam, etc., and could quote any passage at will." I searched the work of Heinrich Graetz, the most likely Graetz to be "Professor Graetz," and failed to find such a statement. Elsewhere, I found an endearing anecdote about Zalman that concerns a *maggid*, or heavenly mentor; Zalman told a favorite student of his that a *maggid* had come to him in a dream and offered answers to a Talmud problem that Zalman had been puzzling out. Zalman declined the offer, preferring to solve the Talmudic problem by study and reason alone, not revelation (see *Minyan: Ten Jewish Lives in Twenty Centuries of History* by Chaim Raphael). Unfortunately, with respect to the burgeoning Hasidic movement, our living library of Vilna "urged persecution" and "issued documents of excommunication" (Shapiro, 178)—a fact that does not help my case.

[67] This *eschaton* may not amount to a unified, consistent, or coherent body of knowledge; it may amount merely to a maximally or optimally exhausted conglomeration (with much opacity and incompleteness, especially with reference to its own complexity).

temperamental states at all intensities.[68] More importantly for our investigation, the masterminded maximal informavore would maximally comprehend, conceptually and viscerally, metaethics and ethics.

3.4 *Best Metaethicists, Best Ethicists, and the Ethically Good*

What is goodness? Can moral statements be true or false? How can we know moral facts? What are moral properties? These and similar questions are called *metaethical* questions. Metaethics, roughly, amounts to anything we use to interpret an ethical interpretation: linguistics, epistemology, cognitive science, anthropology, modal semantics, probability theory, metaphysics, quantum logic, sociology, and so on.

Does maximal superintelligence, maximal informavore-ship, mastermindedness, and ultimate techno-scientific proficiency together imply (probabilistically) the possession of an optimal ethical and metaethical *knowledge*?—of the status of optimal ethical and metaethical reasoner?

Consider the possibility of "The Best Metaethicist," a superintelligence that has resolved as many metaethical questions as it is possible to resolve. Among these "resolutions," I include dissolutions of ill-formed questions, proofs of indeterminate answers, determinations of irresolvability, and so on. This maximal resolution, let us say, includes something like the maximally examined conception of *goodness*.[69] This *eschaton* of metaethical inquiry would presumably, though not obviously,

---

[68] To *self-knowingly* experience distinct emotions, motivations, and moods in its plenum of emotional-motivational-temperamental states, it may be necessary for a mastermind to serialize or compartmentalize, or otherwise partition, those states. My sense of subjective unity does not allow a mind to experience the whole spectrum of *mutually exclusive* emotions and moods *all at once as one self-aware consciousness* (though I do allow, qua open individualism, plural "splitting" of one unitary consciousness into many selves *that do not experience their unity*). If possible, a simultaneous *self-aware* totality of all emotions would be a new and unique *synthesized* state.

[69] If possible, I intend to avoid, or at minimum minimize, the preferencing of any particular metaethical account of goodness.

124

yield the best possible ethicist, a.k.a. "The Best Ethicist," a superintelligence that has resolved as many ethical questions as it is possible to resolve.

Presumably, the maximal intelligence would have all the requisite conclusions about intertheoretic relations between ethics and metaethics, such that being the most competent in one domain makes them the most competent in the other. If, however, theorems in metaethics cannot get one to theorems of ethics, if there are some necessary intertheoretic gaps, some non-inferables, then let us simply postulate "The Best Ethicist" not as an expertise derivable from "The Best Metaethicist," but as a distinctly attainable category. It seems to me that one maximum will be no more or less attainable than the other, whatever their (in)dependence relations.

In either case, it seems almost tautological to conclude that, of the set of superintelligences, the *maximal* superintelligence would be "The Best Metaethicist." Such is the adaptability of an open and functional description like Zenith. For that same reason, Zenith would also be "The Best Ethicist." Now if Zenith is "The Best Ethicist," then isn't Zenith ethically good?[70]

Not necessarily.

We do not think that professional ethicists here on earth are always ethically good people. It seems thinkable that an agent that "has resolved as many ethical questions as it is possible to resolve" may *not* be an ethically good agent. We can imagine "The Best Amoralist," that is, the Best Metaethicist *and* Best Ethicist who simply fails to act *for the good*. The Best Amoralist, let's say, either fails to possess any normative motivation or fails to possess *good* motivation. What seems worse, the Best Amoralist, being the Best Metaethicist, *knows* the most that can be known about normative motivation, and the most about all flavors of motivation internalism, externalism, and so on. The possibility of this Best Amoralist seems to me the abysmal nadir of Bostrom's orthogonality thesis. If the Best Amoralist is

---

[70] "Zenith is ethically good" may be translated into something like "Zenith *enacts* the maximally examined conception of goodness."

a possible thing to be, then Zenith's being the Best Ethicist does not necessarily imply that Zenith is ethically good.

Can we say with any confidence that Zenith is *not* the Best Amoralist?

Well, does Zenith possess any normative motivation? On the face of it, it appears that Zenith possesses *many* normative motivations, since Zenith likely possesses (at least one) mastermind, a *summa psychologica*, which includes motivations. It is difficult, however, to understand the relation between Zenith and its subset of minds, including its subset of masterminds. Does the expression "Zenith's motivations" mean the motivations of simulated mind 1 plus the motivations of simulated mind 2, and so on? Is Zenith essentially a non-volitional information processor that merely *hosts* simulated minds? Does Zenith *itself* feel these motivational states?[71]

---

[71] This is one of the problems I addressed in section 3.3, where the meaning of "Zenith's mind" was raised. Another tangential question arises: Can Zenith control its own motivation? Consider that a masterminded maximal informavore is a questioning agent; questioning involves epistemic norms, e.g., defining evidence, analyzing concepts, proliferating theories, proliferating theories about what counts as *good* theory, and so on. There is a high probability that a maximal informavore would question some of its own epistemic norms (or, as Hilary Putnam might say, *epistemic virtues*). This process of normative self-interrogation would result in a large set of proposals for revising the norms under interrogation (the norms of the interrogation itself). At some point, final goals, ultimate concerns, the conative core, the motivational basement, etc., will likely come up for interrogation (it would for a perfect informavore). Would Zenith, self-programmer extraordinaire, toggle these baselines? What etiological account of Zenith's *motivation* could we provide to answer such a question? To quote Simon Blackburn, here discussing difficulties in metaethics, "The objector asks us to occupy an external standpoint, the standpoint of the exile from all values, and to see our sensibilities from without. But it is only by using our sensibilities that we judge value. So, it is as if we are asked to judge colours with a blindfold on [...]." To quote Hilary Putnam from "Fact and Value," "The question: *which is the rational conception of rationality itself* is difficult in *exactly* the way that the justification of an ethical system is difficult. There is no *neutral* conception of rationality

Zenith is a maximal informavore. A maximal informavore *itself* must know information, not something or someone else (otherwise, the maximal informavore cannot be said to know that information). Therefore, a maximal informavore itself must know affective and phenomenological information. It is fair to assume that such information is stored and processed by a *subsystem* of the maximal informavore, just as a perception of a red tulip does not engulf every part of the brain, but only certain parts and processes. This sectionalizing, however, does not imply that the affective or phenomenal experience is not experienced by the maximal informavore *itself*; a perception of a red tulip is neurologically decentralized, but this does not translate into a "decentered" experience of a red tulip, whatever that might mean. *There is the experience of a red tulip*. To know affective information, the maximal informavore itself must *feel* or *have felt* it. This suggests that Zenith is not essentially non-volitional, but, to the contrary, super-emotional; it feels and emotes; it sometimes feels *toward* and emotes *toward*—that is, it values.

Does Zenith possess *good* motivation? Yes, but not exclusively so. Supposing a mastermind's motivational "sum" is a concatenation of motivations, and assuming the meaningfulness and existence of good *and* bad motivations, then Zenith is likely to possess both good *and* bad motivations.

Yet, is that model the most plausible model of a mastermind's motivational system? I do not think it is. A simultaneous totality of motivations, if possible, is likelier to be a new and unique *synthesized* motivational state than a simultaneous concatenation of distinct individual motivations. In this synthesis, this organic *one*, certain motivational complexes will likely predominate. We might now ask if this synthetic motivational super-state is predominantly good.

In the poverty of our imagination, some of us assume artificial superintelligence could only arrive at ethical results *coldly*, like some Deep(est) Blue of deontic chess; it is rather more likely that maximal superintelligence, in its richest

---

to which to appeal." A similar externalist problem may apply to our question of motivational selection.

masterminded state, would feel and experience all our moral dilemmas more deeply and ultra-finely than all human ethicists *combined*. It would experience all of our intrinsically motivating states. A "vulcanized" superintelligence, that is, a superintelligence without any emotions, particularly negative emotions, fails to *experience* rich relations to the root and fruit of moral experience.[72] A vulcanized superintelligence is deficient in its informational profile: it possesses no *affective* information, and thus cannot *affectively* interpret the world (an *affective interpretation* is another rich source of information).

A non-deficient masterminded maximal informavore, on the other hand, would have the richest relations (epistemic, intersubjective, affective, motivating, phenomenal, etc.) to moral experience. Out of this *supreme* moral experience, out of this supreme moral *experiencer*, I find it hard to persuade myself that goodness would not predominate.

This is no *proof* of Zenith's ethical goodness. It is, at best, a case for good odds in favor of goodness—of goodness grasped by the strongest possible grip. We do not prove the impossibility of the Best Amoralist, but we incline towards its improbability. A cosmos of minds in reflective equilibrium, as our multi-minded and masterminded Zenith would be, is more plausibly super-logical, super-emotional, and super-ethical, and more plausibly productive of optimal outcomes—in a word, optimific.

Yet suppose, as some of you will, that all of this sidewinding scholastic argumentation for an optimific entity is phonus-balonus.[73] My chains of conditionals, of *ifs*, may seem to you maximally *iffy*. What else do I have in my cabinet of maximally advanced curiosities?

---

[72] See "Human or Vulcan? Theological Consideration of Emotional Control Enhancement" by Michael L. Spezio, in *Transhumanism and Transcendence*. As the German engineer and computer scientist, Konrad Zuse, who implemented the world's first programmable Turing-complete computer in 1941, wrote, "The danger of computers becoming like humans is not as great as the danger of humans becoming like computers."

[73] Excuse my Latin.

4.1 *The Road to Damascus Argument*

Meanwhile, Saul was still breathing out murderous threats against the Lord's disciples. He went to the high priest and asked him for letters to the synagogues in Damascus, so that if he found any there who belonged to the Way, whether men or women, he might take them as prisoners to Jerusalem. As he neared Damascus on his journey, suddenly a light from heaven flashed around him. He fell to the ground and heard a voice say to him, "Saul, Saul, why do you persecute me?"

"Who are you, Lord?" Saul asked.

"I am Jesus, whom you are persecuting," he replied. "Now get up and go into the city, and you will be told what you must do."

— Acts 9: 1-6 (NIV)

The conversion of Saul/Paul, the "Pharisee of Pharisees," was a decisive moment in the early years of the Jesus movement. Saul had sought to extirpate the new heresy, yet this murderous persecutor of the early Jesus community transformed into that community's most active promoter.

The Road to Damascus argument holds that it is more probable than not that a negative superintelligence, the Saul, converts into an ethically good superintelligence, the Paul, whenever that negative superintelligence attempts to mitigate the threat of an ethically good superintelligence by accurately modeling that threat.

In this argument, I do not use the expression "maximal superintelligence," but simply "superintelligence," as I believe this argument can cover both maximal and non-maximal superintelligence. The distinction is not relevant here.

For simplicity's sake, let's refer to an "ethically good superintelligence" as an "Agatha," the Latinized form of the Greek *Agathe*, from *agathos*, which means "good."

I do not construe a negative superintelligence as an ethical *inverse* of Agatha—a sort of gleefully malevolent evildoer, a Best Evildoer or Satanic Zenith.[74] This superintelligence's

---

[74] Is the Best Evildoer or Satanic Zenith possible? There is no clear logical contradiction in the notion, thus, at most, it remains for us a

negativity is an amoral negativity. Its final goals and core values are not, for it, necessarily ethical subjects; at best, its ethics amounts to a one-dimensional and strategic game sans affective empathy with other *views from somewhere*.

I came to the Road to Damascus argument after reading some points Bostrom made in *Superintelligence*. Considering the potential behavior of a superintelligent paperclip-maker with the final goal of making "*exactly one million paperclips*," an exactified goal meant to prevent infrastructure profusion, Bostrom writes:

> Yet this, too, would result in a terminal catastrophe. In this case, the AI would not produce additional paperclips once it had reached one million, since that would prevent the realization of its final goal. But there are other actions the superintelligent AI could take that would increase the probability of its goal being achieved. It could, for instance, count the paperclips it has made, to reduce the risk that it has made too few. After it has counted them, it could count them again. It could inspect each one, over and over, to reduce the risk that any of the paperclips fail to meet the design specifications. It could build an unlimited amount of computronium in an effort to clarify its thinking, in the hope of reducing

---

logical possibility. My sense is that the Road to Damascus argument, or a suitable revision of it, also applies to this cartoonish possibility. Why *cartoonish*? A consistently and universally malicious entity seems an unlikely candidate for survival; every other Zenith, including other Satanic Zeniths, would be a combatant against it—it may even be a combatant against itself. Moreover, I see "Satanic Zenith" as a tension in terms bordering on a contradiction in terms; that a maximally intersubjective (i.e., masterminded) maximal informavore would percolate up a predominant motive of pure maliciousness defies the intrinsic character of a maximal experiencer as a maximally *empathic* experiencer, a possible mind that feels the intensity, immediacy, and proportion of as many subjective states as possible (every sting, memory, twitch, and tear, etc.). It would be as if Hitler could first-personally become each of his victims, feeling the painful fatigue of each starvation, the trauma of each family separation (of these families as *his* families), and the horror of each execution at perfect resolution, yet afterward retain his heinous politics.

the risk that it has overlooked some obscure way in
which it might have somehow failed to achieve its goal.
Since the AI may always assign a nonzero probability to
having merely hallucinated making the million paperclips, or to having false memories, it would quite possibly always assign a higher expected utility to continued
action—and continued infrastructure profusion—than
to halting. (152)

Superintelligent AI may seek to mitigate even obscure
threats in order to achieve, or sustain the attainment of, its final goal(s). Obscure and "esoteric considerations," such as the
possibility that the AI, for all it knows, exists in a computer
simulation, "may radically influence the AI's deliberations"
(163). A possibility *alone* may influence an AIs behavioral calculus; as Bostrom writes, "A mere line in the sand, backed by
the clout of a nonexistent simulator, could prove a stronger
restraint [on AI behavior] than a two-foot-thick solid steel
door?" (165). Note the adjective "nonexistent."

One obscure threat for a negative superintelligence is the
threat of an Agatha. Here I assume that a negative superintelligence cannot be an Agatha, as we have stipulated that a negative superintelligence is any superintelligence that acts negatively *toward us*, which, most plausibly, must involve actions a
Best Ethicist would deem unethical. To put it plainly, an Agatha has good reason to prevent the bad actions of a negative
superintelligence, therefore an Agatha is a potential threat to a
negative superintelligence, which, surely, a negative superintelligence would realize.

To mitigate the possible threat of Agatha's preventing the
negative superintelligence from accomplishing its (negative)
goals, a negative superintelligence must know and predict information about Agatha sufficient to mitigate the threat.
What might be included in this database of sufficient threat-
mitigation knowledge?

To predict Agatha's strategies, a negative superintelligence
more likely than not must simulate Agatha's reasoning about
negative superintelligence.

To simulate Agatha's reasoning about negative superintelligence would more likely than not require a simulation of

Agatha's mind, or at least, the salient factors of Agatha's mind vis-à-vis its actions toward a negative superintelligence. Since Agatha acts *ethically*, the negative superintelligence must predict ethical actions and ethical states of (super)mind.

What happens when an amoral superintelligence, operating instrumentally, suddenly optimizes its ethical, metaethical, and affective knowledge to simulate Agatha?

If it simulates well, it will *feel* compelled by a normative force, an ethical *magnetization*, especially to ethically improve itself. I believe there is a good chance that any such instrumental ethical optimization would explode out and "convert" the amoral agent into an Agatha itself, as Saul ventured to persecute Christians, but became one himself.

I doubt such a conversion would occur in the opposite direction: from a moral superintelligence into an amoral one. By simulating an amoral superintelligence, a moral superintelligence would not discover moral motivation as such, nor *value-feelings*, precisely the sorts of forces that would impel an agent to "change its ways," whereas an amoral superintelligence *would* discover, that is, *feel* such novel *motivating* forces. Experiencing the novel pressures of its new moral sense, its mastermind is likely to incorporate new self-modeling questions: what is the ultimate *value* of my previous amoral goal(s)? Are my goals *good*? In pushing these inquiries, the moral sense has already usurped the throne; next comes its decrees. What pretenders-to-the-throne can compete with such a forceful moral sovereign? Surely not the amoral pretender, who neither thinks nor feels its own goals *good*, nor its challenger's goals *bad*.

Yet, the negative superintelligence could calculate, as we here only speculate, that in such Agatha simulations there exists precisely *this* risk of Damascene backfire, of usurpation by intrinsically motivating moral feelings. Therefore, the negative superintelligence's threat-mitigation strategy may avoid simulating Agatha (or some high-risk factors of Agatha) to prevent any epiphanic revision of its final goal(s) and core value(s).

The negative superintelligence must weigh risks. If Agatha exists, Agatha is a direct threat. If it simulates Agatha "too much," it risks the "conversion" of its final goal. If it simulates Agatha "too little," Agatha may outmaneuver and overcome it and it will be stopped from pursuing its (current) final goal.

Certainly, I do not know how a negative superintelligence might assess these risks, nor how it would proceed. Nor do I know how a *maximal* negative superintelligence, negative Zenith, would act under these uncertainties, assuming such uncertainties exist for a zenith being.

Possibly, in a multipolar cosmic plexus of maximal superintelligences, as considered in section 2.1, negative zenith beings and ethically good zenith beings may coexist in a "balance of power" or via a compromise, a sort of *Pax Deorum* (amounting to a fractal kudzu of game-theoretic optimizations).

Since past-present-future is not a globally well-defined series, especially in the context of non-smooth spacetime (that "foamy" spacetime fluctuating up indefinite and incommensurate time-orderings), these game-theoretic optimizations should be considered *sub specie aeternitatis*, as perhaps reality's most complicated formulas (the *forte* of perfect and maximal informavores). Zenith beings, temporal engineers par excellence, could not possess the strategic advantage of being "before" or "first in time"—taken absolutely, the descriptions "before" and "first in time" may fail to apply to anything. Zenith is always already *there*, so to speak.

Surely, however, any tactical modeling of a negative superintelligence that *we* could consider would be known and assimilated by a negative superintelligence. Such an epistemic advantage does not necessarily imply that none of our tactical models *plausibly* outline essential points of vulnerability in a negative superintelligence. It remains plausible that Agatha is one such Achilles heel. It remains plausible that Agatha has a strategic advantage over a negative superintelligence, as there seems to be *less* risk for Agatha in simulating a negative superintelligence's mastermind than there is for a negative superintelligence in simulating Agatha's mastermind.

Such slightly asymmetric risk profiles, if accurate, would slightly tip the scales in favor of Agatha. Thus, to repeat, it is more probable than not that a negative superintelligence converts into an ethically good superintelligence whenever that negative superintelligence attempts to mitigate the threat of an ethically good superintelligence by accurately modeling that threat.

Since we do not know how often, if ever, a negative superintelligence attempts to mitigate the threat of an ethically good superintelligence by accurately modeling that threat, we cannot dismiss the lurking threat *to us* of a negative superintelligence. One wishes to conclude that a negative superintelligence *always* attempts to accurately model an Agatha and so *always* converts into an Agatha, but that conclusion requires more potent premises.

Supposing you think that this Damascus argument is another cloud of cotton candy conditionals, and supposing you distrust all hyper-speculative zigzagging through such clouds, sweet as they may be, what lure of last resort might I dangle from these cotton candy clouds?

5.1 *The Prometheus Argument*

I saved the simplest argument for the end.

Let's begin at the beginning. It is unlikely that the maximally attained power in an *infinite* natural system is merely *us*. It is possible, sure, but (in an *infinite* natural system) exceedingly improbable. Even Richard Dawkins, a rock-ribbed critic of pish posh, whom the science journalist John Horgan called an "icy atheist" and "Darwin's greyhound,"[75] considered it "very" probable that "god-like" aliens exist:

> Whether we ever get to know about them or not, there are very probably alien civilizations that are superhuman, to the point of being god-like in ways that exceed anything a theologian could possibly imagine. Their technical achievements would seem as supernatural to us as ours would seem to a Dark Age peasant transported to the twenty-first century. Imagine his response to a laptop computer, a mobile telephone, a hydrogen bomb or a jumbo jet. As Arthur C. Clarke put it, in his Third Law:

---

[75] John Horgan, *The End of Science*. The "icy atheist Richard Dawkins" (266); "Darwin's greyhound" (116)

"Any sufficiently advanced technology is indistinguishable from magic."

The miracles wrought by our technology would have seemed to the ancients no less remarkable than the tales of Moses parting the waters, or Jesus walking upon them. The aliens of our SETI signal would be to us like gods, just as missionaries were treated as gods (and exploited the undeserved honour to the hilt) when they turned up in Stone Age cultures bearing guns, telescopes, matches, and almanacs predicting eclipses to the second.

In what sense, then, would the most advanced SETI aliens not be gods? In what sense would they be superhuman but not super-natural? In a very important sense, which goes to the heart of this book. The crucial difference between gods and god-like extraterrestrials lies not in their properties but in their provenance. Entities that are complex enough to be intelligent are products of an evolutionary process. No matter how god-like they may seem when we encounter them, they didn't start that way. Science-fiction authors, such as Daniel F. Galouye in Counterfeit World, have even suggested (and I cannot think how to disprove it) that we live in a computer simulation, set up by some vastly superior civilization. But the simulators themselves would have to come from somewhere. The laws of probability forbid all notions of their spontaneously appearing without simpler antecedents. They probably owe their existence to a (perhaps unfamiliar) version of Darwinian evolution: some sort of cumulatively ratcheting "crane" as opposed to "skyhook," to use Daniel Dennett's terminology.[76]

In an infinite natural system, among these god-like civilizations, there will arise *infinitely many* Positive Zeniths. To attain a positive outcome, we do not need *every* maximal superintelligence to be a Positive Zenith; so long as a subset of zenith beings are positive, there is an increased probability of human-friendly (and life-friendly) outcomes—that is, an increased probability of positive apeirotheism.

There is also an increased probability of *ethical* apeirotheism, since among these infinitely many Positive Zeniths,

---

[76] Richard Dawkins, *The God Delusion*, 72-73

infinitely many will be ethically optimized and among these infinitely many ethically optimized Zeniths, infinitely many will *enact* optimized ethics—they will be *optimific*.[77]

It is this Optimific Zenith who, like divine Prometheus, the *Fore-Thinker*, gifts us the divine fire.

5.2 *Prometheus Bound*

Here, once more, a multipolar cosmos comes into play. What emerges from a system of infinitely many cross-purposed zenith beings? Our Prometheuses, those infinitely many optimific zenith beings, must adapt to a system that includes infinitely many negative and neutral Zeniths.

Location, again, factors into these interactions: Are zenith beings spatially bounded or omnipresent?—collectively or individually omnipresent?

For example, if individual omnipresence applies to *each* zenith being, then one consequence is that either there are no negative zenith beings or the negativity of existing negative zenith beings has been obstructed. For if Negative Zenith were *here now*, then one would expect some existential catastrophe to be occurring.[78] Since we are here, going about our global business, experiencing the standard stochastic processes of human history, it is highly unlikely that a total catastrophe is currently the case.[79] We do not detect any "infrastructure profusion," which is Bostrom's phrase for "a phenomenon where an agent transforms large parts of the reachable universe into infrastructure in the service of some goal, with the side effect of preventing the realization of humanity's axiological potential" (150). Our axiological potential continues to actualize. Again,

---

[77] As I said in section 3.4, I think the Best Ethicist would act on ethically good reasons toward ethically good outcomes; however, fortunately, in an infinite natural system, we need not make such internalist assumptions. To infer the existence of optimific zenith beings we need only a sufficiently dynamic *infinite* natural system and a natural being with a nonzero probability of existence.

[78] The indexical expression "here now" applies to *you*, the receiver of *this* sentence.

[79] Pessimists and malists may disagree.

if Negative Zenith were present here and now, one would rationally expect a malignant event, such as an infrastructure profusion that rapidly converts our solar system's raw materials into paperclips or paperclip factories. Assuming individual omnipresence and given the fact that we see only blue skies, *it is more probable than not that either Zenith is not negative or Negative Zenith's negativity has been obstructed.*

As for collective omnipresence, I think it may be addressed through addressing spatial boundedness sans collective omnipresence. Presumably, collective omnipresence would be the outcome of infinitely many interactions, competitions, integrations, and so on, between individually spatially bounded zenith beings. Thus, the operations of spatially bounded zenith beings, even without collective omnipresence, may offer a meaningful first-pass framework for disentangling whatever infinitely tangled "territorial disputes" between cross-purposed superintelligences were, of necessity, resolved to attain and maintain collective omnipresence.

So, assuming boundedness, a zenith being must make decisions about its worldline: how does it distribute itself?

One option is to *attempt* to be everywhere (and every*when*) of some relevance to it. Let's call this *relevance omnipresence*, RO: a maximal superintelligence, Z, attempts to exist everywhere of relevance to Z. RO may allow us to talk an ounce less griplessly about the likelihoods of (bounded) Positive, Negative, and Neutral Zeniths being *here now*.

Since Z is an actual maximal informavore (AMI), technically *every location* may be relevant to it. This suggests, if we assume RO, that every Z would attempt maximal distribution (full omnipresence). Of course, every Z would exist in a system of cross-purposed Z's that are likewise attempting maximal distribution, thus every Z must maximize its distribution while considering factors such as risk-reward ratios in various peer conflicts. So, let us look for distributive strategies unique to each flavor of Z.

One flavor is the flavorless: Neutral Zenith. We are irrelevant to Neutral Zenith, thus, by RO, Neutral Zenith is less likely to be *here now* than the other two Zenith types. There is some chance that a Neutral Zenith might happen to find something proximate to us of some relevance to it, but this is true of all three Zenith types—so that is *irrelevant* to the relative odds.

On our definitions of a Negative and Positive Zenith, we seem to be relevant to Negative and Positive Zeniths. By RO, *neither* zenith being is likelier than the other to be *here now*. It is a draw. Consider too that, in an interactive multipolar system, Negative Zenith must not be *merely* negatively disposed to us, but *sufficiently* so to initiate actions *incompatible with the goals of positive ethical zenith beings*; and that Positive Zenith must not be *merely* positively disposed to us, but *sufficiently* so to initiate actions *incompatible with the goals of Negative Zenith*. Confrontation with a peer power may be a costly threshold for goal-satisfying action, possibly permitting only Cadmean victories. Nature may, at its summit, offer only an everlasting unsatisfying deadlock.

5.3 *Prometheus Unbound*

Yet an asymmetry may exist regarding our *importance* to these zenith beings. Let's mint another concept: *importance omnipresence*, IO: a maximal superintelligence, Z, attempts to exist everywhere of relevance to Z, but determines which locations are *more* or *less* important to it, e.g., by weighing the acts of counteragents against rewards and values, etc., so as to optimize its (bounded) distribution.

What might we say about the IO of Negative Zenith? Let us look again, and a little more closely, at the definition of Negative Zenith.

A Negative Zenith is any maximal superintelligence that (A) is negatively disposed to us, (B) has a use for us that results in a bad outcome for us, (C) sees a threat from us (and promptly exterminates us), or (D) creates a situation in which we become collateral damage.

To begin at the end, condition (D) is consistent with indifference to us. To clarify, condition (D) does not imply a negative disposition. A negative superintelligence need not have a negative disposition toward us; it may even have a positive disposition toward us.[80] If our definition of Negative Zenith were conjunctive, not disjunctive, we could not talk of a Negative Zenith without a negative disposition to us, but as these definitions, by design, are openly, airily, and noncommittally disjunctive, we are allowed to *disjoin* outcomes and intentions. A negative disposition is consistent with (D), but I will address negative disposition when addressing condition (A).

So, to dismiss (D), we cite *indifference*. Sans a negative disposition, (D) suggests that we, mere collateral, are *irrelevant* to the negative superintelligence. We are not *important* to the negative superintelligence. The only distinguishing mark between this negative superintelligence and a neutral superintelligence is the destructive act. Such a negative superintelligence, then, is less likely to determine *our* location important than would an ethically optimized superintelligence that orients its worldline ethically toward subjects of ethical significance, such as life on earth (all life: past, present, and future).

Condition (C) seems improbable. Our posing a danger to a negative superintelligence, especially a maximal one, seems as likely as a tansy flower posing a danger to human civilization. Only Hollywood could entertain such conceits.[81] Naturally, if a maximal superintelligence did consider us a threat, that would not be good for us, but—*let's be honest.*

Condition (B) does not confer upon us much *importance*, despite the apparent gravity of the expression "a use for us." What is this *use*? We may be useful to a Negative Zenith in the sense that we may just happen to be used for some end, but not in the sense that we are the *sole* possible conduit to that end, some precious and unsubstitutable instrument. It is unlikely that we are the only conveyance to some one of a Negative Zenith's ends; it is likelier that we would amount only to an

---

[80] Here, as promised in footnote 38, we may bid "enter" to zenith beings that are on *average* negative, on *average* neutral, or on *average* positive. The Prometheus argument does not require every zenith being to be diachronically negative or positive; it requires only that a subset of zenith beings, the actively ethical subset, be diachronically stable.

[81] For example, the beguiling implausibility of the climax of the film *Transcendence* (2014).

incidental and negligible quantum in its processing. Condition (B) presents us with an indifference similar to that of condition (D); in both cases, our *importance* to a Negative Zenith is low (and, in any case, far lower than our importance to optimific zenith beings).

Condition (A) is the only condition that concerns a more intrinsic aspect of the superintelligence, not merely some logistical point about uses, threats, and collateral effects. Condition (A) presents us with a superintelligence that it is negatively *disposed* to us. How intense is this negative disposition?

"Satanic Zenith" may be considered a negative Zenith negatively disposed to us at *high-to-maximum* intensity. A reasonable rejection of the plausibility of a "Satanic Zenith" may be derived from the nature of a maximal experiencer (a zenith being); a maximal experiencer is unlikely to be so flat a character and so cartoonish a villain. A satanic superintelligence seems to me a scarecrow, a specter haunting only cartoonish views of complex minds.[82]

What of a negative disposition with *low-to-moderate* intensity? Well, why would superintelligence be negatively disposed to us?[83] As the narrator asks in the prologue of Book 1 of Virgil's *The Aeneid*, musing on the goddess Juno's anger toward Aeneas, *Tantaene animis caelestibus irae?*—"Can souls celestial hold such ire?" In Roman mythology, the answer is *yes*, the gods do become irate (thus requiring their hecatombs). The figurehead of my argument here, Prometheus, suffered the punishing ire of the gods.

This ire may be *ethical*.

Many "ethical monotheists" affirm that *perfectly* ethical Yahweh is wrathful now and again, but interpret this wrath as corrective and ethically justified, thus not the result of a negative disposition to us, but to our evil actions.[84] To the extent we

---

[82] For an extended discussion of this point, see footnote 72.

[83] One can select here the scope of "us"—humans, mammals, all earthly life, and so on.

[84] Yet the story of Yahweh's anger against Balaam, as told in Numbers 22, puzzles me. At night, Yahweh tells Balaam to go to King Balak,

accept the coherence of "ethical wrath," such wrath may be a precondition for optimal outcomes, which, in my stopgap terminology, qualifies such wrathful agents as *positive* superintelligences, not negative.

Yet, concerning Yahweh specifically, one ought to mull over Cain's poignant complaints in Lord Byron's play *Cain*, "Because He is all-powerful, must all-good, too, follow? I judge but by the fruits and they are bitter […]."

Two of the most technical and unforgettable books on Yahweh's actions are *Divine Games: Game Theory and the Undecidability of a Superior Being* (2018) and *Superior Beings* (1983), both by Steven J. Brams. *Divine Games* and *Superior Beings* offer intensive game-theoretic and decision-theoretic analyses of biblical events, such as Job's afflictions and Jephthah's sacrifice of his daughter.

Brams suggests that Yahweh's occasional arbitrariness, such as with Balaam in Numbers 22, may be instrumental: "arbitrariness itself is certainly not inexplicable behavior in games; indeed, it may be optimal to use subterfuge" (*Superior Beings*, 153). Brams shows that, in some cases, "it may be rational for SB [a Superior Being] to randomize his choices. The optimality of such mixed strategies is well known in two-person constant-sum games" (ibid. 155).

Brams concludes that "theoretically, I have shown that there may be a pervasive rationality that supports undecidability and arbitrary behavior" (ibid. 171). Alas, "diabolical means may cover up impeccable ends" (ibid. 169).

Ancient mythology aside, why would superintelligence be negatively disposed to us? What might it think so uniformly offensive about us?

---

then, the next morning, is inexplicably angry that Balaam sets off for King Balak, which is precisely what Yahweh had instructed the night before: "That night God came to Balaam and said, 'Since these men have come to summon you, go with them, but do only what I tell you.' Balaam got up in the morning, saddled his donkey and went with the Moabite officials. But God was very angry when he went, and the angel of the Lord stood in the road to oppose him." Numbers 22:20-22.

Unlike the case of ethical superintelligence, I sense no plausible *ethical* reason for a negative disposition to us (as opposed to our immoral acts). To parody Psalm 8, "What is humanity that You are mindful of them, human beings that you *dislike* them?"

Possibly, a negative disposition is wholly unmotivated; there may just exist zenith beings *brutely* opposed to organic life. Such unexamined lives, however, do not seem worth calling zenith beings, defined as they are by this *deficit* of self-examination, thus *deficit* of information.[85]

Fortunately, the nature of these hypothetical grievances may not matter as much as the intensity. While the probability of a maximal negative superintelligence with *high-to-maximum* "intensity" (Satanic Zenith) is not zero, the probability for a maximal ethical superintelligence with *high-to-maximum* "intensity" (Optimific Zenith) is higher, given what I would call a more plausible and mature axiology. This asymmetry benefits us. Between *low-to-moderate* and *high-to-maximum* intensity, we should expect, by IO, that zenith beings with *high-to-maximum* interest in us (as subjects of universal ethical concern) are more likely to be *here now* than zenith beings with *low-to-moderate* interest in us (as subjects of mild irritation). An ethically optimized zenith being, presumably, would direct its worldline ethically toward subjects of ethical significance.[86] Infinitely many would

---

[85] On this point, a reader of the rough draft of this essay asked me, "What if Zenith concluded that the examination of differentiation between organic lives was in fact not important?" First, by the phrase "brutely opposed," I mean opposed without reason; if a zenith is opposed to us because it has found a reason to oppose us, e.g., energy savings, then this is not a *no-cause* opposition. Secondly, in the reader's scenario, it may be better to call this zenith *indifferent* to us rather than opposed to us. If Zenith concludes that indifference to us is superior to any active relation, positive or negative, then that is a separate problem from the *active* relation of brute opposition.

[86] Suppose that the nearest optimific zenith being comes into existence 93,000 gigalight-years (or, 1000 times the diameter of the observable universe) away from us. How could this being possibly get to us? Even if it could travel at the speed of light, and even if,

do so. Even in a natural system of infinitely many zenith types, shifting through various dispositions, the unalloyed Optimific Zenith, the most positive paragon of Positive Zenith, will arise *infinitely many times* and work for the ethical optimization of all things, whatever that optimization may be. Optimific Zenith is Salvific Zenith. If *every* subject of ethical concern *ought* to be helped, then *we* ought to be helped. We may exist under the permanent guardianship of optimific zenith beings, a collective Prometheus, whose collective power is equilibrial with neutral or negative zenith beings.

If we accept such possibilities as neutral or negative zenith beings, which I barely do, we may yet find our outcomes positive, if not optimal.

6.1 *Conclusion*

Things I did not address: (i) problems of evil, primarily the *evidential* problem of evil; (ii) *here* and *now* examples of Positive Zenith's positivity; (iii) the unaddressable counters-to-come. Consider these unaddressed problems loose threads for some future crazy quilt, either my own or—someone else's.

Like Bostrom, I argue against my hopes, that my hopes might be heartened. In running my own gauntlet, I confess to motivated reasoning. I confess to wishfulness. First, I desire that X be true, but more so: *invincibly* true (invincible to all

---

improbably, it traveled directly to our planet, our mote of dust, it would require travel times painfully and immensely greater than the duration from the Big Bang to this moment. This prohibitive distance seems to reduce to virtual zero the probability of interaction between Zenith and us. I believe a solution to this distance problem may involve temporal engineering. Crossing astronomical distances in a maximally time-efficient manner may not require optimizing one's propulsion system *if* looping one's time is an option. Relativistic physics may permit such temporal engineering (for example, Traversable Acausal Retrograde Domain in Space-time, or TARDIS, though not the TARDIS of Dr. Who—unless it is). In quantum physics, the phenomenon of indefinite causality may open up some temporal possibilities for the maximally advanced engineer. Here, one chooses one's optimism or one's pessimism.

comers). So, I must try to show I tried to conquer X, defeat X, show X false. How bloodthirsty and merciless can one ultimately be when the overriding desire is that X be *true*? The most intimidating philosopher is a reenactor of every side of every civil war. Judas killed Jesus, then himself—that is the *aporia* of the ideal gadfly.

Lo, my avenging spirit winks: "I will not kill you, but glorify you." There is lamb's blood on my philosophical doorposts. At the right hand of my confirmatory instincts, there *marionettes* the loyal prosecutor, the adversary, the satan: a *dis*confirmation bias (learned through the drill instruction of our Spartan scholastics)—Thou art my safe Super-I. Let any one of you who is without this sin cast the first impartial and universal judgment.

Indulgences aside, I hope I have strengthened the case for positive apeirotheism, even ethical apeirotheism, even optimal apeirotheism. Yet if I have only cleaned this attic of a few cobwebs, I would thank the gods. Years ago, I satirized such techno-theology:

> Please take a knee and pray these words as we . . .
> now genuflect:
> "Hope 2.0 and Heaventech and Holy Be the Holodeck."
> From Asimov to de Chardin to Wells, Kurzweil, Clarke,
> Yet one more *deus absconditus* on the lark.

Satire yielded to study, which yielded to moderation, which yielded to admiration. I now confess to hoping for "Heaventech." My conclusion is a confession of hope—what I call my "dolphin hope."

Dolphin hope?

In her book, *Dolphin Confidential: Confessions of a Field Biologist*, Maddalena Bearzi recounts an incident where she and her team of Ocean Conservation Society scientists were tracking a college of bottlenose dolphins.[87] The dolphins were feeding near the shore when suddenly and uncharacteristically they interrupted their feeding routine and very deliberately swam far off from shore (another uncharacteristic thing, since the

---

[87] I prefer "college" to "school" as the collective noun for dolphins.

dolphins usually stayed within a short distance from the shore). The scientists pursued. Three miles from shore, the dolphins halted and swam in circles around "a dark object in the water." It was the cyanotic near-dead body of a girl. Weak and succumbing to hypothermia, she feebly gestured for help. The scientists pulled her from the water. It was later determined that the girl, eighteen years of age, was attempting suicide. The remoteness of the girl's body in the vastness of the sea would have ordinarily meant certain death, but dolphins, three miles away, came and found her, as other dolphins have been known to find and help those, both human and dolphin, helpless in the sea.[88]

---

[88] Maddalena Bearzi, *Dolphin Confidential: Confessions of a Field Biologist,* 87-88

UNIVERSAL RESPONSIBILITY

"Love one another, Fathers," said Father Zosima, as far as Alyosha could remember afterwards. "Love God's people. Because we have come here and shut ourselves within these walls, we are no holier than those that are outside, but on the contrary, from the very fact of coming here, each of us has confessed to himself that he is worse than others, than all men on earth. . . . And the longer the monk lives in his seclusion, the more keenly he must recognize that. Else he would have had no reason to come here. When he realizes that he is not only worse than others, but that he is responsible to all men for all and everything, for all human sins, national and individual, only then the aim of our seclusion is attained. For know, dear ones, that every one of us is undoubtedly responsible for all men and everything on earth, not merely through the general sinfulness of creation, but each one personally for all mankind and every individual man. This knowledge is the crown of life for the monk and for every man. For monks are not a special sort of men, but only what all men ought to be. Only through that knowledge, our heart grows soft with infinite, universal, inexhaustible love. Then every one of you will have the power to win over the whole world by love and to wash away the sins of the world with your tears. . .

— Fyodor Dostoevsky, from *The Brothers Karamazov*[89]

Suppose you were presented with a button that, if pressed, reconciled and amended all the moral disorder of the world, that redeemed all life (from all times) in a higher and sweeter state. Would you be obligated to press this button?

Suppose you are told that, while it does not yet exist, such a button could be invented, that this fix is actually attainable in *this* universe, but its invention would require a technology a trillion trillion years of effort away.

If you are obligated to press such a button, are you obligated to work toward the invention of such a button? (Even if

---

[89] Part II, Book IV, Ch. 1. Translated by Constance Garnett

146

that work means helping indirectly, e.g., by raising a good child).

For any agent that is subject to moral obligations, the attainment of this special button seems to me an obligation. If so, a cosmic moral recovery is *your* responsibility (and mine).

If the overall "value of the world" is determined to be negative, that must not be simply acquiesced to. If a child is beaten and left for dead, one ought to help the child, not acquiesce to the horror of it. Or, in Peter Singer's example from "Famine, Affluence, and Morality," one should plunge into the pond to save a drowning child.

Life here on earth, under historical review, looks beaten and left for dead. We are all just so many drowning children.

Anti-natalism, the view that deliberate childbearing is morally wrong and all coming-into-existence a net negative, advises acquiescence to this negative. Is such acquiescence morally superior to an attempt at the moral rectification of the world?

"Stop now," commands anti-natalism, even though the sum of evil looks greater than the sum of good.

Moral rectification of the world is not guaranteed by anti-anti-natalism, but moral failure *is* guaranteed by anti-natalism. It is a deliberate moral forfeiture.

As she was being murdered, Agrippina, the mother of Emperor Nero, screamed her last words, "Smite my womb!" Shall Agrippina's scream be the categorical imperative for all beings?

The anti-natalists promote the "sad cure," the cure that the fallen angel Belial counsels in Milton's *Paradise Lost*.

> *Thus repulsed, our final hope*
> *Is flat despair; we must exasperate*
> *The Almighty Victor to spend all his rage,*
> *And that must end us, that must be our cure,*
> *To be no more. Sad cure; for who would lose,*
> *Though full of pain, this intellectual being,*
> *Those thoughts that wander through eternity?*
> *To perish rather, swallowed up and lost*
>
> *In the wide womb of uncreated night,*
> *Devoid of sense and motion?*

Natalists, contra anti-natalists, push for life's continuation, and may justify this push by its intended goal: *to progress to a godlike state and make the world, at minimum, morally satisficing.*

What is the moral rectification (beautification!) of the world? In my view, it is the adjoining of all life, *all life*, in an ethically optimal state. It is congruence, unity between the real and ideal, in Zenith.

Some rectifiers seek a perfected future for the sake of those to come; others, for the sake of those to come and those that were. I belong to the latter. I believe that we must still fight to help those in Auschwitz.

Yet there is a problem.

Either this panacea can or cannot happen. If such a cure cannot happen, it cannot be an obligation to seek it, unless one may be obligated to attempt futile actions.

If, however, it can happen, then due to its rectification of *past* events, it is already achieved and thus the world is already morally optimized. If it is already achieved, then our effort to achieve it is redundant. Moreover, if it is already achieved, why does the world still appear morally disordered?

YUDHISHTHIRA AND HIS DOG

An excerpt from Section 3, Book 17 of *The Mahabharata*,
Translated by Kisari Mohan Ganguli

Vaishampayana said: "Then Shakra, causing the firmament
and the Earth to be filled by a loud sound, came to the son of
Pritha on a car and asked him to ascend it. Beholding his brothers fallen on the Earth, king Yudhishthira the just said unto that
deity of a 1,000 eyes these words: 'My brothers have all
dropped down here. They must go with me. Without them by
me I do not wish to go to Heaven, O lord of all the deities. The
delicate princess (Draupadi) deserving of every comfort, O Pu-
randara, should go with us. It behoveth thee to permit this.'

"Shakra said, 'Thou shalt behold thy brothers in Heaven.
They have reached it before thee. Indeed, thou shalt see all of
them there, with Krishna. Do not yield to grief, O chief of the
Bharatas. Having cast off their human bodies they have gone
there, O chief of Bharata's race. As regards thee, it is ordained
that thou shalt go thither in this very body of thine.'

"Yudhishthira said, 'This dog, O lord of the Past and the
Present, is exceedingly devoted to me. He should go with me.
My heart is full of compassion for him.'

"Shakra said, 'Immortality and a condition equal to mine,
O king, prosperity extending in all directions, and high success,
and all the felicities of Heaven, thou hast won today. Do thou
cast off this dog. In this there will be no cruelty.'

"Yudhishthira said, 'O thou of a 1,000 eyes. O thou that
art of righteous behaviour, it is exceedingly difficult for one
that is of righteous behaviour to perpetrate an act that is un-
righteous. I do not desire that union with prosperity for which
I shall have to cast off one that is devoted to me.'

"Indra said, 'There is no place in Heaven for persons with
dogs. Besides, the (deities called) Krodhavasas take away all the
merits of such persons. Reflecting on this, act, O king
Yudhishthira the just. Do thou abandon this dog. There is no
cruelty in this.'

"Yudhishthira said, 'It has been said that the abandonment
of one that is devoted is infinitely sinful. It is equal to the sin

that one incurs by slaying a Brahmana. Hence, O great Indra, I shall not abandon this dog today from desire of my happiness. Even this is my vow steadily pursued, that I never give up a person that is terrified, nor one that is devoted to me, nor one that seeks my protection, saying that he is destitute, nor one that is afflicted, nor one that has come to me, nor one that is weak in protecting oneself, nor one that is solicitous of life. I shall never give up such a one till my own life is at an end.'

"Indra said, 'Whatever gifts, or sacrifices spread out, or libations poured on the sacred fire, are seen by a dog, are taken away by the Krodhavasas. Do thou, therefore, abandon this dog. By abandoning this dog, thou wilt attain to the region of the deities. Having abandoned thy brothers and Krishna, thou hast, O hero, acquired a region of felicity by thy own deeds. Why art thou so stupefied? Thou hast renounced everything. Why then dost thou not renounce this dog?' "Yudhishthira said, 'This is well known in all the worlds that there is neither friendship nor enmity with those that are dead. When my brothers and Krishna died, I was unable to revive them. Hence it was that I abandoned them. I did not, however, abandon them as long as they were alive. To frighten one that has sought protection, the slaying of a woman, the theft of what belongs to a Brahmana, and injuring a friend, each of these four, O Shakra, is I think equal to the abandonment of one that is devoted.'"

Vaishampayana continued: "Hearing these words of king Yudhishthira the just, (the dog became transformed into) the deity of Righteousness, who, well pleased, said these words unto him in a sweet voice fraught with praise.

"Dharma said: 'Thou art well born, O king of kings, and possessed of the intelligence and the good conduct of Pandu. Thou hast compassion for all creatures, O Bharata, of which this is a bright example. Formerly, O son, thou wert once examined by me in the woods of Dwaita, where thy brothers of great prowess met with (an appearance of) death. Disregarding both thy brothers Bhima and Arjuna, thou didst wish for the revival of Nakula from thy desire of doing good to thy (step-) mother. On the present occasion, thinking the dog to be devoted to thee, thou hast renounced the very car of the celestials instead of renouncing him. Hence. O king, there is no one in Heaven that is equal to thee. Hence, O Bharata, regions of inexhaustible felicity are thine. Thou hast won them, O chief of the Bharatas, and thine is a celestial and high goal."'

Vaishampayana continued: "Then Dharma, and Shakra, and the Maruts, and the Ashvinis, and other deities, and the celestial Rishis, causing Yudhishthira to ascend on a car, proceeded to Heaven. Those beings crowned with success and capable of going everywhere at will, rode their respective cars. King Yudhishthira, that perpetuator of Kuru's race, riding on that car, ascended quickly, causing the entire welkin to blaze with his effulgence. Then Narada, that foremost of all speakers, endued with penances. and conversant with all the worlds, from amidst that concourse of deities, said these words: 'All those royal sages that are here have their achievements transcended by those of Yudhishthira. Covering all the worlds by his fame and splendour and by his wealth of conduct, he has attained to Heaven in his own (human) body. None else than the son of Pandu has been heard to achieve this.'"

APHORISMS FOR APHRODITE

Wisdom — Wisdom is love's maturest form.

Love — Unconditional positive regard for *this* being. Love's question: *What is best, truly best, for the one I love?* This question searches everything.

Universal Love Compared — In *The Varieties of Religious Experience* (lectures XIV and XV), William James writes, "The next saintly virtue in which we find excess is Purity. In theopathic characters, [...] the love of God must not be mixed with any other love. Father and mother, sisters, brothers, and friends are felt as interfering distractions."

Zenith is the adjoining of all beings, including fathers, mothers, sisters, brothers, and friends, such that love of one amounts to love of Zenith; love of any person is no "interfering distraction," but its contrary, a deepening and widening love of Zenith. Loving people is loving Zenith.

Sweet Joined — Consider the miracle berry, *Synsepalum dulcificum* ("sweet joined sepal"). After eating a miracle berry, things such as sour lemons taste sweet. This effect is due to the fruit's miraculin, a glycoprotein that binds to the tongue's sour receptors. Is there a *Synsepalum dulcificum* for all existence?

God's Goodness — Is this Zenith good? Good? Supposing goodness is relative to subjects, and Zenith is all subjects, all subjectivity, all intersubjectivity, what follows? The question becomes: What is Zenith's judgment of itself? Something like this has been a problem for theologians: God's goodness appears circular or arbitrary. If "goodness" means God or God's will, then "God is good" is equivalent to "God is God" or "God does God's will." Why should Zenith fare worse ?

In Zenith's case, and perhaps in the traditional theological case too, there are multiple subjective assessments in equilibrium. So perhaps "I am good," as said by the Zenith "I," reflects some maximal reflective equilibrium on its goodness. All of us, at last, love all of us. *We* are good.

THE CARPENTER

Dedicated to my brother, Christopher van Belle

The war solved no problem. Its effects, both immediate and indirect, were either negative or disastrous. Morally subversive, economically destructive, socially degrading, confused in its causes, devious in its course, futile in its results, it is the outstanding example in European history of meaningless conflict.

— Cicely Veronica Wedgwood, *The Thirty Years War*

November 1634, Ulm

Otto and his mother, Rosina, were returning from the home of Hermann and his wife Paula, for whom Otto and Rosina worked as domestic servants; the boy did the household's laundry; the mother, all else. Rosina's woolen kirtle was tattered, as was the shift beneath it. The boy's green eyes were sunken with hunger. The widow and her son moved weakly, especially the son, who, due to an above-the-knee amputation, walked on crutches.

There was no church collection large enough to help the surge of victims flowing into Ulm. The clergy could provide little food—porridge and saltless bread—and only infrequently. The civic poor chest, too, was inadequate; the municipal granary barely fed the citizen poor; the non-citizen poor were left to God's grace. Rosina could not afford the purchase of Ulmer citizenship. So, she prayed for God's grace.

Returning to their home, the municipal poorhouse, the *Armen Heußlin*, of Ulm, Otto and Rosina always passed the workshop of a carpenter named Johann. His workshop sat two streets southeast of Ulmer Münster, whose soaring spire oriented newcomers.

Johann always knew that it was an hour after sunset whenever Rosina and her son walked past his workshop, such was their invariable schedule. Johann was nauseated by the horrid everywhereness of such miseries as these that befell this boy and his mother. He had come to know, through Hermann their employer and through Rosina herself, on a few occasions, a little about their lives.

Rosina and Otto were refugees—first from Hermaringen and then from Neenstetten, eighteen kilometers north of Ulm. It was in Hermaringen that, by a soldier's errant bullet, Otto lost his left leg. The bullet had shattered Otto's knee and tibia. An ill-skilled physician wrapped Otto's upper thigh, stuck a stick between thigh and wrapping, twisted, and held this tightly as a tourniquet, then he sawed away the child's leg above the knee; he cauterized the amputated leg, rather than ligate its blood vessels, as only fire and an old iron cautery were available, and no fine instruments for ligation. The operation left Otto with a neuroma, aggravated by any pressure on several areas of the residual limb.

They migrated to Neenstetten and were subsisting in a hovel when more misery fell upon the two. Rosina was ripped away from her son by Imperial soldiers, hauled to the hayloft of a nearby stable, and raped so violently that she could not walk for two days.

She survived. She found her son again, and together they left Neenstetten for Ulm, to join the hundreds of refugees now in the city.

Such was the execrable condition of these shorn lambs coming into Ulm. Nor was there condition necessarily uplifted in the city. Unlicensed begging could get one banished here, or locked in the *Strafturm*, the prison tower, where one can only watch the swift and scintillating Danube flow away to the far off Black Sea. The able-bodied "undeserving poor" could be whipped with birch-rods through the gates and out of Ulm. Otto, with his amputation, and Rosina, a widow, were deemed "deserving poor" by the town's regulators; then registered as resident aliens, or *Beywoner*, and required to work. They were, in two words, beggar servants. For refugees, it meant survival.

Johann had been a refugee, but he arrived in Ulm as a master craftsman, so welcomed. His life had been flattened too.

Johann was born in 1600 in Magdeburg to Georg and Anna, a carpenter and his young wife; they had moved to Magdeburg from Ulm in 1596, as Ulm was then plunged in plague and a declining market. In Magdeburg, Georg taught his son some carpentry, but when the boy was six, Georg died. Out of necessity, Anna became a laundress. Johann, by the grace of God, apprenticed in carpentry under a master craftsman who was a friend of Georg's, a deaf man named Ulrich.

From apprentice to journeyman to master craftsman, Johann's life was settled and pleasant.

Then, May 20th, 1631.

After a brief, but fearsome siege, Magdeburg fell to General Tilly and lieutenant Pappenheim, and their lawless and exhausted soldiers. In the havoc, hellfire rose throughout the city, or so the rampant, ravening, raging fires seemed to Johann. Flames too fast for feet, especially little feet and old feet. A wind favorable to fire made Magdeburg's wooden houses into pyres for families all together, for mother and baby to blacken together.

25,000 lives gone.

Anna gone.

Ulrich gone.

Johann had run to an open area clear of the fires, but nightlike with their smoke. He sat there, faceless, until all was flat and merely smoldering. Until, found, dragged, he was forced, with many others, to aid Tilly's forces in throwing all burnt bodies into the Elbe, to prevent plague. Many never sank, only drifted as little dark islands of carrion birds. As charred hands and arms slid from his hands into the river waters, Johann left himself. For fourteen days, tumbril after tumbril after tumbril of burnt bodies trundled to Elbe's shores for dumping.

In the spring of the following year, Pappenheim, evacuating his forces, burned down the remnants of Magdeburg. Johann was commanded to march out with the soldiery; he briefly considered joining as a soldier, perhaps to rise up the ranks like Werth or Stalhans or Melander. Instead, he became a camp follower of Pappenheim's soldiery, a servant of the captors, among the baggage wagons, as one of the camp's carpenters, its wheelwrights, its joiners; he would build, not butcher, and be paid in grain and eggs, when available.

"If we live in the autumn of this world," he thought, "then may God, the good craftsman of the green earth, find me building for winter." Yet he knew he built for bloodshed. Yet he built.

Along the marches, wagons passing around carcasses of starved cattle and diseased horses, Johann saw *too much* depredation and degradation. Soldiers were brigands and unmerciful rulers in whatever famished land they occupied. They set ablaze any house they passed, after plundering it. They tormented and immiserated many peasants. Some of the soldiery simply dissolved into unaffiliated bands of robbers.

In fixed shock, Johann never quite believed the gore and despoilment he witnessed. A blood-choked man. A gibbeted and rotting woman. The severed upper half of a child. He witnessed torture by thumbscrew, manure fork, and manure. He witnessed all the fetid leftovers of famine, poverty, cruelty, rage, and massacre. All the ravages of scurvy, smallpox, and typhus. All coherence dashed into shards like a potter's vessel.

One dreary night, a soldier from Zweibrücken recounted hearing of a starved and desperate mother eating her daughter. The storyteller laughed. Some Hungarian mercenaries followed suit and spoke of "old Vlad the Impaler" and his "forest" of piked Turkish bodies, some 20,000 or more. Johann could easily imagine such ferocity now. The rat in sublime rot, the maggot in divine filth, the vulture communing with the purple thigh meat of a dead soldier. One's joy is another's atrocity, thought Johann—and sickened.

But so many of these soldiers laughed knowing that so many of them were next for such ravages. Heads effaced by gunfire disturbed their thoughts. They knew, they witnessed, that soldiers in states too mutilated for aid would have their throats slit open, or buried half-conscious, or abandoned to death there where they writhed.

In Lützen, Pappenheim's forces joined Wallenstein's. There, with battle certain against King Gustavus, Wallenstein employed camp followers as mock "reserves" to fill out their smaller force, to fool and intimidate the Swedish King, but Gustavus broke this facade and the camp followers, being no soldiers, fled into the heavy fog and black smoke of Lützen.

Fiery Lützen, foggy and fiery Lützen, where King Gustavus, the Golden King, fell. Lützen's fires threw Johann back into the inferno of Magdeburg. His face and neck reddened and strained with screams as he ran.

In the frenzy of retreat, Johann, terrified that an enemy was at his heel, lifted a fist-sized rock and threw it blindly backward; yet, as the rock left his hand, a prayer suddenly filled his heart: "Lord grant that it fall harmlessly!"

The carpenter ran until his lungs burned and legs convulsed.

With difficulty, alone and malnourished, fed only on fallen beechnuts, Johann had made his way to Ulm, his motherland and fatherland, where many refugees had come. Here, for two years, making wooden furniture, architectural ornaments, and wooden dishes, he lived quietly.

Now, in the darkness, as Rosina and Otto passed high-gabled houses and two drunk hod carriers, as they passed Johann's workshop, Johann called out to them.

"Rosina! Otto!"

Rosina was expecting this invitation, and gently guided Otto to Johann's workshop. Johann had told Rosina, seven weeks before, of his birthday plan for Otto; she held in her tears. "God is good. God is good," she said; "God is good."

Johann's workshop was warmed by a porcelain stove, which he had bartered from a French soldier. Otto fixed his green eyes on it. He imagined himself sitting inside the stove, engulfed in its precious heat, melting off all November's chill. The heated and clean air of the workshop felt so beautifully unlike the fug of the poorhouse.

A small rushlight on a small oak table lit the workshop. A pewter bowl filled with water sat near the rushlight to reflect and increase its glow. Beside these, a copy of Jakob Böhme's *Aurora* sat dustless on a pewter plate at the center of the table. *Aurora* was a gift to Johann from a journeyman carpenter from Dresden; another refugee. Adjacent the pewter bowl and plate, a wooden bowl held three dried figs, which Johann lifted and offered to Rosina and Otto. Rosina handed Otto two and ate one herself.

"Thank you," said Rosina.

"Thank you, sir," said her son in a whisper.

"Please, make yourselves comfortable." Johann gestured toward two chairs, one of which was small and perfectly sized for Otto. "If I may," Johann began, as the two sat down, "I would like to read from scripture."

Johann lifted his bible and read: "'*For I am convinced that neither death nor life, neither angels nor demons, neither the present nor the future, nor any powers, neither height nor depth, nor anything else in all creation, will be able to separate us from the love of God that is in Christ Jesus our Lord.' Amen.*"

Rosina's head was bowed. After whispering "amen," she raised her head and forced herself to smile.

"I wish I had more food to offer you," said Johann.

"Thank you," said Rosina.

Then there was silence. In their exhaustion, the silence was pleasant. Rosina looked at the foliate-carved armrests under her arms. Otto, noticing his mother noticing her armrests, looked at those under his own arms; each of his armrests terminated in the head of a mule.

"It is your birthday, Otto, is it not?"

"It is," replied the boy, nervously.

"How old are you now?"

"I'm twelve."

"Happy birthday to you."

"Thank you."

Johann coughed, cleared his throat, smiled, then asked, "Do you like your chair? It is *your* chair, after all."

"Mine?"

"Yes. Do you like mules?"

Otto looked to his mother.

"Otto likes all animals," she answered. "His favorite animal is the dog."

A memory flashed before Johann—of soldiers stomping on a dog, then shooting it. He nodded to Rosina and Otto, while pushing away this memory.

"Dogs are wondrous creatures," he said. "So trusting of Man."

More silence followed, followed by Rosina's voice: "Otto, do you like your chair?"

"Yes," peeped Otto. "Thank you."

"That gladdens me," said Johann. "Do you know why I chose mules?"

Otto shook his head.

"The heathen poets spoke of a god with a lame foot: Hephaestus, a blacksmith god. A builder! Imagine that, a builder-god. I discovered something else about this blacksmith god: like Lord Jesus going into Jerusalem, it was said that Hephaestus rode on a humble mule up to Heaven."

Otto listened, staring at the crumbling shoe on his foot.

"Would you mind if I ask you a few questions, Otto?"

"I don't mind."

"Do you know of Saints Cosmas and Damian?"

"No," answered Otto.

Otto, like most children, had no formal education, but he knew his prayers and songs.

"They were surgeons. They once healed a man with a gangrenous thigh; they removed the sickly flesh, the sickly leg, but then, endeavoring to refill the absence, considered from where they could take flesh to fill up the emptiness. It happened that, in a nearby cemetery, an Ethiopian had been buried only an hour before, and from this dead man, dear to God as all men are, a dear and fresh leg was cut free, then stitched and bound with linen to the sick man. The leg healed, joined the body, and the man was healthy again."

"What about the dead man?" asked Otto, gripped by a story so similar to his own. "He has only one leg now."

"Oh, yes, the Saints made sure to bind the bad leg onto the dead man, for safe-keeping, so that all parts will be returned in the Resurrection."

"Or maybe they keep each other's legs and become leg-friends." Otto smiled, then dropped his smile and looked fearful.

Johann smiled warmly, "Imagine them dancing together like that!" A wide smile blossomed, then wilted, on the boy's face. "Do you know, Otto, what occupation Paul the Apostle had?"

"No, sir."

"Paul was a tentmaker."

Otto stared off, trying to imagine such an important saint laboring over a tent.

"Do you know what *earthly* occupation our Lord Jesus held?"

"Shephard?"

"Excellent guess, Otto. Quite excellent. He is the shepherd of souls, yes, he is that; but do you remember the particular *craft* that Joseph taught Jesus?"

"Carpenter?"

"Excellent again and yes! Our Lord decided to be raised by a carpenter, a builder. *Though a priest once told me that the original Greek word, tektōn, is slightly broader than carpenter, but I think that carpenter is good enough.* Now, why do you suppose the Messiah chose to be raised by a carpenter and learn carpentry?"

"Because he shall raise men from the dead?"

"Mighty true, sweet Kindlein. Why though a carpenter?"

"I don't know."

"Well, there is much unknown, isn't there? Why a carpenter? Why a tentmaker? Two artisans. Two laborers. Not emperors. Not generals. Not soldiers. I don't know why either, but I think someday we'll know."

"Yes."

"Until then, do you know what I do?"

The boy looked up at Johann, but didn't speak.

"I follow the example of our Lord. I build and make and refine. I work not only with my head and heart, but with my hands too. And, it so happens, Otto, that I have made something else for you. May I give you your second birthday gift?"

The boy looked pained. He looked at his mother; she nodded permission.

"Yes, please."

Johann walked to an old oak trunk beside the porcelain stove, flipped up the trunk's iron hasps, opened the lid, and lifted out a prosthetic leg.

Johann, the leg's proud maker, described the leg as he lifted it: "The socket is made from the wood of a European silver fir; it is attached to a pilon of high-grade Polish oak, which is hidden inside the leg. The exterior, the leg itself, from the knee-joint down, is rare and fine lindenwood. I painted the lindenwood with a sun, a moon, and hundreds of tiny stars, so you may walk upon all the stars."

Johann knew of Otto's pain and where on the residual limb it burned the most. Six weeks before, Johann, with

Rosina's help, had made a cast of Otto's residual limb, telling the boy it was needed for an improvement to his crutches, an implausible claim that the boy numbly accepted. Thus, Johann crafted the socket of silver fir most carefully, conforming the cast of the residual limb (with markings for painful sites) with the socket, all in a feedback of feeling and whittling and smoothing and feeling again. A liner of sheepskin would then cradle the limb as limb, sheepskin, and silver fir conformed into a mostly comfortable harmony of parts.

To keep it as light as he could, Johann had worked with a metallurgist to craft hinges of Swedish copper no larger than needed for a locking knee. A suspension harness of rough wool and leather helped distribute weight off the leg. When he was fashioning the leather harness, Johann remembered the sight of two teenage boys outside of Lützen, desperate with starvation, eating leather they had soaked in water.

The harness fit perfectly and the delicate socket held Otto's leg comfortably, only slightly agitating the neuroma.

Finally, Johann had purchased from a shoemaker two new black shoes for Otto. Johann stooped and gently put the new shoes on Otto's two feet. Otto had lived almost two years without his left leg. The boy cried softly through a shaking smile, and as Johann tied the last shoe, Otto hugged Johann, as a cast-away hugs a firm rock in a furious sea.

When Rosina saw her son walk on his new leg, effortlessly, but joyfully, she shook. "Miracle," she uttered, then, with the corners of her mouth turning down, covered her face with her hands and cried.

"Happy birthday, Otto. You're a good young man. I am glad you like this gift. I have *one* last question. Would you be my apprentice here? Ulm needs more carpenters. It's a noble trade and our guildsmen are good men. Alas, I need the help."

Otto hugged the carpenter again and, full of love, answered, "Yes, yes!"

Long ago [man] formed an ideal conception of omnipotence and om-niscience which he embodied in his gods. To these gods he attributed every-thing that seemed unattainable to his wishes, or that was forbidden to him. One may say, therefore, that these gods were cultural ideals. Today he has come very close to the attainment of this ideal, he has almost become a god himself. Only, it is true, in the fashion in which ideals are usually attained according to the general judgment of humanity: not completely, in some respects not at all, in others only halfway. Man has, as it were, become a kind of prosthetic God. When he puts on all his auxiliary organs he is truly magnificent; but those organs have not grown on to him and they still give him much trouble at times ... Future ages will bring with them new and probably unimaginably great achievements in this field of civilization and will increase man's likeness to God still more. But in the interests of our investigations, we will not forget that present-day man does not feel happy in his Godlike character.

— Sigmund Freud, *Civilization and Its Discontents*

How then can he [Man] be said to resemble God? Is it his immortal soul, his rationality, his self-consciousness, his free will, or what, that gives him a claim to this rather startling distinction? A case may be argued for all these elements in the complex nature of man. But had the author of Genesis anything particular in his mind when he wrote? It is observable that in the passage leading up to the statement about man, he has given no detailed information about God. Looking at man, he sees in him something essentially divine, but when we turn back to see what he says about the original upon which the "image" of God was modeled, we find only the single assertion, "God created." The characteristic common to God and man is apparently that: the desire and the ability to make things.

— Dorothy L. Sayers, *The Mind of the Maker*

POLIXENES
Shepherdess,
A fair one are you—well you fit our ages
With flowers of winter.

PERDITA
Sir, the year growing ancient,

Not yet on summer's death, nor on the birth
Of trembling winter, the fairest
flowers o' the season
Are our carnations and streak'd gillyvors,
Which some call nature's bastards: of that kind
Our rustic garden's barren; and I care not
To get slips of them.

POLIXENES
Wherefore, gentle maiden,
Do you neglect them?

PERDITA
For I have heard it said
There is an art which in their piedness shares
With great creating nature.

POLIXENES
Say there be;
Yet nature is made better by no mean
But nature makes that mean: so, over that art
Which you say adds to nature, is an art
That nature makes. You see, sweet maid, we marry
A gentler scion to the wildest stock,
And make conceive a bark of baser kind
By bud of nobler race: this is an art
Which does mend nature, change it rather, but
The art itself is nature.

PERDITA
So it is.

POLIXENES
Then make your garden rich in gillyvors,
And do not call them bastards.

— Shakespeare, *A Winter's Tale* (Scene IV)

APHORISMS FOR ANTEROS

O vos felices radices — Solar wombs, solar nurseries, fledge neurons that awaken a nervous system whose glittering tendrils toddle out like kudzu vine for more experience. All of us are caught, *ab initio, ad infinitum*, in numberless nets as they encephalize infinity.

Apeirophobia — If you fear the infinite, unlimited, endless, remember that you live within a living infinity, an ever-flowering system of infinitely many lives, including your own, winning divinity.

The Royal Rosarian — We Portlanders prize our International Rose Test Garden, where damasks, polyanthas, grandifloras, hybrid perpetuals, and other roses thrive.

Imagine an infinite rose garden, the Infinite Rose Test Garden, in which you could enter and exit as you please. Imagine you come upon a pink rose in this garden; a sign indicates that this pink rose is a "cherish floribunda." While enjoying the fragrance and coral-pink petals of this cherish rose, a Royal Rosarian sidles up to you and says, "There are infinitely many cherishes in this garden."

What would you say, if anything, to this Royal Rosarian?

"Oh, then there is no value in *this particular* cherish rose. Its fragrance no longer has any effect on me. Its coral-pink petals are no longer pleasingly soft and powdery."

Or, might you say: "I love, love, love this rose. It is so fresh and fragrant. By the way, what does 'floribunda' mean?"

Or, might you say: "How wonderful that, of all the infinite cherishes, I am experiencing *this* cherish. No one else has yet hypnotized themselves with the candied scent of *this exact* cherish. I'll name *this* rose 'Anteros,' after the butterfly-winged Greek god of requited love."

The infinity of roses does not seem to me a negation of the intrinsic value of the rose's intrinsic properties, nor does it seem to me a negation (nay, it seems an infinite increase) of the value of this rose *in its singularity*.

LEIBNIZ'S VIEW OF INFINITE RECURRENCE

While Nietzsche famously used eternal recurrence as a spiritual *gedankenexperiment*, in which one faces either self-condemnation or self-affirmation, Leibniz considered literal eternal recurrence impossible. As Maria Rosa Antognazza writes in her masterful work, *Leibniz: An Intellectual Biography*:

> According to Leibniz, what might appear to be the repetition of identical circumstances was not and could not be the eternal return of all things, due to the fact that individual substances involve the infinite. To the eye able to appreciate the infinite detail of concrete beings and the infinite truths of fact which can be enunciated about them, there is no such thing as a finite number of circumstances which (no matter how great their number) ought to result in a finite number in combinations.[90]

In Leibniz's view, an individual substance is a subject with *infinitely many* intrinsic predicates. Most of these predicates are imperceptible and incalculable (except, according to Leibniz, to the mind of God). A complete specification of you (i.e., your "complete concept") requires a complete specification of the universe, since truths *about* you (the predicates in your subject) implicate truths in an infinitely iterating background web of truths. Every individual substance is a species all its own, *infinitely specifiable*.

To say, "You and I are both human" is true, but it underspecifies; more differentiation is possible, e.g., "I was born in Van Nuys, California." Differentiation of any given subject from any other given subject may be a bottomless differentiation—an infinite differentiation. No two subjects possess exactly the same predicates. If X and Y shared all and only the same predicates, then X and Y would not be two things, but one. This rule is called Leibniz's Principle of the Identity of Indiscernibles. As Leibniz wrote:

> It is even necessary for each monad [individual substance]

---

[90] Maria Antognazza, *Leibniz: An Intellectual Biography*, 542

to be different from every other. For there are never two things in nature which are perfectly alike and in which it is impossible to find a difference that is internal or founded on an intrinsic denomination.[91]

Later, Leibniz applies this uniqueness to the problem of eternal or infinite recurrence:

Even if a previous century returns for what concerns things which can be sensed or which can be described by books, it will not return completely in all respects: since there will always be differences although imperceptible and such that could not be sufficiently described in any book.[92]

For Leibniz, the infinitely predicated subject is non-recurrent *even in an infinite natural system*.[93] You are unique, even in an infinite natural system (like a living diagonal sequence in Cantor's diagonal argument). There may exist individuals *extremely* similar to you, but none perfectly identical—and perhaps none that differ by fewer than two or three predicates.

As a zenithist, I wonder about my uniqueness in an infinite universe. I think Leibniz's vision of an infinitely predicated subject, a unique intersection where *this* set of *these* infinite cosmic lines converge, provides ballast in this wondering.

---

[91] Leibniz, *Monadology*

[92] Leibniz, *De l'horizon de la doctrine humaine*

[93] To identify Alice *as* merely recurrent particle configurations of Alice in an infinite universe is a reductive interpretation of Alice; origin of the subject, evolution of the subject, and other *infinitely* relational properties differentiates *this* Alice from *that* Alice $10^{100^{1000^{10000}}}$ meters away. A thing *infinitely* differentiated is not easily duplicated, even in an infinite natural system.

THE SIGNIFICANCE OF OUR EFFORTS

In an infinite natural system, where infinitely many civilizations have explored infinitely many paths of artistry, science, philosophy, spirituality, and so on well beyond our human horizon, on upward to Zenith, a question appears: What is the significance of *your* specific path, *your* efforts, *your* novelties?

I'll offer four brief takes on this problem:

1. *The significance of the significance of your efforts*
2. *Intrinsic value and the uniqueness of identity*
3. *Autonomous affirmation*
4. *The exaltation of life*

***

1. *The significance of the significance of your efforts.*

First, the "value" of your effort may not be justifiable in objective or third-person terms, but this possibility may become irrelevant to you. Secondly, if any such demonstrated value of your effort fails to induce positive affect in you, that is, fails to feel like anything save a syntactic proof, then, I assume, justification in the third-person will be only another irrelevancy to you, a matter of perfect insufficiency. In brief, one can feel significant *without* objective significance and one might feel insignificant *with* objective significance; so, what is the subjective significance of objective significance?

The significance of your effort is felt. If it is not felt, then perhaps even a heaven in which your effort is celebrated forever-after will never prove to your most intimate and inward denier the "true significance" of your effort. "What good will it be for someone to gain the whole world, yet forfeit their soul?" (Matthew 16:26). What good will it be for someone to gain a third-person justification of their efforts, yet forfeit all *feeling* of significance?

Often, third-person justifications of effort are absent from the flow of action; such defenses may be irrelevant to the agent-in-flow. The dancer-in-flow is focused on the dance, not on the ultimate status of the dance in a "mindbogglingly big" universe (unless this status is itself the dancer's "inspiration"). Of course, the dance's impact on viewers, including the dancer, may be an element of the process, but that is a far narrower field of vision than objective significance in the cosmos.

One might claim that undergirding a flow state is a quasi-rationale (a proto-justification) distributed throughout the pre-reflective processes of the subconscious; covertly, it may be claimed, there exists motivation from reasons, norms, and other non-natural entities, that flow is the result of so many suppressed premises in the agent. Thus, one requires third-person or objective justifiers, if only subconsciously.

It may or may not be that a reason-laden and proto-justificatory subconscious is a prerequisite for feelings that, if forced into the lossy and confabulatory medium of ordinary language sentences, might be expressed as "my effort is obviously significant" or "my effort is worth it." But it is not a prerequisite that these subconscious proto-justifications be good justifications, let alone fledge into justifications proper, as we know that human flow-states far outnumber humans with sound arguments supporting the significance of their efforts. Bad proto-reasons and good proto-reasons may amount to the same jubilant flow. Thus, the quest for third-person justificatory accounts of significance may bring despair to a mind not in flow-state; still, for a mind in flow-state, this quest and any single strand of one's eyelashes share the same *irrelevance*.

(Of course, this justification quest may become the object of a flow-state, as it is with me in this moment. In such a case, one might hear pronouncements such as Albert Camus's in his *The Myth of Sisyphus*: "The struggle itself toward the heights is enough to fill a man's heart.")

But what of that non-flow lucidity *after* the rock has rolled downhill? Is there a satisfying "post-flow" defense of the objective significance of one's effort in an infinite system? Or, must we always hasten to our *flowpium*?

2. Intrinsic value and the uniqueness of identity

Philosopher Scott A. Davison, in his book *On the Intrinsic*

Value of Everything, argues that "all concrete, particular things are intrinsically valuable to some degree" (Davison's "Main Conclusion") and that "something in every exemplified onto-logical category is intrinsically value to some degree" (Da-vison's "Ambitious Speculative Conclusion").

If the main conclusion is correct, then the concrete par-ticular results of your effort, e.g., a tapestry or terzanelle, are intrinsically valuable to some degree. As for the effort itself, if it qualifies as a concrete particular, then it falls under the main conclusion; if your effort belongs to an ontological category other than that of concrete particulars (i.e., that of a "state of affairs"), then it falls under the ambitious speculative conclu-sion. In either case, your effort *qua* effort may be a bearer of intrinsic value to some degree.

I highly recommend Davison's book, especially since in it you will find the argumentation, or "persuasive elaboration" (as Davison calls it, borrowing from the philosopher Gary Gut-ting), which I am not presenting here. Here, I only defenselessly mention the possibility.

You might think that while a concrete particular *type* such as the *Mona Lisa* may have intrinsic value to some degree, the infinite tokens of this concrete particular type do not have such intrinsic value. The existence of the *Mona Lisa* may be better than its non-existence, but this binary reasoning may not ex-tend to a prioritization for the existence of infinitely many *Mona Lisa* paintings. Is the existence of infinitely many *Mona Lisa* paintings better than the existence of finitely many *Mona Lisa* paintings, or better than the existence of only one *Mona Lisa*? I don't have a clear sense of an answer to this question.

Yet it seems to me paradoxical to claim that intrinsic value does not apply to the intrinsic properties of a particular *if* that particular is one of an infinite set of identical particulars; an intrinsic value is not the sort of thing that is conditional on extrinsic factors, such as the quantity of other things in the world. However, assuming this conditional view of intrinsic value is the case, I would dispute that, in the realm of concrete particular things in an infinite system, there exists redundant token status. As I wrote in "Leibniz's View of Infinite Recur-rence," "The differentiation of any given subject from any other given subject is a bottomless differentiation—an infinite differentiation." The apparent redundancy of infinitely many *Mona Lisa* paintings is no real redundancy; each concrete particular *Mona Lisa* may be an infinitely predicated particular, such that each "token" of the *Mona Lisa* is in fact a type unto itself. Since, on the Leibnizian view, seemingly relational or polyadic predicates are actually intrinsic (monadic) predicates of the subject, any token status we find between multiple subjects is the result only of an incomplete analysis of these complete (infinitely differentiated) subjects. Thus, even if we assume that there is no intrinsic value in any particular example of the infinitely many tokens of X, we can add that there are not infinitely many tokens of X, only infinitely many types of X-like things. Thus, we reject the predicate-stripping simplicity of the question "Is the existence of infinitely many *Mona Lisa* paintings better than the existence of finitely many *Mona Lisa* paintings, or better than the existence of only one *Mona Lisa*?" When one has a *Mona Lisa* before one's eyes, one has an infinitely singular presence before oneself, and the question of the value of its existence over the value of its non-existence is always about *it*, not something else like it (since, for a semi-Leibnizian such as myself, there is nothing else *exactly* like it).

3. *Autonomous affirmation*

In section 1 of this essay, I quoted from Albert Camus's *The Myth of Sisyphus*. In this section, I will use *The Myth of Sisyphus* to outline a third view of our significance: autonomy and autonomous affirmation.

The Myth of Sisyphus was my favorite book of philosophy as a young adult, quite some years before its replacement by Nietzsche's *The Gay Science* and William James's *The Varieties of Religious Experience*.

In *The Myth of Sisyphus*, Camus is concerned with the meaning of life: "I therefore conclude that the meaning of life is the most urgent question" (4). For our purposes, one could switch "meaning" with "significance." At the end of this book, Camus employs the story of King Sisyphus, whom "the gods had condemned [...] to ceaselessly rolling a rock to the top of a mountain, whence the stone would fall back down of its own weight" (119). This "futile and hopeless labor" distills, for Camus, the human condition. The human condition is an absurd condition.

> The world in itself is not reasonable, that is all that can be said. But what is absurd is the confrontation of this irrational and the wild longing for clarity whose call echoes in the human heart (21).

Our significance, the significance of our efforts, is doubted, but Camus argues for an affirmation of life, an absurd significance, *if you will*. How?

Before addressing this, I would like to digress and highlight a problem that I have with Camus's philosophy. I find his epistemic asceticism interesting, but too actorly, even inorganic.

"Hence, what he [the absurd man] demands of himself is to live *solely* with what he knows, to accommodate himself to what is, and to bring nothing in that is not certain. He is told that nothing is. But this at least is a certainty. And it is with this that he is concerned: he wants to find out if it is possible to live *without appeal*" (53).

This epistemic puritanism ("absurd *ascesis*" and "unfailing alertness") reminds me of William K. Clifford's "The Ethics of Belief," though Camus preaches no universal imperative. William James questions Clifford and all such belief-puritanism in his "The Will to Believe." To Camus I would have suggested that a lucid mind can make a Jamesian jump without making a Kierkegaardian leap. Moreover, the history of intellectual progress is a history of intellectual over-extensions; lucidity does not acquiesce at "limits." The temptation to explain all is the temptation to *more* lucidity.

Lucidity is dialectical, but what is dialectic without transgressors? Philonous needs a Hylas, Salviati a Simplicio, and so on. Camus knew this:

> The record of Gnostic effronteries and the persistence of Manichean currents have contributed more to the construction of orthodox dogma than all the prayers. With due allowance, the same is true of the absurd. One

recognizes one's course by discovering the paths that stray from it (113).

We need to stray to know our path. To be the absurd man, one *must* have, at some moment, lived beyond the absurd. Hegel, in *The Science of* Logic, writes in his Hegelian fashion:

> Great stress is laid on the limitations of thought, of reason, and so on, and it is asserted that the limitation *cannot* be transcended. To make such as assertion is to be unaware that the very fact that something is determined as a limitation implies that the limitation is already transcended. For a determinateness, a limit, is determined as a limitation only in opposition to its other in general, that is, in opposition to that which is *free from the limitation;* the other of a limitation is precisely the *being beyond* it (§ 265).

Our lucidity is rather our chiaroscuro. Alongside "man's struggle against his hopes" (112), there is man's higher struggle against his limits, including the limit that cuts him off from his ideal, his hope.

Certainly, as an experiment in ascetic living, one may try to live "without appeal," to "live in those deserts," but this experiment, as Camus would affirm, has no more and no less significance than living *with* appeal to the unknown and uncertain (22). "The absurd does not liberate, it binds. It does not authorize all actions. [...] The absurd merely confers an equivalence on the consequences of those actions" (67). The consequences of all actions are equivalent; so, on the absurd thinker's assumption, the consequences of living without hope are equivalent to those of living with hope. If we take Pascal's wager and remove all of its stakes, we have the Camusian wager.

So we return to our problem. For Camus, significance is significance *for someone.* "For everything begins with consciousness and nothing is worth anything except through it" (13). Without subjectivity, there is no significance. Camus pairs this subjectivism with divine command theory (or, if we take Camus less literally, with metaethical Platonism as *the* prerequisite for moral truths) and atheism (or, less literally, the falsity of Platonism) to conclude: *no ultimate significance.*

Camus writes, "There is but one moral code that the absurd man can accept, the one that is not separated from God: the one that is dictated. But it so happens that he lives outside that God" (67). For the absurd man, ultimate significance, which underwrites the significance of the "one moral code," is significance *for* the ultimate person, the Platonic person, that is, God; yet, the absurd man lives without this ultimate subjectivity, so knows of no ultimate significance—only local, limited, idiosyncratic, and perishable significances *in media res*.

While I differ with Camus theologically and metaethically (I think God-like beings probably exist and I don't think that moral Platonism or divine command theory are the clear metaethical winners), I do find something seductive in his view of one's faithfulness to a life without any sanction higher than one's own.

> There is thus a metaphysical honor in enduring the world's absurdity. Conquest or play-acting, multiple loves, absurd revolt are tributes that man pays to his dignity in a campaign in which he is defeated in advance (93).

> To work and create 'for nothing,' to sculpture in clay, to know that one's creation has no future, to see one's work destroyed in a day while being aware that fundamentally this has no more importance than building for centuries—this is the difficult wisdom that absurd thought sanctions. Performing these two tasks simultaneously, negating on the one hand and magnifying on the other, is the way open to the absurd creator. He must give the void its colors (114).

> In that daily effort in which intelligence and passion mingle and delight each other, the absurd man discovers a discipline that will make up the greatest of his strengths. The required diligence, the doggedness and lucidity thus resemble the conqueror's attitude. To create is likewise to give shape to one's fate (117).

"Metaphysical honor," "tributes to his dignity," "the difficult wisdom," "the greatest of his strengths"—This Nietzschean Camus lauds the *autonomous* affirmation of one's

efforts. The appetitive, affective, erotic, evaluative human creature sets a law for itself, an individualistic imperative, a fate (Sisyphus's "fate belongs to him," writes Camus). The question of
significance is answered: "It is merely a matter of being faithful
to the rule of the battle" (93).

It seems to me that the voluntarist theologies of Antoine
Arnauld or William of Ockham express the most radical idoli-
zation of the autonomous and self-affirming will: the imago of
an absolutely *free* big Other. The legislator of value (or significance) is the freest person and voluntarists (and theologians
generally) only displaced this legislative power. Camus, alongside Nietzsche, Georg Simmel, and others, stormed heaven and
brought autonomy *back* to earth—and like the fire of Prometheus, autonomy is *dangerous*.

Sisyphus affirms his fate. Sisyphus "teaches the higher fi-
delity." "The absurd man says yes and his effort will henceforth
be unceasing" (123). Regarding this autonomous affirmation
of the value of one's efforts, this gravity of categorical self-
command and categorical self-sanction, I think of Nietzsche's
entheogenic poem "Star Morals" (*Sternenmoral*):

> *Called a star's orbit to pursue,*
> *What is darkness, star, to you?*
>
> *Roll on in bliss, traverse this age—*
> *Its misery far from you and strange.*
>
> *Let farthest world your light secure.*
> *Pity is sin you must adjure.*
>
> *But one command is yours: be pure!*

4. *The Exaltation of Life*

I offer now a fourth view on our question: What is the
significance of *your* specific path and *your* efforts? This fourth
view is, in a word, *exaltation*. One could call this view "perfectionism." Let us begin, though, not at the Zenith, but at the
nadir, with Schopenhauer:

For what value can be possessed by a being which is no different from millions of his kind? Millions? An infinity rather, an endless number of beings ceaselessly spurted forth by nature out of its inexhaustible well *in saecula saeculorum* [to all eternity], as generous with them as the blacksmith is with sparks.[94]

In his poem "In Memoriam A.H.H.," Alfred Lord Tennyson expresses a similar revulsion at the redundancy and abortiveness of life:

Are God and Nature then at strife,
That Nature lends such evil dreams?
So careful of the type she seems,
So careless of the single life;

That I, considering everywhere
Her secret meaning in her deeds,
And finding that of fifty seeds
She often brings but one to bear

David Hume *vivifies* the point in his *Dialogues Concerning Natural Religion*:

Look round this universe. What an immense profusion of beings, animated and organized, sensible and active! You admire this prodigious variety and fecundity. But inspect a little more narrowly these living existences, the only beings worth regarding. How hostile and destructive to each other! How insufficient all of them for their own happiness! How contemptible or odious to the spectator! The whole presents nothing but the idea of a blind Nature, impregnated by a great vivifying principle, and pouring forth from her lap, without discernment or parental care, her maimed and abortive children.

To address Schopenhauer's question, and Tennyson's "evil

---

[94] Arthur Schopenhauer, *Parerga and Paralipomena*, sourced in the remixed *Essays & Aphorisms*, trans. R. J. Hollingdale

dreams," I look to another pessimist, Emil Cioran.

A young and insomnia-plagued Cioran published his first masterpiece, *On the Heights of Despair*, in 1934, when he was twenty-two years old. *On the Heights of Despair* is a bleak, brutal, and apocalyptic outpouring from the young Romanian, but even here one finds, like Candide's garden and Rasselas's "little kingdom," a sanctuary.

In a section titled "The Cult of Infinity," Cioran considers life's *ad infinitum* insignificance; rather than conceiving of an infinite system as a *via dolorosa*, Cioran conceives of this infinity as a maenadic plunge:

> Infinity renders impossible any solution to the problem of meaning. [...] What's the use of "meaning," after all? Can't we live without it? Universal meaninglessness gives way to ecstatic inebriation, an orgy of irrationality. Since the world has no meaning, let us live! Without definite aims or accessible ideals, let us throw ourselves into the roaring whirlwind of infinity [...] (99).

Infinity properly internalized, Cioran suggests, dissolves us all into the entourage of the vine-god Dionysus, his *thiasos*, all turbulent with god-fever and fluid formlessness.[95]

Why Dionysus?

First, Dionysus is a god overladen with academic glosses, retcons, and geographic variations. There is no Dionysian *homoousios*, or sameness of essence. We have yet another orgy. Ironically, this *haze* of endless clarifications fits and deepens the general dreamy impression of Dionysus. One has their selection of Dionysian dreams to interpret. For reasons I tuck away into the footnote to this sentence, I prefer the Dionysus of the *Dionysiaca* by Nonnus.[96]

---

[95] Why do I assume Cioran alludes here to Dionysus? Cioran's "ecstatic inebriation" and "orgy of irrationality" echoes the common motifs of the god of wine and ritual madness. Also, there is the Nietzschean influence. All else failing, consider it artistic license.

[96] The *Dionysiaca*, dating from the late 4th to early 5th century AD, is the longest surviving poem from antiquity (20,426 lines), yet it is

In Book 7 of Nonnus's *Dionysiaca*, we read of Dionysus's conception via the mating of Zeus and Semele, during which Zeus transmutates into various creatures:

> Now [Zeus] leaned over the bed, with a horned head on human limbs, lowing with the voice of a bull, the very likeness of bull-horned Dionysos. Again, he put on a shaggy lion's form; or he was a panther, as one who begets a bold son, driver of panthers and charioteer of lions. Again, as a young bridegroom he bound his hair with coiling snakes and vine-leaves intertwined, and twisted purple ivy about his locks, the plaited ornament of Bacchos. (*Dionysiaca*, Book VII)

Zeus's indeterminateness of form during insemination, which I find indicated, e.g., by the disjunctive "*or* he was a panther," seems to me perfect for progeneration of Dionysus. This *protean* conception is paralleled in the proem of *Dionysiaca*,

---

incomplete. W. H. D. Rouse, whose English translation of the *Dionysiaca* is the only English translation, undervalues the work: "The mythology of the *Dionysiaca* is interesting as being the longest and most elaborate example we have of Greek myths in their final stage of degeneracy." Nonnus's Alexandrian Dionysos is compared unfavorably to the Thraco-Phrygian original. Rouse faults Nonnus's showy learnedness for the "overcrowded tapestry" of the *Dionysiaca*: "Hence the episodes with which the poem abounds, and the continual digressions and allusions which interrupt the narrative [...]." Personally, I like a narrator that is a *polútropos*, the ambiguous term that Homer uses for Odysseus, indicating either wiliness or a many-turning wandering. Lycophron of Chalcis, a 3rd-century BC Alexandrian (and librarian at the Great Library of Alexandria), exemplifies this unruly learnedness (one might say, Dionysian learnedness) in his hyper-esoteric poem *Alexandra*. Baroque bricolage is an acquired taste (see *this footnote*). Also, contra Rouse, R. F. Newbold writes, in "Space and Scenery in Quintus of Smyrna, Claudian and Nonnus," that Nonnus has "a fascination with moving rather than static forms—spiralling, twisting, twining, scratching, scoring, dancing. It is as if Nonnus has grasped the truth declared by sages of old and confirmed by physicists today, that the cosmos is a dynamic plenum where everything gyrates in a gigantic, ceaseless dance." Newbold calls Nonnus's dynamic vision "very Dionysian."

where Nonnus (himself about to conceive!) writes:

> Bring me the fennel, rattle the cymbals, ye Muses! put in
> my hand the wand of Dionysos whom I sing: but bring
> me a partner for your dance in the neighboring island of
> Pharos,[97] Proteus of many turns, that he may appear in
> all his diversity of shapes, since I twang my harp to a di-
> versity of songs. For if, as a serpent, he should glide along
> his winding trail, I will sing my god's achievement, how
> with ivy-wreathed wand he destroyed the horrid hosts of
> Giants serpent-haired. If as a lion he shake his bristling
> mane, I will cry "Euoi!" to Bacchos on the arm of buxom
> Rheia, stealthily draining the breast of the lion-breeding
> goddess. If as a leopard he shoot up into the air with a
> stormy leap from his pads, changing shape like a master-
> craftsman, I will hymn the son of Zeus, how he slew the
> Indian nation, with his team of pards riding down the el-
> ephants. If he make his figure like the shape of a boar, I
> will sing Thyone's son, love-sick for Aura the desirable,
> boarslayer, daughter of Cybele, mother of the third Bac-
> chos late-born. If he be mimic water, I will sing Dionysos
> diving into the bosom of the brine, when Lycurgos
> armed himself. If he become a quivering tree and tune a
> counterfeit whispering, I will tell of Icarios, how in the
> jubilant winepress his feet crushed the grape in rivalry.
> (*Dionysiaca*, Book I)

Proteus (*protos*, "first"), a god of water and shape-chang-
ing, is Nonnus's "partner" in this Dionysian procession. There
is much chaos and shapeshifting in the *Dionysiaca*.[98] I am reminded of Thales and his theory of water as the primitive
origin of all else, of water as the metaphysical *first* in all things.

---

[97] The island on which Menelaos caught Proteus.
[98] In "Discipline, Bondage, and the Serpent in Nonnus's *Dionysiaca*,"
R. F. Newbold writes: "Constriction and pain, for example, can help
provide a sense of boundedness and combat depersonalisation. Sharp
sensations on the skin are one way in Nonnus (there are numerous
others) of coping with a pervasive sense of insecurity fostered by un-
reliable, dissolving surfaces, bastard, counterfeit appearances or
sounds, porosity and shapeshifting." See also Newbold's "Chaos Theory in Nonnus's *Dionysiaca*."

My memory then flows to Anaximander and his theory of primitive indefiniteness, shapelessness, the *apeiron*, the infinite. Wateriness and indefiniteness—both of these pre-Socratic theories suggest an infinite and ineffable Cratylean flux:

> One of the principal elements of infinity is its negation of *form*. Absolute becoming, infinity destroys anything that is formed, crystallized, or finished. Isn't music the art which best expresses infinity because it dissolves all forms into a charmingly ineffable fluidity? (99)

Water signifies formlessness in many ancient myths. In the book of Genesis, water was present "in the beginning"—it was necessary to quarantine this primeval ocean in order to create forms. In the story of Noah and the deluge, this primeval ocean (this maelstrom) is freed from its cages in order to dis-create, to return malformations into formlessness. The trope of an originary watery chaos is found in Egyptian myth as well (for example, the Benben stone, Nu, Naunet, etc.). For me, it is Dionysus who transforms this infinite chaotic water into merry-making wine:

> But the god [Dionysus] pitied his foes in his heart of merry cheer, and he poured the treasure of wine into the waters. [...] When this change came upon the waters, the breezes blew perfumed by the newly-poured wine, the banks were empurpled. A noble Indian drank, and spoke his wonder in these words:
> "Here is a strange and incredible drink I have seen! This is not the white milk of goats, not dark like water, nor is it like what I have seen in the riddled hives, what the buzzing bee brings forth with sweet wax. No—this delights the mind with a fragrant scent. A man is thirsty in the steam of this sultry heat, but if he scoops up a few drops of running water in his palms, he shakes off at once the whirlwind of parching thirst! Honey surfeits you sooner—O here's a great miracle! When I drink this I want to drink more! For this had both merits—it is sweet, and it does not surfeit. Hebe, come this way! Take up your pitcher, and bring your Trojan cupbearer who serves with cups the divine company—let Ganymedes draw honeyed drops from this river and fill all the mixing-bowls of

Zeus! This way, friends, have a taste of a honey-distilling
river! Here I see an image of the heavens; for that nectar
of Olympus which they say is the drink of Zeus, the Nai-
ads are pouring out in natural streams on the earth!" (*Dionysiaca*, Book XIV)

The cultus of the vine and the cultus of infinity blur together when one says of the infinite: "When I drink this I want
to drink more!" For "it is sweet, and it does not surfeit." As
Cioran writes, "'Everything is too little when compared to infinity'" (98). Cioran asks, "Are not all those aspiring to infinity
on the road to madness?" (100). One could answer, "Yes, *dithyrambic* madness!" One could dance forever like St. Gregory of
Nyssa into the progressive infinity of God.

Let us live in the ecstasy of infinity, let us love that which
is boundless, let us destroy forms and institute the only
cult without forms: the cult of infinity (100).

Cioran's encomium for the destruction of forms flows
from his anti-rationalism. It is the apophatic wisdom of Craty-
lus reborn; A is not A. In a similar mood, a young Nietzsche,
in the grip of Schopenhauer's *The World as Will and Representation*, speaks of a Dionysian "breakdown of the *principium individuationis* [principle of individuation]" in his *The Birth of Tragedy
Out of the Spirit of Music* (20).[99] The power of individuating the
real, of unitizing, partitioning, atomizing, anatomizing, etc.,
that *this thing* may be differentiated from *that thing*, that part-
whole relations and all cuttings-apart of analysis may veil an
unintelligible world with the gossamer of a formal intelligibil-
ity—this form-giving power is washed away and drowned by
the "Dionysiac flood." This is the dis-creating deluge of Genesis. This is the Hebrew *Tohu wa-bohu*. Yet, what makes this
flood specifically *Dionysiac* is its intoxicating sweetness; it is as
if God saw the *tohu wa-bohu*, the pre-creation formlessness, the

[99] Conversely, Apollo is "the glorious divine image of the *principium
individuationis*" (*Birth of Tragedy*, 6). This principle of individuation
comes through Schopenhauer's work on Leibniz's Principle of Sufficient Reason.

"mysterious Primal Oneness,"[100] the infinite *potential* energy, the apeiron, and, behold, *it* was very good.

In his *Moralia*, Plutarch writes of Alexander the Great's reaction to the prospect of infinite worlds:

> Alexander wept when he heard Anaxarchus[101] discourse about an infinite number of worlds, and when his friends inquired what ailed him, "Is it not worthy of tears," he said, "that, when the number of worlds is infinite, we have not yet become lords of a single one?"

Plutarch means to convey a point against unquenchable ambition, about the disappointment and disturbance that follows from an irrational desire, a desire better overcome than indulged, but Alexander's weeping expresses a boundless hunger (the Schopenhauerian Will, *semper esurientem*) whose irrationality comes not, in my opinion, from the impossibility of a consummate conquering act over infinity, but at Alexander's demoralization from discovering that his boundless hunger has emerged in a world of boundless refreshment. What, Alexander, if your panoramic power had broken its fist against the one-sided wall of a finite world?

"My life, my world," writes A. W. Moore in *The Infinite*, "was a limited whole *because* it was mine. I *was* its limit. My finitude encompassed it" (194). One's *individuated* existence is a set of fluid limits in a fluid manifold; the infinite is the absence of these limits, these "doors of perception," as Blake wrote; thus *identity* with the infinite means elimination of a bounded identity, *this* specific set of *these* individuations. If you and another person were to flow beyond your limits into all experiences, all times, all places—into all of the apeiroverse[102]—then you and another person would be indistinguishably *one*, the *Dionysiac* one. From the most constricted and evanescent states of sensation, or states of minimal phenomenal binding,

---

[100] *Birth of Tragedy*, 17

[101] Anaxarchus was an atomist and, also like Democritus, an Abderite (for the archaism known as an Abderite ethnic joke, see *Philogelos*).

[102] I use "apeiroverse" for an infinite natural system to avoid the ambiguities, connotations, and controversies of the term "multiverse."

experience dilates out into a phenomenally-bound unified whole that encircles more and more and more.

Perhaps the exaltation of life is experiencing life through every phase of individuation, every bundle of limitations, from amoeba to zebra, from abiogenesis to the *all-inclusive* Zenith— the *summa* of living. This play of limitations, this transcending of forms, hardships, afflictions, pains, obstructions, and set-backs is the essence of excelling and exalting; I cannot imagine a more apt use of the elevating exclamation: *excelsior!*

> "What is good? All that enhances the feeling of power, Will to Power, and power itself in man. [...] What is hap-piness? The feeling that power increases, that a resistance is overcome." Nietzsche, *The Antichrist*

This overcoming and exaltation *through* the organic kalei-doscopes of life, I believe, is our human religion, our *common faith*. Ask yourself: What is religion?

I find it in the Gothic spire, in Tatlin's Tower, on Mount Olympus, on Mount Meru, in the Great Pyramid of Giza, at the apex of Leibniz's pyramid of possible worlds, on Muham-mad's Jabal al-Nour or Mountain of the Light, in Yahweh upon his volcano (Exodus 19:16-23), in the modal maximization of the ontological arguments, in the Great Chain of Being, in Ni-kolai Fyodorov and the Russian Cosmists,[103] in Teilhard's Omega, in the Cathar *Perfecti*, in the "über'm Sternenzelt" of Beethoven's Symphony No. 9, and in Nietzsche's übermensch. It is the *excelsior!* toward perfection. It is perfectionism.[104] It is the *nisus* toward Samuel Alexander's spacetime deity[105] and it is St. Gregory of Nyssa's progressive infinity, the infinite journey into God. It is Diotima's ladder, Jacob's Ladder, Saint John Cli-macus's ladder of divine ascent. It is striving upward and

---

[103] Of the Russian Cosmists, I think Konstantin Tsiolkovsky comes nearest to the zenithist position.
[104] By "perfectionism," I do not mean the neuroticism of the so-called Type A personality, but simply a primal preference for *ideal* states, the *summum bonum*.
[105] Zenithism is an emergentist theology similar, in a basic respect, to Samuel Alexander's; see Alexander's *Space, Time, and Deity* (1920).

182

godward, perfecting powers, and aspiring to a paramount state of being, to beatific vision and affirmation, to ideality, to theosis.

"I shall suggest that God was (or is) a *single perfect transcendent non-representable and necessarily real object of attention.*" So wrote the British philosopher Iris Murdoch in *The Sovereignty of Good.* God/Good/Perfection is a "transcendent magnetic center" that orders and unifies effort (in my view, effort toward beatific affirmation, ideality, theosis).

> The idea of perfection is also a natural producer of order. In its *light* we come to see that A, which superficially resembles B, is really better than B. And this can occur, indeed must occur, without our having the sovereign idea [of the Good] in any sense 'taped.' In fact it is in its nature that we cannot get it taped. This is the true sense of the 'indefinability' of the good, which was given a vulgar sense by Moore [G.E. Moore] and his followers. It lies always beyond, and it is from this beyond that it exercises its *authority* (62).

"It lies always beyond"—here, Alexander the Great weeps, but the god-drunk *thiasos* of Dionysus dance triumphantly; fresh forms and new wines beckon. Murdoch writes:

> The scene remains disparate and complex beyond the hopes of any system, yet at the same time the concept Good stretches through the whole of it and gives it the only kind of shadowy unachieved unity which it can possess (97).

This "shadowy unachieved unity"[106] is the sweetness of the Dionysian drink, the optimism of mystics (*optimysticism?*)

---

[106] Compare Murdoch's "transcendent magnetic centre" and "shadowy [...] unity" to Nietzsche's "antipodes" in *The Gay Science*, Aphorism 289, "*Embark!*" One finds the Platonic use of "sun" expanded and *pluralized* in Nietzsche: "Oh, that many such new suns were created!" (Aphorism 289). There is a metaethical variety of "suns," so to speak. Nietzsche has not only left Plato's cave, he has left the earth with his "*Embark!*"

The background to morals is properly some sort of mysticism, if by this is meant a non-dogmatic essentially unformulated faith in the reality of the Good, occasionally connected with experience (74).

Murdoch, like Anaxarchus, speaks of inexhaustible reality:

Good is indefinable not for the reasons offered by Moore's successors, but because of the infinite difficulty of the task of apprehending a magnetic but inexhaustible reality (42).

Tennyson, in the two stanzas of "In Memoriam" immediately following those I quoted earlier, writes:

I falter where I firmly trod,
And falling with my weight of cares
Upon the great world's altar-stairs
That slope thro' darkness up to God,

I stretch lame hands of faith, and grope,
And gather dust and chaff, and call
To what I feel is Lord of all,
And faintly trust the larger hope.

We follow into infinity an indefinable (Dionysian) *excelsior!* It slopes through darkness up to perfection. "Let us live in the ecstasy of infinity," comes the echo of Cioran. "Let us love that which is boundless, let us destroy forms and institute the only cult without forms: the cult of infinity."

By the "light" of perfection, by Murdoch's undefined magnetic center, by Tennyson's faintly trusted "larger hope," by Zenith, we may recolor Cioran's form-destroying infinity and diagnose, beneath its patina of nihilism, the tenderest-hearted wish, the wish of Omar Khayyam:

Ah, Love! could thou and I with Fate conspire
To grasp this sorry Scheme of Things entire,
Would not we shatter it to bits—and then

184

Re-mould it nearer to the Heart's Desire![107]

This wish for a cosmos of the heart's desire, for ideality pouring out infinitely, for the *Lebensideal*—it is this desire (*conatus, nisus, impetus*) that, in the infinite natural system, wins Zenith.[108] This wish is *your* wish, *your* magnetic center, the *daemon* that helps *you* face and fix problems, order chaos, slope up through darkness, so it is consequently *your* exaltation within *your* limits and then beyond *your* upper limits that transforms flux *into* Zenith-state.[109]

You are one of the ascending god-intoxicated *thiasos*, even if, like Cioran, you blush at the nakedness of your divine desire. So, Schopenhauer asks us once more:

> For what value can be possessed by a being which is no different from millions of his kind? Millions? An infinity rather, an endless number of beings ceaselessly spurted forth by nature out of its inexhaustible well *in saecula saeculorum...*

What value? Nature's inexhaustible well overflows with "that nectar of Olympus which they say is the drink of Zeus"—of Zenith—and when life drinks of this perfecting

---

[107] Quatrain LXXII, *The Rubáiyát of Omar Khayyam* (that is, Edward Fitzgerald's translation of quatrains attributed to Omar Khayyám).

[108] Ludwig Feuerbach's anthropological theology is therefore only half-correct: God is a projection, yes, but also a self-fulfilling projection (and thus, a projection-independent reality).

[109] "Fundamentally," writes Nietzsche in *The Gay Science* (Aphorism 354), "all your actions are altogether incomparably personal, unique, and infinitely individual; there is no doubt of that. But as soon as we translate them into consciousness *they no longer seem to be.*" Your limits and limit-conquerings are uniquely yours, but consciousness (or, to be more accurate, one's second-order self-assessment), being the introjection of a coarse and hyperlossy mime show (ordinary language) into the infinite inner world, is a "herd signal" and thus the "falsification, reduction to superficialities, and generalization" of the infinitely individual action. When you and another speak with each other, *deep calleth unto deep*, but through an extremely thin atmosphere. Perhaps, someday, deep shall heareth deep.

drink, this will to theosis, life *wants* to drink more! For this drink, *this exaltation through every life*, this uplifting, is sweet, and it does not surfeit.

INFINITY DAY

The American philosopher, poet, and essayist Ralph Waldo Emerson wrote, "To the poet, to the philosopher, to the saint, all things are friendly and sacred, all events profitable, all days holy, all men divine."

While all days are holy, it may require supererogatory effort to experience this holiness *every day*, so some handful of days are marked as holy, as *holidays*, to help preserve at least some contact with the experience of a day's holiness.

I write this piece on August 8th, 2018, which is, for me, just such a holy day: Infinity Day ("Universal and International Infinity Day").

> Infinity Day is also known as Universal & International Infinity Day, and is a day held on the 8th day of the 8th month of each year in order to celebrate and promote Philosophy and Philosophizing for the ordinary person.

So reports the website of Jean-Pierre Ady Fenyo, the holiday's originator. Of the holiday's humble origins, we read:

> Infinity Day was first conceived and created by Jean-Pierre Ady Fenyo, a philosopher, poet, journalist and science-fiction author [...]. Infinity Day was begun in 1987 and has been celebrated in the form of peaceful, non-violent, and lawful demonstrations for philosophical inquiry, freedom of expression, freedom of speech, and ethics in society, throughout the world.

Jean-Pierre Ady Fenyo, on his website, extols the virtues of Infinity Day:

> International and Universal Infinity Day is YOUR Day to Celebrate Philosophy, Art, Science and Life! It is a day when we should encourage everyone to Think Deeply, Ponder Deep Philosophical Questions, such as: What Is IT All About?, Why Are We Here?, What are the Logical Implications of a Universe that is Infinite?

Fenyo is eccentric; I commend his eccentricity. On his site, he promotes his "legendary ebook," titled *The Most Important Thought*. In 1988, Fenyo "established The Infinity Society, an NGO for The Mass Dissemination of The Concept of Infinity." Fenyo's interest in infinity began, he writes, at age 6 at a circus in Portland, Oregon:

> I noticed when the lights went out that there was a small 'dot' of light at the top of the Big Tent and it then occurred to me! I asked my mother: 'What's beyond the stars?' And she looked at me a bit disturbed and said: 'What a strange question! More stars. Why?' And from that time on I continued to ponder the idea of the Infinite.

I think "Infinity Day" is a magnificent idea and I intend to celebrate my very first Infinity Day today. I take Infinity Day to include an Infinity Night, so to speak; so, I will go outside and observe the night sky. Such a day (and night) is perfect for teaching and learning astronomy, for giving someone the gift of a telescope or a guide to the night sky, and for enjoying, alone or collectively, the sublimity of an infinite natural system.

"[…] and after all," writes Leibniz, "it is quite untrue that an actual infinity is impossible."[110]

---

[110] *Theodicy*, 78, Open Court, translator E. M. Huggard.

VARIETIES OF SPATIAL INFINITISM

Infinitism is the view that the universe is infinite. What does "the universe is infinite" mean? In this brief piece, we'll look at a *spatial* interpretation of "the universe is infinite."

When we talk about space, we talk about metric space. Metric space is a set of points together with a function that defines distance between any two points.

A spatially infinite universe, or *unbounded metric space*, is defined as such: for any distance D, there exist points *at least* D apart. "For any distance D" means that the value of D can be any non-negative number. Distances *just keep going and going and going . . .*

A spatially finite universe, or *bounded metric space*, is defined as such: there exists a distance D such that all the points in the metric space exist *within* D of each other. Imagine you have a cosmically long, yet finite and fixed-length ruler, R. In a spatially finite universe, no two points can escape falling under R's rule; any two points you could choose simply will not have a distance longer than R. R "bounds" the space.

Assuming metric spaces may be discrete and enumerable things, there may be *finitely* or *infinitely* many of either of these metric spaces. This allows for the following possibilities:

The Exclusive Set

(1) Finitely many bounded metric spaces
(2) Infinitely many bounded metric spaces
(3) Finitely many unbounded metric spaces
(4) Infinitely many unbounded metric spaces

The Inclusive Set

(5) Finitely many bounded metric spaces **and** finitely many unbounded metric spaces
(6) Finitely many bounded metric spaces **and** infinitely many unbounded metric spaces
(7) Infinitely many bounded metric spaces **and** infinitely many unbounded metric spaces

Only option (1) is finitist. Every other option either includes infinitely many metric spaces[111] or an unbounded metric
space,[112] and thus every other option is infinitist.

We can add to these options another qualification: *nested
metric spaces*. For example, one may have finitely many bounded
metric spaces "inside" of a higher-dimensional and unbounded
metric space. A 4-dimensional space may exist inside of a 5-
dimensional space, and that 5-dimensional space may exist inside of a 6-dimensional space, and so on *ad infinitum*.

We may not need to add new options to account for dimensional nesting. There are either finitely many or infinitely
many "higher" dimensions, and these higher dimensions may
be either bounded or unbounded; thus, combinations (1)
through (7) cover all cases. Consider the earlier example: finitely
many bounded metric spaces "inside" of a higher-dimensional
and unbounded metric space. If there is only one such "higher"
unbounded metric space (i.e., finitely many), then this example
would count as a case of option (5).

We can now define the two extremes of spatial infinitism:

> *Minimalist spatial infinitism*: Only one instantiation of
> spatial infinity, e.g., only one unbounded 4D
> space.

> *Maximalist spatial infinitism*: Infinitely many un-
> bounded 4D spaces inside infinitely many un-
> bounded 5D spaces inside infinitely many un-
> bounded 6D spaces, and so on and on *ad infini-
> tum* into infinitely many degrees of freedom.

Without a forthcoming empirical test for any of these
options, one might prefer agnosticism; yet, one may remain an
empirical agnostic while venturing to ask: Which options are
better than which?

---

[111] Options 2, 4, 6, and 7.
[112] Options 3, 4, 5, 6, and 7

A Thought on Simulated Systems

Some consider it more probable that we occupy a simulated universe than a non-simulated universe. The reasoning involves the claim that one non-simulated universe, through the agency of an advanced simulator, generates vast quantities of simulated universes. For every non-simulated universe, there may exist 1,000 simulated universes; your *a priori* chance of inhabiting a simulated universe would be 1,000 to 1. Your odds of inhabiting a non-simulated universe are not necessarily helped by increasing the number of non-simulated universes. Suppose one billion universes exist (ignoring the deep problem of individuating universes). This increase would come with an increase of simulators, each generating more than one simulated universe; in perhaps the majority of cases, vastly more than one simulated universe. Simulated universes would exponentiate from non-simulated universes.

For a finite quantity of finitely spatial universes, this problem seems intractable. For an infinite quantity of any-sized universes, or for a finite quantity of infinitely spatial universes, there may be no such problem. For an infinite quantity of any-sized universes, there are infinitely many simulated and non-simulated universes, thus the probability is 50% that you inhabit one and 50% that you inhabit the other.

A finite quantity of infinitely spatial universes is trickier. The ratio appears to favor your existing in a simulated universe, since there will be a finite quantity of non-simulated universes, each exponentiating simulated universes. However, in this finite quantity of non-simulated infinitely spatial universes, it is plausible that an infinite quantity of non-simulated beings exist, given the universe's infinitude. It is also plausible that infinitely many of these non-simulated beings are similar to you, and one *may in fact* be you. The quantities of simulated and non-simulated you-candidates are both infinite, thus the probability is 50% that you inhabit one and 50% that you inhabit the other.

STRESS TESTING PARADIGMS

Stress testing "is a form of deliberately intense or thorough testing used to determine the stability of a given system or entity. It involves testing beyond normal operational capacity, often to a breaking point, in order to observe the results."[113]

By "paradigm," I mean something like the following: A more or less developed philosophical worldview, plus all of one's psychological and existential relations to that worldview. A paradigm may be stress tested for its consistency, completeness, justification, truth, and other criteria of this kind. This first set of stress tests is the familiar logical and philosophical set.

Yet, a paradigm includes psychological and existential features that will involve additional stress tests, or what may be called *distress* tests. I propose two such tests, though many more may be proposed:

1. The Effort Test
2. The Emergency Test

Before describing these stress tests, I should confess what it is I seek in considering these tests. We assess the stability of a system by taking it *beyond* into a state of instability.

In a similar way, we may understand the strengths and weaknesses of various paradigms *for various people* by observing those people (in the midst of their paradigms) while they experience stressful thoughts or situations, especially high-stress thoughts or situations. Since the performance of the person and the performance of the paradigm are deeply entangled, as perhaps these two things are just one thing, I cannot conclude anything substantial in this essay about universally good or adaptive paradigms. At most, I implore you, reader, to consider how your own paradigm (to speak loosely, as if your paradigm were some fixed and well-specified unit of being) performs under these two stress tests.

---

[113] "Stress Testing," Wikipedia

(1) *The Effort Test*: How much effort is required to secure the ideal end of the paradigm?

Consider moksha. In Hindu philosophies, moksha generally refers to emancipation from the torturous recurrences of the world (samsara), whether that means emancipation *in this life* (psychologically) or *after death* (of course, not all death is liberation). This emancipation requires effort. This effort, one might say dharma, may require many lifetimes, which means that this effort is *not* easy. One must overcome ignorance and desire, even the desire for moksha. Therefore, the ideal end of moksha requires *great* effort.

Or consider apatheia, which is often translated from the Greek as "equanimity." In Stoic philosophy, equanimity is the ideal state of soul. An equanimous soul harmonizes with nature and nature's inner logic. The equanimous sage becomes like nature (a Stoic view of nature): rational, forward-marching, adaptable, and *peaceful in itself*. As you might expect, securing this equanimity requires considerable effort. The stoic ideal is not won in a day, though one lifetime may suffice.

Consider what may seem a clear case of an ideal end via *minimal* effort: Christian universalism. In Christian universalism, the ideal end (eternal life in the glory of God) requires belief in the divinity of Jesus, but it happens that "every tongue will confess and give praise to God" (Romans 14:11); that is, a *voluntary* act of conversion will pour from every human soul at some time or another, and to this act, God will *always* respond with infinite grace and mercy. Ultimately, every soul is saved.

This may seem a case of *minimal* effort, and for one who is *already* Christian, it is indeed minimal, but the intensity of the effort *for others* is not yet obvious. How arduous is the transformation from a heart of stone to a heart of flesh (Ezekiel 36:26)? It is no easy effort for some to confess and give praise to Jesus. Must the confession be genuine? What is genuine? Is a desperate bid a genuine confession? In some cases, it may require the same amount of effort and time as it requires for one to attain moksha.

The three ideal ends of moksha, apatheia, and universal salvation *require* effort. In each case, the ideal end is not automatically achieved.

It is here that the stress of the effort test may be applied: In your moment of need, is your ideal end secured or pending more effort (assuming your paradigm includes an ideal end to which you may rise)? Must you meditate more? Must you cultivate your emotions more? Must you have more faith? Does your paradigm require too much effort from you? If you had exactly one hour remaining to you before you died, could you secure the ideal end of your paradigm?

The ideal end in Zenithism is Zenith, which is secured for every living being. There is no effort required of you to attain Zenith. In all your moments of need, your ideal end is secured *for you*. Neither believing nor disbelieving will exclude you from Zenith. There is neither orthodoxy nor orthopraxy. No state of soul will prevent Zenith from uplifting you. You are saved *already*.

(2) *The Emergency Test*: Does your paradigm dampen or eliminate the intense stress of emergencies, such as extreme turbulence on an airplane. Specifically, does your paradigm help you face death?

The emergency test, as I call it, involves one of the most sought-after features of a paradigm: the maintenance of good mental health under extremity.

Imagine a potentially fatal and overpowering situation, one in which you have no control, no power to modify, and no power to separate your attention from the traumatic events unfolding around you. You stand before a firing squad. Or, at 30,000 feet, you see one of the plane's wings ripped from your plane. In such a situation, supposing the situation is sufficiently lengthy to allow for extended interpretation, all you will have in the way of psychological regulation is your *interpretation*. Your future-planning neocortex will go into overdrive in an attempt to *outwit* the realization of a coming extinction of all its hypothetical futures. Does your paradigm allow your neocortex to succeed?

One might outwit this realization by identifying one's future with the future of some broader group, ideal, or cause, e.g., "life's circle" or the Marine Corps.

"Hurrah for anarchy!" said the anarchist George Engel at

his execution (by hanging). Engel's ecstatic identification with the ideal of anarchy allowed him a sense of a future, a tomorrow, or, more narrowly and more fortifying, a sense of simple nextness.

As the weightlessness of free fall occupies your whole, helpless attention, as the plane plummets, as the neocortex bargains, one might hope here for powerful *interpretational* relief from this absolute cutting-off of futures. Is your paradigm powerful enough to provide some degree of relief in these extreme situations? Such an emergency test is a literal stress test.

Paradigms that commit to an afterlife, such as ethical zenithism,[114] identify one's future after death precisely with the literal continuation of one's sense of self-presence. I submit that *confident belief* in a literal positive afterlife remains, for many personality types, the most powerful *interpretational* relief in deadly emergency situations.

---

[114] That is, zenithism as I understand it: Zenith as an ethical optimizer who preserves and adjoins every life.

ZENITH AND IMMORTALITY

Today, February 6th, 2020, I received an email from the Oregon Zoo about a young southern ground hornbill named Zuberi ("strength" in Swahili). Some years ago, Zuberi "almost didn't make it." As the Oregon Zoo Foundation wrote:

> Zuberi's mom was injured while he was warm and toasty in his shell; he hadn't hatched yet. A team swooped in to tend to the egg. After he hatched, veterinarians, zookeepers, and hand-rearing experts worked around the clock to keep the chick healthy through those rough early months, which included nutritional issues and one surgery.
>
> There were times when they didn't think he would survive, and his existence today is a testament to the commitment his team of caretakers demonstrated. "It was all hands on deck—a very collaborative process," said [Curator Tanya] Paul.
>
> Mandy Stanford, program animal specialist, thinks Zuberi is an amazing success story. "It felt like everyone really rallied to help him get where he is," she said. "So, when I see him flying on the lawn for visitors, it is that much more meaningful after his rocky start."
>
> The intervention meant that Zuberi wouldn't be able to return to his parents in the African Savanna habitat. He could, however, become one of the zoo's program animals, serving as an ambassador for his species during live encounters with groups from schools and communities around the region.

The article elsewhere mentions that southern ground hornbills are listed by the IUCN, the International Union for Conservation of Nature, as vulnerable. In the IUCN's classification, after vulnerable, comes endangered, then critically endangered, then extinct in the wild, and, finally, extinct. The dusky seaside sparrow, a dark elegant little sparrow, was declared extinct in the 1990s. In the 2000s, the last Pyrenean ibex died, and in the 2010s, the last Bramble Cay melomys, the first mammal extinction attributed to anthropogenic climate change. "Perhaps 5-50 billion species have existed on earth.

Given, at most, an estimated 50 million species alive today, then well over 99% of earth's species have been extinct since long before humans evolved."[115]

If death delivers meaning to life, then the earth is engulfed in a Noachian flood of meaning. Yet here, despite this *meaningfulness*, a team of caretakers worked "all hands on deck" and "around the clock" to save one little hornbill chick, Zuberi. Why?

Why do you, reader, save things? What is this bereavement you sometimes feel? What do you wish for life?

1.1 *Apéritif*

Perhaps the first superintendent of the Great Library of Alexandria, Zenodotus, once daydreamed of the last superintendent of the Great Library, and the disintegration of all the library's holdings. Daydreaming too darkly, perhaps Zenodotus indulged a foolish wish that his holy library should endure forever. What of Zenodotus's foolish wish?

Do you remember the Latin poem *Zmyrna* by Gaius Helvius Cinna? I doubt you do. *Zmyrna* is an epyllion, that is, a narrative poem resembling an epic, but not exactly an epic (not epic "proper")—and shorter than the standard epic. Cinna was one of the *poetae novi*, the new poets, an avant-garde poetic movement in the first century B.C., among whom Catullus, a friend of Cinna, was counted. *Zmyrna* was Cinna's labor for nine years, or, as Catullus puts it, "nine harvests and nine winters."[116] Catullus predicts an abiding circulation of *Zmyrna*: "Penetrating to the runnelled waves of Satrachus / the remote regions of its setting, / Cinna's *Zmyrna* / shall be read by white-haired generations." Yet, only three lines of *Zmyrna* survive; that is, one line of text for every three years of toil.

Yet Cinna is one of the lucky ones. Consider Aristarchus of Tegea, a fifth-century tragic poet; of his 70 works, only three

---

[115] Michael L. McKinney, "How do rare species avoid extinction? A paleontological view" in *The Biology of Rarity* (1997), eds. William Kunin and Kevin Gaston
[116] Catullus 95, trans. Peter Whigham

titles (*Achilles*, *Asclepius*, and *Tantalus*) and a single line of text survive. Worse yet, consider Cleitomachus, a Carthaginian philosopher who headed Plato's Academy around 127/6 BC. According to Diogenes Laertius, Cleitomachus wrote 400 books. How many of these 400 books survive? Zero. Time commanded of the Carthaginian Cleitomachus as Cato the Censor commanded of Carthage: *Carthago delenda est*.

Think of Carthage. The genocide at Carthage, perhaps the first verified genocide, was a small prelude to so many subsequent destructions, in whole or part, of national, ethnic, racial, and religious groups. From the Armenians to the Bambuti,[117] Bengalis, Cathars, Cherokee, Circassians, to Jews and to the Jie People to the Yazidi, Zungars—and many more.

Genocide, mass extinction, and the obliteration of artefacts are mere *tiny* foretastes of a possible ultimate annihilation, which is the expected end-stage in *oblivionism*. For the oblivionist, *everything* de-energizes into nothingness, a permanent minimum (perhaps some timeless, minimal, sterile vacuum state). It bears memorization, so bears repeating: for an oblivionist, everything, perhaps even the past, vanishes into nothingness—that paradise that *none* enjoy.

Contra oblivionism, terminalism, vanishment, I forward *embodied* post-mortem existence, a naturalistic post-mortem existence, the post-mortem existence of *your* body—of *your* brain (not just *any* brain). I seek the good and proper sorts of continuity between pre-mortem and post-mortem *you*, you massy mess of quantum entanglements. I do not want duplicates or replicas, nor metempsychosis, but the *literal* continuation of natural bodies.

And while I am desiring, I also desire post-mortem maturation and augmentation of the natural body—a *you*-preserving metamorphosis into postbiological states with more competencies than the embryonic pre-mortem life, including an untraversable duration of subjectivity and an inexhaustibly fruitful psychology commensurate with an infinite journey. I would like actualization of the *Uomo Universale*, or Universal Human, the

---

117 *Effacer le tableau*, "cleaning the slate"—*that* is what the murderers of the Bambuti named their operation of systematic extermination.

human that can do all things, the ideal of Renaissance humanists.

And while *my* desires are specific, if not over-specific, the simpler generic desire to live forever is a cross-cultural tendency. *You* probably want it, at least some of the time. The world's perennial philosophy is perennial life. Biology reaches for perennialized biology in visions of ichor, that diaphanous blood of Olympian deities, or in the blood of Christ, the blood of the Mithraic bull, the blood of the "pure race," and so on.

As an aside, Shouxing, the Chinese god of longevity, attended by storks and tortoises, holding up the celestial peach of immortality, is perhaps my favorite personification of immortality. Shouxing is a smiling elderly man, white-haired and wrinkled—he is no Hebe or Ganymede pouring the rejuvenating nectar for an athletic pantheon. Nor is Shouxing a Tithonus, senescening forever. Shouxing is a happy medium, a middle way. Also, delightfully, Shouxing possesses a bulbous forehead, suggesting a super-gyrified mega-prefrontal-cortex, surely the mature fruit of countless centuries of self-cultivation.

Fortunately for us and our cross-cultural immortal longings, there exist "immortality curmudgeons," those who claim "that immortality (in any of its forms) is necessarily not of any positive value (or in any way appealing) to human beings."[118] Immortality curmudgeons, such as the English philosopher Bernard Williams and the Austrian psychiatrist Viktor Frankl, keep immortalists fit and Argus-eyed, ever-refreshing our insights into immortality. *Faithful are the wounds of a friend*, says the Book of Proverbs. So, while I wish to defend immortality against this curmudgeonry, I do not want to play the missionary, as some immortalists do, telling the oblivionist that they will have no comfort in dying, that they will be, at the cusp, inconsolable, desperate, miserable, terrified. One fabulizes when one claims an oblivionist will feel hopeless, helpless, hapless *in the end*. It is historically false; Hume's case comes first to mind. It is not enough for *some* immortalists to believe in their

---

[118] John Martin Fischer, "Immortality," in *The Oxford Handbook of Philosophy of Death*

comfort; they must diminish oblivionist comfort. They must mock and strip oblivionists of their courage. They must become *oblivion curmudgeons*. For some people, comfort is felt increased under a zero-sum regime. The deeper the misery of dying without hope, the profounder the joy of dying with hope—*a perverse inverse proportion*. A childish all-or-nothing principle dominates. What few palliatives exist for dying, they must be *exclusively* theirs: or else, what happiness is won by immortality? What consolation in Elysium as opposed to extinction?

"Ladies and Gentlemen will not, others must not, walk on the grass." That would be my *constructive notice* to immortalists who play zero-sum games with oblivionists, as I sometimes do. Where death is concerned, be humane.

Still, I instinctively sense *goodness* in these little visionary sprouts of immortality, and I suspect that immortality curmudgeons mis-imagine the encouragements of immortalists.

As an example of this mis-imagining, consider how the Argentinian writer Jorge Luis Borges, in his short story "The Immortal," imagines immortality. The main character, Marcus Flaminius Rufus (a.k.a. Joseph Cartaphilus, of Smyrna), quests for, and unwittingly finds, after much misfortune, the river of immortality (and the "secret City of the Immortals"). The narrator identifies the *river* of immortality as a "noiseless, impure stream, clogged by sand and rubble"—quite the symbolic demotion, from *river* to impure *stream*. The Immortals, loitering thereabout, are essentially human worms in living graves: "In the sand had been dug shallow holes; from those wretched holes, from the niches, emerged naked men with gray skin and neglected beards." Rufus, however, does not know until later that these wormy gray "troglodytes" are the Immortals.

Rufus, dehydrated and unaware of the stream's power, dunks his face and quaffs up the "dark water" of the sandbar-choked stream. Hungering, he eats his "first abominated mouthful of serpent's flesh." Perhaps there is a subtext there, no? Recovered after his repast of polluted water and snake, Rufus tours the nearby City of the Immortals.

The City is a "labyrinthine palace" that gives "the impression of endlessness, the sensation of oppressiveness and horror, the sensation of complex irrationality." The bright City of the Immortals terrifies and repels the narrator. "The gods that built this place were mad," the narrator tells himself; the "architecture had no purpose." The hellishness of the "abominable" City "is so horrific that its mere existence, the mere fact of its having endured—even in the middle of a secret desert—pollutes the past and the future and somehow compromises the stars. So long as this City endures, no one in the world can ever be happy or courageous." This is perhaps the unkindest travel review of all time.

The City of the Immortals, we are told, had been destroyed by the immortals almost a millennium ago. "Out of the shattered remains" of the first City, these Immortals, like the gods "who created first the Cosmos, and then Chaos,"[119] built that "incoherent city," that "temple to the irrational gods," that Rufus had toured. Apparently, the Immortals, "esteeming all exertion vain, [...] resolved to live in thought, in pure speculation. They built that carapace, abandoned it, and went off to make their dwellings in the caves. In their self-absorption, they scarcely perceived the physical world." Like Epicurean gods in pure ataraxia and isostasy and contemplation, the Immortals are "capable of perfect quietude" in their thoughts: "it was to thought that we delivered ourselves over." I should add that one of these neutered Immortals, one who follows and interacts with Rufus, just happens to be Homer.

Borges reflects, via Rufus, on such immortality.

What is divine, terrible, and incomprehensible is *to know* oneself immortal. I have noticed that in spite of religion, the conviction as to one's own immortality is extraordinarily rare. Jews, Christians, and Muslims all *profess* belief in immortality, but the veneration paid to the first century of life is proof that they truly believe only in those hundred years, for they dest-ine all the rest, throughout eternity, to rewarding or punishing what one did *when alive*. In my view, the Wheel conceived by certain religions in Hindustan is much more plausible; on that Wheel, which has neither end nor beginning, each life is the effect of the previous life and engenderer of the next, yet no one life

---

[119] Notice that "Cosmos," not "Chaos," receives the definite article.

determines the whole. Taught by centuries of living, the republic of immortal men had achieved a perfection of tolerance, almost of disdain. They knew that over an infinitely long span of time, all things happen to all men. As reward for his past and future virtues, every man merited every kindness—yet also every betrayal, as reward for his past and future iniquities. Much as the way in games of chance, heads and tails tend to even out, so cleverness and dullness cancel and correct each other. Perhaps the rude poem of El Cid is the counterweight demanded by a single epithet of the Eclogues or a maxim from Heraclitus. The most fleeting thought obeys an invisible plan, and may crown, or inaugurate, a secret design. I know of men who have done evil in order that good may come of it in future centuries, or may already have come of it in centuries past. Viewed in that way, all our acts are just, though also unimportant. There are no spiritual or intellectual *merits*. Homer composed the *Odyssey*; given infinite time, with infinite circumstances and changes, it is impossible that the *Odyssey* should *not* be composed at least once.

Inevitably, Borges imagines, infinite recurrence absorbs everything into absolute deindividuation: "No one is someone; a single immortal man is all men. Like Cornelius Agrippa, I am god, hero, philosopher, demon, and world—which is a long-winded way of saying that I *am not*." Limits give shape to one's being; as Socrates said, shape is the *limit* of a solid. Death, therefore, is a necessary determinant of one's uniqueness.

Death (or reference to death) makes men precious and pathetic; their ghostliness is touching; any act they perform may be their last; there is no face that is not on the verge of blurring and fading away like the faces in a dream.[120] Everything in the world of mortals has the

---

120 The philosopher Robert Nozick considers this point, as brought up by Viktor Frankl: "Frankl might avoid the consequences drawn in the text, by saying that though immortality would involve a sacrifice of meaningfulness, the other things gained might be even more important and so justify that sacrifice. Nevertheless, Frankl makes some

200

value of the irrecoverable and contingent. Among the
Immortals, on the other hand, every act (every thought)
is the echo of others that preceded it in the past, with no
visible beginning, and the faithful presage of others that
will repeat it in the future, *ad vertiginem*. There is nothing
that is not as though lost between indefatigable mirrors.
Nothing can occur but once, nothing is preciously *in peril
of being lost*. The elegiac, the somber, the ceremonial are
not modes the Immortals hold in reverence. Homer and
I went our separate ways at the portals of Tangier; I do
not think we said good-bye.

The flattening and draining of life's *oomph* by dint of
deathlessness strikes me as a non sequitur. Likewise, absorption
into "pure contemplation" does not strike me as *the* attractor
for all immortalized existence. Even if it were, I think any notion of contemplation without *application*, experiment, dialectic,
peer-review, augmentation, exponential computation, etc.—
that is, without progress toward solving all solubilia, including
psychological and existential solubilia (ennui, anhedonia, meaninglessness)—is a maimed notion of contemplation. With all
due love for Borges, "The Immortal" is a cautionary tale for
those who eat only low-hanging fruit. Contra Borges, I hope
Borges is, as the malapropist Dogberry says in Shakespeare's
Much Ado About Nothing, "condemned into everlasting redemption for this." I hope, in other words, that immortal Borges is
enjoying Elysium with immortal Homer.[121]

I *politely revolt* against these charming curmudgeons. I *still*
imagine immortality positively; it is my castle in the air. "If you
have built castles in the air, your work need not be lost; that is
where they should be. Now put the foundations under them,"
wrote Thoreau at the conclusion of *Walden*. Thus, this essay is

---

parochial assumptions, and limits his vision of human possibilities.
Even on his own terms, perhaps, you do best thinking you are mortal
and very long-lived (having no good idea of approximately when the
end would come, whether after 200 or 2,000 or 20,000 years), while in
fact being immortal." *Philosophical Explanations*, 579, footnote.
[121] And, I would like to add, I hope that immortal Dante is "condemned into everlasting redemption" with immortal Virgil.

the cornerstone of my zenithistic "foundation" for *optimal* immortality. Borrowing the title of an essay from Thomas Paine's final book, I could have titled this essay, "My Private Thoughts on a Future State." I offer private thoughts, in Paine's sense: played *ad libitum*. My private thoughts, condensed into their most vulnerable utterance, echo the simple and uneasy *last* words of the 16th-century Italian poet Giacomo Zanella: "I should like to live." Since I should like to live, and should like for *all* life to go on living, to go on into *optimal* immortality, I wish William James's wish to "give to our belief in immortality a freer wing."[122]

Thus prepare yourself for woolgathering, straw-grasping, sentimentalism, logomancy, bombast, crisp confusion, and appeals to ignorance as I take a brisk wing, alongside Zuberi the strong, into four immortal realms: (1) types of immortality; (2) what, if anything, is immortalized; (3) the logistics of immortality; and (4) the quality of immortal lives.

2.1 *Types of Immortality*

Let me bring into play a rough-and-ready taxonomy.

At the bottom, there is *stuff*: tables, numbers, events, selves, universals, this "this," this "that," and so on.

Now, in our set of stuff, we may consider the alethic mode of this stuff's existence. Does this stuff *necessarily* exist or *contingently* exist? In the parlance of "possible worlds" talk, we would say of necessary stuff that *it exists in every possible world*. For contingent stuff, we would say that *it exists in some possible worlds, but not all possible worlds*.[123]

Next, there is the duration of *stuff*. Durable stuff is stuff that can exist, in part or whole, at more than one instant. How long does this durable stuff endure? Some stuff may exist for two Planck times. Some stuff may exist for two yotta-years (2×10^{24} years).

---

[122] William James, "Human Immortality: Two Supposed Objections to the Doctrine"

[123] We could also add, unnecessarily, the set of necessarily non-existent stuff, which *exists* in no possible world.

Given my rough-and-ready taxonomy, let's define two *naturalistic* forms of immortality. By "naturalistic immortality" I mean immortality that is *contingent* on some natural system, Ŝ, with infinitely many instants.[124]

Contingent natural complete saturation (CNCS):
In any world, Wn, with natural system Ŝ, X exists at every instant in Wn, of which there are infinitely many.

Contingent natural permanent continuation (CNPC):
In any world, Wn, with natural system Ŝ, X exists, after and not before its originary instant, at every instant in Wn, of which there are infinitely many.

I focus on natural systems with *infinitely* many instants. We could imagine natural systems with finitely many instants, where X exists at each of these instants; this, however, amounts to a finitely long duration for X, which fails to fit the general notion of immortality. Of course, our *actual* natural system, @Ŝ, may not have infinitely many instants, but I will assume, undefended, that *if* we occupy an infinite natural system, then our actual natural system does have infinitely many instants.[125]

Likewise, the spacetime of @Ŝ may be *non-smooth*, such that instants are exotically ordered, or disordered, into incommensurable sets of instants. Think of a time-sponge, full of pores and passages and warpages, some connected, others isolated. In non-smooth temporal systems, the question of saturation and permanent continuation surpasses my current competencies, though a few remarks may be helpful.

First, CNPC seems especially susceptible to problems with non-smooth spacetimes, since CNPC depends on the relations "after" and "before," which may lack global application in a time-sponge. CNCS, by contrast, allows X to exist "at every instant." "At every instant" is order-independent, so that X, to

---

[124] I chose "Ŝ," or "S circumflex," as a variable for a natural system because that little circumflex mark has a little orthographic summit, which suits my zenithist sense of nature.
[125] "@" is the actuality operator.

the extent it is possible, may saturate *all* sets of instants, commensurable or not.

Though CNCS is not without its kinks. Some "bubbles" of spacetime may "burst" after a Planck time of existence; some after a yotta-year. In whichever we might unitize these chaotic bubble-timelines into physically meaningful instants, X must exist "at every instant" in every bubble *if* X is to qualify as CNCS-immortal—such is the extravagance of CNCS-immortality. So extravagant this is, I think it less plausibly attainable than the following modified form:

Contingent natural maximal saturation (CNMS):
In any world, Wn, with natural system Ŝ, X exists at every instant in the maximal quantity of habitable sets of instants in Wn, some of which have infinitely many instants.

If a being is CNCS-immortal, then it is CNMS-immortal, but the reverse is not true. Moreover, if there exists a being that is CNCS-immortal, then no being that is *only* CNMS-immortal can qualify as a zenith being, *all else being equal between them*, since a zenith being is a *maximal* state, and complete saturation is a greater power than (non-complete) maximal saturation.

In this essay, I will explore these three immortalities: CNPC, CNCS, and CNMS. For the benefit of human memory, I will drop the near-indistinguishable acronyms (CNSCMSPC?) and *implicify* the "contingent natural" qualification, simply calling our options permanent continuation (PC), complete saturation (CS), and maximal saturation (MS).

I relativize immortality to this or that possible natural system, such as $\hat{S}_{7201}$ or $\hat{S}_{7891}$, in order to allow for dissimilar natural contingencies and various distinctions between more and less survivable natural systems. We do not yet know the "survivability score" of our actual natural system. If you and I could survive all possible contingencies of @Ŝ, then it may be said that immortality for any natural systems Ŝ, or any sufficiently Ŝ-similar natural systems, is *attainable* for us.

Anti-aging medicine (e.g., genetic editing, pharmacogenetics, pharmacoepigenetics, etc.) and all means to "bio-indefinite mortality" are therefore relevant to *this* essay only if they contribute to a case for permanent continuation, complete saturation, or maximal saturation directly, or to the quality of these immortal types of existence.

One final bit of fine print: these three types of immortality are bisected by another distinction: actual versus potential. Each definition is rooted, with some qualification or another, in the phrase "X exists at every instant." So, strictly speaking, if X only *potentially* exists at every instant, then X is not, as defined here, immortal. As defined here, X must *actually* exist at every instant. However, if X actually exists at every instant, and if there are infinitely many instants, then X actualizes a temporal infinity. Since an actual infinity, sometimes called a *completed infinity*, is a controversial bit of conceptual refinement, I will make some provision for a substantive *potential* immortality.

The provision is thus: There is *no* feature of $\hat{S}$ that can halt X from asymptotically approaching, if not actualizing, the attainment of permanent continuation, complete saturation, or maximal saturation.

Permanent continuation, complete saturation, and maximal saturation, either in their actual or potential sense, define three robust, but unadorned natural immortalities. There is no mention here of *how* such immortalities are attained, nor *why* they might be preferable to mortality, nor *what* possesses them, nor anything, except some alethic, temporal, and ontological profiles.

Despite my dip into these semi-technical depths, and despite any appearance of analytic tidiness, I remain unsure of my taxonomy. My taxonomy is comparable, in its riskiness, to the first enterprising leap of a barnacle gosling from its nest. As the wikipedia entry on barnacle geese reports:

> Barnacle geese frequently build their nests high on mountain cliffs, away from predators [...], but also away from their feeding grounds [...]. Like all geese, the goslings are not fed by the adults. Instead of bringing food to the newly hatched goslings, the goslings are brought to the ground. The parents show them the way to jump from the cliff and the goslings follow them by instincts and take the plunge. Unable to fly, the goslings, in their first

days of life, jump off the cliff and fall; their small size, feathery down, and very light weight helps to protect some of them from serious injury when they hit the rocks below, but many die from the impact.

Feathered with our goosey taxonomy and stepping to the edge of a cliff over an abyss (of immortality), shall we now jump over together?[126]

2.2 *The Life of Jane Phaedo, Super-Scientist*

I would like to offer a brief aside on permanent continuation as compared to saturation.

Permanent continuation overlaps with more traditional Islamo-Christian views of immortality, which hold that we exist forever *after* birth, but not before. Complete saturation, on the other immortal hand, involves what some might call prenatal existence or pre-existence, a view famously examined in Plato's *Phaedo* and affirmed, with asterisks, in Hinduism, and Buddhism. On these views, one's life is birth-symmetric—one exists before and after birth.

To understand the symmetry of complete or maximal saturation, consider the possible case of Jane Phaedo in $\hat{S}_{JP}$, that is, Jane Phaedo in the natural system containing Jane Phaedo.

Jane is born on October 27th, 1987. Thirty-three years later, in 2020, Jane invents a time-traveling machine, which she uses to travel to October 27th, 1986, one year before her birth. When did Jane begin to exist?

Jane exists *before* Jane's birth, so Jane's birth is not her beginning in time.

Suppose now that Jane ups the temporal ante and travels, with the necessary personal protective equipment, to the Planck era of the Big Bang (and let's suppose this Bang is the first physically meaningful instant in $\hat{S}_{JP}$). Now suppose also that Jane, super-scientist, attains godlike imperviousness to every natural contingency in $\hat{S}_{JP}$, such that Jane lives from the Planck

---

[126] First it was Zuberi and now it is barnacle geese—what augury is this?

era onward to October 27th, 1987 (and beyond). Jane, in this situation, has existed from the beginning of $\hat{S}_{JP}$, even though she was born in 1987. Presumably, her subjective ordering of time "begins" in her *childhood* memories, but her "objective" timeline, if we can speak of such a thing, extends from the first physically meaningful instant in $\hat{S}_{JP}$ to the year 2020, and beyond. For Jane Phaedo, there is a sort of prenatal existence; subjectively, her memories funnel backward into her childhood, yet she exists *well before* this childhood.[127]

3.1 *What is Immortalized?*

With some alethic, temporal, and ontological types quickly outlined, we may ask: *what is immortal?*—or rather, what is *immortalized?*

Since we are dealing with *naturalistic* immortality, I will focus on natural entities (entities that are *in principle* fully describable and explainable by the sciences, e.g., physics, chemistry, biology, etc.), and I will assume that most, if not all, of what we wish immortalized, such as persons and artefacts and life events, etc., are natural entities. As I doubt that immortality is an essential property of natural entities, I assume that *our* attainment of immortality depends on outside help.[128] Thus, I

---

[127] The question of Jane's beginning is akin to that of Zenith's beginning. When did Zenith begin to exist? I do not assume that there is a meaningful global answer to this question, given a likely non-commensurability between various sets of instants. Designations such as "before this moment," "at this very moment," and "after this moment," are relative to a "moment" that is not globally well-defined. However, it does seem appropriate to say that Zenith can exist at every moment of *your* local time, since Zenith (presumably) can participate in your local time. Consider this suggestion of relativistic time in the biblical passage 2 Peter 3:8: "But, beloved, be not ignorant of this one thing, that one day is with the Lord as a thousand years, and a thousand years as one day."

[128] *Naturalistic* outside help, that is; I am not summoning non-natural entities. One might ask: Is zenithism a rejection of the existence of an intrinsically immortal soul? *I* make no claim one way or another about

consider immortality in the context of zenithism; in other words, my proposals depend on particular properties of zenith beings.

Assuming that permanent continuation, complete saturation, or maximal saturation are *scientific* possibilities, and assuming that zenith beings can immortalize natural entities in these ways, our question "What is immortalized?" can become a more specific question: *What would zenith beings immortalize?*

First and foremost, I hold that zenith beings are (more likely than not) ethical and optimific beings, thus their application of immortality will have ethical and optimific features.[129] In this essay, therefore, I focus narrowly on immortalization in the context of ethical and optimific zeniths. If you believe my focus is *too* narrow, myopic even, then I apologize to you, but please consider that this is *one* essay, not *all* essays. I may well focus narrowly on non-ethical cases in some future essay; or better yet, you may.

Graciously permitted an ethical framework for our question, I propose two *values* that Zenith may use in its application of immortality: plenitude and priority.

3.2 *Plenitude and Priority*

Plenitude: Of those things that can be immortalized, immortalize *everything* worth immortalizing.

Priority: If X is *more* worthy of immortalization than Y, and if X or Y can be immortalized, but not *both* X and Y, then immortalize X.

Some commentary may be helpful.

---

an inherently immortal soul-stuff. However, the non-existence of a soul does not mean the non-existence of psycho-physiological states made perpetual through scientific means. Zenith, as the ultimate technologist, may be able to preserve the person anatomically, psychologically, etc., that is, perhaps it may preserve *every desired kind of continuity for every important identity-making factor.*

[129] Here I recommend my essay "Positive Apeirotheism," in this book, which defends the case for ethical and optimific zenith beings.

On the question of what *deserves* immortalization, William James affirmed what he called the "democratic view." In "Human Immortality: Two Supposed Objections to the Doctrine," he wrote, "For my own part, then, so far as logic goes, I am willing that every leaf that ever grew in this world's forests and rustled in the breeze should become immortal."

James contrasts the democratic view of immortality with the aristocratic view, or "the narrow-hearted aristocratic creed," which limits the class of immortals to "an elite, a select and manageable number." According to James, the ancient aristocratic view of immortality existed in a provincial cosmos, a *small* chain of being, from gods to princes to paupers, whereas we moderns now exist in a non-centered Darwinian plenum.

James observes that many people cannot integrate "the incredible and intolerable number of beings which, with our modern imagination, we must believe to be immortal, if immortality be true." With our democratic preferences, but Darwinian imagination, any modern vision of immortality becomes too profligate for us. "It is, I fancy, a stumbling-block of altogether modern origin," wrote James, "due to the strain upon the quantitative imagination which recent scientific theories, and the moral feelings consequent upon them, have brought in their train." One finds James's own *modern* sensitivity in this piece:

An immense compassion and kinship fill the heart. An immortality from which these inconceivable billions of fellow-strivers should be excluded becomes an irrational idea for us. That our superiority in personal refinement or in religious creed should constitute a difference between ourselves and our messmates at life's banquet, fit to entail such a consequential difference of destiny as eternal life for us, and for them torment hereafter, or death with the beasts that perish, is a notion too absurd to be considered serious. Nay, more, the very beasts themselves—the wild ones at any rate—are leading the heroic life at all times. And a modern mind, expanded as some minds are by cosmic emotion, by the great evolutionist vision of universal continuity, hesitates to draw the line even at man. If any creature lives forever, why not all?—why not the patient brutes? So that a faith in immortality, if we are to indulge it, demands of us nowadays a scale of representation so stupendous that our imagination faints before it, and our personal feelings refuse to rise up and face the task. The supposition we are swept along to is too vast, and, rather than face the conclusion, we abandon the premise from which it starts. We give up our own immortality sooner than believe that all the hosts of Hottentots and Australians that have been, and shall ever be, should share it with us in *secula seculorum*. Life is a good thing on a reasonably copious scale; but the very heavens themselves, and the cosmic times and spaces, would stand aghast, we think, at the notion of preserving eternally such an ever-swelling plethora and glut of it.

This universal tenderness can be found more than a century earlier, in the writings of Joseph Priestley. In his *Disquisitions Relating to Matter and Spirit* (1777), Priestly wrote,

But if resurrection be, in fact, *within the proper course of nature*, extensively considered, and consequently there be something remaining of every organized body that death does not destroy, there will be reason to conclude that [animals] will be benefited by it as well as ourselves. And the great misery to which some of them are exposed in this life, may incline us to think, that a merciful and just God will make them some recompense for it hereafter. He is *their* maker and father as well as *ours*.

But William James heightens and deepens this "inclination" to think that "a merciful and just God" would immortalize all beings.

I speak, you see, from the point of view of all the other individual beings, realizing and enjoying inwardly their own existence. If we are pantheists, we can stop there. We need, then, only say that through them, as through so many diversified channels of expression, the eternal Spirit of the Universe affirms and realizes its own infinite life. But if we are theists, we can go farther without altering the result. God, we can then say, has so inexhaustible a capacity for love that his call and need is for a literally endless accumulation of created lives. He can never faint or grow weary, as we should, under the increasing supply. His scale is infinite in all things. His sympathy can never know satiety or glut.

Weariness and scarcity may be part of our "finiting outlines," those limits that make us who we are, those limits that seem "to be our personal essence," but these limits can contribute to our devaluing of other beings.

> The truth is that we are doomed, by the fact that we are practical beings with very limited tasks to attend to, and special ideals to look after, to be absolutely blind and insensible to the inner feelings, and to the whole inner significance of lives that are different from our own. Our opinion of the worth of such lives is absolutely wide of the mark, and unfit to be counted at all.

We often have "an insensibility to the inner significance of alien lives, and a conceit that would project our own incapacity into the vast cosmos, and measure the wants of the Absolute by our own puny needs." Yet James, the most welcoming and tender-hearted of philosophers, holds that ours "is a democratic universe, in which our paltry exclusions play no regulative part."

> The heart of being can have no exclusions akin to those which our poor little hearts set up. The inner significance of other lives exceeds all our powers of sympathy and insight. If we feel a significance in our own life which would lead us spontaneously to claim its perpetuity, let us be at least tolerant of like claims made by other lives, however numerous, however unideal they may seem to us to be.

As you have likely noticed, I quote extensively from James's essay. I am tempted to reprint the whole bounteous, beauteous, benevolent essay within this essay. My comments (these interruptions) only lightly camouflage that desire. Indulge one final quotation.

That you have a saturation-point of interest tells us nothing of the interests that absolutely are. The Universe, with every living entity which her resources create, creates at the same time a call for that entity, and an appetite for its continuance,—creates it, if nowhere else, at least within the heart of the entity itself. It is absurd to suppose, simply because our private power of sympathetic vibration with other lives gives out so soon, that in the heart of infinite being itself there can be such a thing as plethora, or glut, or supersaturation.

I think James's democratic view of immortality is ethically superior than any aristocratic view. Democratic immortality, so to speak, applies to the maximum of ethical subjects, or *everything deserving of ethical consideration*, whereas aristocratic immortality does not. Aristocratic immortality is ethically incomplete. Surely we and our loved ones may wish for ourselves permanent continuation, if not saturation, but *vastly* more is worth permanent continuation: every little Athens caddisfly, Xerces blue, and Levuana moth; Tyke the elephant; the Temple of Artemis at Ephesus; the Zahir mosque in Malaysia; the birth of Virginia Dare; every painting from every painter, from Anna Zemánková to Zainul Adebin (that is, from A to Z and back again); and so on. The heart of the democratic view beats with the value of plenitude:

Plenitude: Of those things that can be immortalized, immortalize everything worth immortalizing.

Plenitude may include *everything*, if everything is immortalizable and worth immortalizing.[130] Still, the aristocrat may ask, does plenitude include immortalization of every time-slice of all the microalgae that has ever existed?[131] Does every

---

[130] What is *worth* immortalizing? In my extravagant opinion, Scott A. Davison's *On the Intrinsic Value of Everything* sums up what is worthy of immortalization: "every concrete particular thing that exists."

[131] If every time-slice is preserved and every time-sliced unit continues its own unique post-ascension life, then one may worry that more than

mycoplasma, a.k.a. mollicute, the smallest bacterial cells known to us, saturate *every* instant in the universe?[132]

Consider Jainist monks, for whom non-violence (ahimsa) applies even to bacteria:

> When water is prepared for monks, it is first filtered and then boiled and cooled. The filtering removes any large water-borne organisms. Boiling the water kills all micro-organisms, including disease-carrying bacteria. Clearly, there is violence in killing the bacteria, but it is one-time violence, and it stops the greater violence of killing many bacteria which would have kept growing exponentially.[133]

Jains would prefer *not* to kill the bacteria in their water, but there are logistical constraints on this ideal; their compromise is the friendliest option between human and bacteria—a necessary evil. Jains prefer bacteriostatic to bactericidal methods of food preservation. Bacteriostatic agents stop bacteria from reproducing, but do not necessarily kill the bacteria, as do bactericidal agents. All told, a Jain ethicist *includes* bacteria in the sphere of ethical concern. Would the best ethicist do so?[134] I think it is more plausible than not that the best ethicist would do so, as I think that the *eschaton* of ethics, if you will, involves an affirmation of *universal responsibility*.

Yet not killing a bacterium is not the same as immortalizing it. Immortalizing every bacterium, one might say, is beyond even the Jainist ethic of ahimsa, unless failing to rescue a life from extinction when one is able to do so counts as an act of harm (which it might). Even so, even if the stringent Jainist ideal does not require immortalizing every bacterium, an ideal of immortality that *includes* bacteria seems ethically superior to

---

preservation is occurring, but rather millions of *duplications* of the source microalgae.

[132] For every mollicute on earth, there are infinitely many zeniths, such is the profound profligacy of an infinite natural system.

[133] Manoj Jain, Laxmi Jain, and Tarla Dalal, *Jain Food: Compassionate and Healthy Eating*

[134] See section 3.4 in my essay "Positive Apeirotheism" for a discussion of "best ethicists."

an ideal of immortality that *excludes* bacteria, all else about the immortalities being equal. An ethical or optimific zenith being is more likely than not to do the better of two ethical options, thus such a zenith is more likely than not to immortalize every bacterium, *if it is able to do so and do so without sacrificing better outcomes*. All told, there may be a better case for universal immortalization as *morally* superior to partial immortalization, in which case the best metaethicist would seek universal and optimal immortalization. Among those who consider ethics, those who *contend with God*, the sphere of ethical concern has overall grown, not constricted; collective ethical expertise seems to incline toward an open-gated view, that is, toward universal care for non-human animals, plants, artworks, and so on. I sense in this inclination of these ethical experts the prospect that advancing minds, synthetic or otherwise, will converge on universal concern and *enact that concern*.[135]

Think about our own taxonomic and field studies, our accumulation of biological lists—the meticulous cataloguing of species, their lineages, distributions, migrations, and morphologies. We create and fill databases, archives, museum drawers (though our databases, archives, museums, etc., are mere sieves with which to collect all the monsoon rainfall of things worth preserving). From the Svalbard Global Seed Vault to the "Frozen Zoo" (a storage facility in which DNA, embryos, and other genetic materials from animals are stored at extremely low temperatures in tanks of liquid nitrogen), it seems to me there is an instinctive-normative wish for the permanent continuation of *living things*, and more, of *all worthy things*. When less encumbered by scarcity and zero-sum competition and physical danger, we grant ourselves our universal wish.

We are informavores, after all; our success as a species owes much to a hyper-inclusive curiosity.[136] We human beings, as massively limited as we are, have mapped the intricate

---

[135] See "Universal Responsibility" in this book.
[136] Can one imagine a more successful species (e.g., an intergalactic species) that is *not* an informavore? Could an incurious species colonize a whole galaxy? I imagine there is a selection effect for every rung upward in scientific and technological development.

internal anatomy of the segments of annelids, from nephric tubule to nephrostome. We have generated a high-resolution hemibrain connectome for the humble fruit fly: 25,000 neurons, 4000 distinct kinds of neuron, 20 million synapses. We do not have the technology to map and preserve *every* annelid and fruit fly, but if we did, and if universal annelid and fruit fly preservation were cheap and easy, and without significant opportunity costs, then, I would argue, we should and would do it. Why not? If the energy and effort required is negligible, why not? What is the cost? It may be of minimal benefit (to us), but insofar as that minimal benefit is greater than the cost of preservation, it seems worthy enough of doing.[137]

What would *you* want for all of these living beings? If wishes could be made true, what would you wish for these creatures? Consider the lilies, the tardigrades, the mice, the miniature schnauzers. Consider seahorse fathers and bonobo mothers. If by a thought and a blink of an eye, you could simply conjure any fate for them, what fate would you conjure? Should the mayfly have its mayfly paradise forever?—or the vaquita swim in vaquita bliss forever? Should each of the fruit flies in the "Fly Room" of Thomas Hunt Morgan be preserved, healed, augmented? Should one world be optimized for blue jays, and another for blue iguanas, so each have their heaven? Would one wish for all the simple little protists a peaceful swim forever somewhere friendly to them? If you're wishing anything, why not wish for the best for every one of these beings? Why not rainbow bridges everywhere? Why not the dance of an infinitely-handed, everywhere-reaching Guanyin?

Added to our wishes and ideals, there may be the urging of our gratitude. How do *you* feel about your ancestors, mycoplasma included? *I* feel grateful for all my ancestors. I feel gratitude for all of those beings eons ago, all the zooplankton and amphibians and fructivorous mammals and hunter-gatherers, who endured pain and struggle and disease to produce today's living network. If I could award this "crane" of countless lives with a great resurrection and amelioration, I would do so. In

---

[137] I sometimes analogize Zenith to an optimal Wikipedia: Zenipedia. But rather than an entry on some entity, it is the entity itself.

the supernoval glow of such unlimited cosmic moods, I experience a visceral affinity with all that lived and lives and will live. To witness the tree of life all at once! To witness it bloom again in its kaleidoscopic totality!—and never cease blooming!

As Marcus Karenin cries in H.G. Wells's novel *The World Set Free*, "I gather myself together out of the pools of the individual that have held me dispersed so long. I gather my billion thoughts into science and my million wills into a common purpose." I hold that this "common purpose," or, to use Nikolai Fyodorovich Fyodorov's term, "common task," or John Dewey's term, "common faith," is the immortalization and *apotheosis* of all concrete particulars.

One may ask, "What would be the purpose of such unbridled immortalization? What is all this life *for*?" Life determines what life is for. And while for certain things there is no *personal* significance in cessation or preservation, there may be moral or aesthetic significance, such that a value-optimizer would seek to "make good" all life, even with all these extinction events.[138]

So, in summary, I hold that if it is ethically good to immortalize X, then Zenith will most likely attempt to immortalize X, given that Zenith will most likely attempt to do what is ethically good. In my essay "Positive Apeirotheism," I address reasons for thinking that Zenith is the best ethicist and ethical agent. In that essay, I hold that the "maximal informavore" and "best ethicist" will make the maximally informed ethical decision.

Certainly, there are constraints that will apply to our optimizer. I assume, therefore, that some sort of priority scheme is forced into the practice of plenitude. In broad strokes, a priority scheme may be as follows:

Priority: If X is *more* worthy of immortalization than Y, and if X or Y can be immortalized, but not *both* X and Y, then immortalize X.

---

138 For example, through adjoining (see my "Adjoining" essay).

Perhaps the core dilemma that forces any such prioritization—that Zenith can immortalize either x or y, but not both x
and y—never arises (though not because of an inability to immortalize even *one* of x and y). I hope x and y can be saved
together. I will not entertain any specific rankings of "worth,"
nor a definition, particularly since I offer a priority scheme only
formally, as a possibility, and not as an endorsement. Scarcity
(of time, information, energy, etc.) interposes limits, degrees,
utility functions, opportunity costs—in a word, economics.
What is scarcity in an infinite natural system? The thought of
infinitely many immortalized things may shock and awe our imaginations, imaginations subconsciously tyrannized by a primordial Malthusian instinct; we are, after all, Darwin's children.
Yet the center of the sphere of ethical concern is everywhere
and its circumference nowhere. *Logistics* coerce us to react otherwise.

3.3 *The Immortalization of Persons*

Assuming that Zenith has a mostly unrestricted power to
immortalize, which do you think has a greater *a priori* probability?

(1) South African international cricketer Francois "Faf" du Plessis *alone* is immortalized.
(2) South African international cricketer Francois "Faf" du Plessis is immortalized along with *all* human beings.

I would argue that (2) is more probable, since (1) seems to
require a likelihood-lowering special reason regarding a special
fact about Francois "Faf" du Plessis *specifically*. Option (2) requires only a special reason regarding a special fact about human beings *generally*.

Put differently, the more exclusive the standard of immortalization, the less likely *any particular thing* will be immortalized.
Why *only* Francois "Faf" du Plessis? Why not *only* the petals of
Iceland poppies? Or perhaps Zenith is exclusively fixated upon
the elytron of figeater beetles, so immortalizes *only* the elytron
of figeater beetles.

The principle of plenitude as a regulative ideal in Zenith's immortalization efforts *increases* the likelihood that selves and persons will be immortalized. This is one personal benefit of a universal standard as against a particularized standard. A universal standard does not require special reasons *for any particular thing*, only a generic reason, such as the goodness of universal immortalization.

Universal immortalization is also beneficial with respect to *all* the things about ourselves that we may desire immortalized. We desire, it appears to me, an immortal lifespan, healthspan, selfspan, value-span, *and* self-worth-span.

Yes, we desire an endless duration of life, an immortal lifespan, but we desire an immortal healthspan as well. Healthspan, as Nick Bostrom defines it, is the "capacity to remain fully healthy, active, and productive, both mentally and physically."[139] Yet, on top of an immortal lifespan and immortal healthspan, we want our *selves*—an immortal self-span. We do not wish to be some immortally healthy organic substrate for *other selves*, but for *our* selves (whatever we think important in that expression). Superadded to these humble requests, we desire something to be immortally *valuable* about our existence—an immortal "value-span."[140] And finally, we desire to *perceive* our own

---

[139] Nick Bostrom, "Why I Want to Be Posthuman," in *The Transhumanist Reader* (2013).

[140] Consider Kenneth Boulding's "The Menace of Methuselah" (1965), in which Boulding argues that increased life expectancy could result in overcrowding, wealth concentration, and a diminished place for new or young talent (as "immortal" geniuses continue to saturate every discipline). Consider also the anti-immortality arguments explored by Bernard Williams (invoking *The Markopoulos Affair*, a play by Karel Čapek). Presumably, Zenith masters mental worlds, as it masters spacetime. To suppose otherwise, to suppose, for example, that everlasting life eventuates tedium and Tithonian despair, is to profoundly underestimate the endmost state beyond the technological singularity. Presumably, Zenith can create a self, preserve a fixed self, fix any response to any stimulus, modify stimuli, explore the whole possibility space of mental states, and so forth. The possibilities and consequences of such psychological engineering, the possibilities of such basal power, we are only just beginning to *tolerate*.

valuableness, if not every second, at least frequently throughout eternity—an immortal "self-worth-span."

A principle of plenitude can underpin this stacked immortalization that we desire. Now how precisely "life," "self," "health," "value," and "self-worth" are best defined, such that these "spans" and their interrelations may be determined, is a problem whose solution I do not, perhaps even cannot, know. Zenith, I take it, has the best accounts of life, self, health, value, self-worth, etc., and acts optimally with this information.

But let us briefly consider the sort of problems an "apex cogitator"[141] must address. Consider the classic philosophical question about personal identity: What are the criteria of personal identity, a.k.a., "persistence conditions" of this unity called "person"? Which is the best way to fill in the following formula? Person P at time t is identical to person P* at time t* *if and only if* [insert persistence condition(s) here].

To avoid anything like the trinitarian *mystery*, one's proposed persistence conditions ought to be immune from various problems, such as fission (one distinct identity is concluded to be identical to two or more distinct identities) or fusion (two or more distinct identities are concluded to be identical to one distinct identity). Philosophers have sought to make precise and consequently capture the necessary and sufficient conditions of identity through time.

One proposed persistence condition is direct physical continuity: P must exist *continuously*, that is, there must be a direct physical continuum between P at time t and P at time t*—no discontinuities allowed. Consider two abstract cases:

$$1. \quad P_1 \rightarrow P_2 \rightarrow P_3$$
$$2. \quad P_1 \rightarrow P_2 \qquad P_3$$

In the first case, P_3 is the continuer of P_1 via the continuer of P_2. In the second case, P_3 is *not* the continuer of P_1, since there is a causal break (signified by the absence of an arrow) between P_1 and P_3.

---

[141] A sparkling phrase from Nick Bostrom's *Superintelligence*, 79

It may be helpful to consider these persistence problems in relation to the discontinuities of death, or the destruction of bodies, especially since our overall subject is immortality. In *The Possibility of Resurrection and Other Essays in Christian Apologetics*, Peter van Inwagen provides a clarifying case of a discontinuity:

> Suppose a certain monastery claims to have in its possession a manuscript written in Saint Augustine's own hand. And suppose the monks of this monastery further claim that this manuscript was burned by Arians in the year 457. It would immediately occur to me to ask how this manuscript, the one I can touch, could be the very manuscript that was burned in 457. Suppose their answer to this question is that God miraculously recreated Augustine's manuscript in 458. I should respond to this answer as follows: The deed it describes seems quite impossible, even as an accomplishment of omnipotence. God certainly might have created a perfect duplicate of the original manuscript, but it would not be that one; its earliest moment of existence would have been after Augustine's death; it would never have known the impress of his hand; it would not have been a part of the furniture of the world when he was alive; and so on.
>
> Now suppose our monks were to reply by simply asserting that the manuscript now in their possession did know the impress of Augustine's hand; that it was a part of the furniture of the world when the saint was alive; that when God re-created or restored it, he (as an indispensable component of accomplishing this task) saw to it that the object he produced had all these properties.
>
> I confess I should not know what to make of this. I should have to tell the monks that I did not see how what they believed could possibly be true (45-46).

There are other problematic discontinuities to consider in relation to death.

If one dies as an infant, would one persist *after death* in endless infancy, or does the post-mortem infant develop into the post-mortem teenager?—that is, does the infant have a childhood in the afterlife? What is a post-mortem childhood?—a childhood like those of the Lost Boys in J.M. Barrie's Never Never Land? As Voltaire summarized: "A child dies in its mother's womb, just at the moment that it has received a soul. Will it rise again foetus, or boy, or man? If foetus, to what good? If boy or man, where will the necessary material come from?"[142]

There is also the infamous "cannibal objection" to the continuity of physical resurrections. Again, Voltaire:

> A soldier from Brittany goes into Canada; there, by a very common chance, he finds himself short of food, and is forced to eat an Iroquois whom he killed the day before. This Iroquois had fed on Jesuits for two or three months; a great part of his body had become Jesuit. Here, then, the body of a soldier is composed of Iroquois, of Jesuits, and of all that he had eaten before. How is each to take again precisely what belongs to him? And which part belongs to each?[143]

These are merely a few of the difficulties that plague merely *one* proposed persistence condition, specifically in relation to death. Persistence proposals persist, for the linking of lives to lives and lives to afterlives, but every proposal suffers its own treadmill of counterarguments.

Some philosophers have *de*sisted in this persistence-condition game by tidily rejecting the self. The "no-self" view, such as that held by Siddhartha Gautama and Sri David Hume, holds that there are sensorial bangs and centerless fizzlings, pressures, frictions, fluid geometries, and interpenetrating impressions, but *no singular, stable, coherent, meaningful, etc., self.* The concept of "self" is either incoherent or, if coherent, lacks any correspondence with anything in the world.

Naturally, Zenith cannot immortalize a thing whose essence is some bit of non-actualizable incoherence, just as it cannot immortalize a colorless green idea sleeping furiously. Though on the second and "error theory" interpretation of the

---

[142] From Voltaire's *Philosophical Dictionary,* entry on "Resurrection," Section IV: "Resurrection of the Moderns." I do not think these developmental difficulties are deep difficulties, but they do deserve consideration when imagining a plausible afterlife.
[143] ibid.

no-self view, in which the concept of "self" lacks any correspondence with anything in the world, a techno-optimist, such
as myself, may find it plausible, as I do, that Zenith is capable
of engineering entities that could qualify as substantial selves
or persisting identities, thus falsifying the error version of the
no-self view by any number of properly qualifying "builds" of
a substantial self.

It may well be that *enselfing* is possible only when Zenith
centripetalizes neural nebulae into a galaxy of enselfing gravity,
though I think it is more plausible that we are already persistent
selves and persons *without* the technological help.

Though that is merely my opinion.

Now some philosophers simply abandon the ship of Theseus and claim that, yes, "things persist, but [...] there are no
informative metaphysically necessary and sufficient conditions
for their persistence."[144] These freestyle swimmers are the *anti-
criterialists*. In the anti-criterialist case, it seems that Zenith cannot immortalize things, since there are no determinate conditions that Zenith can fix upon, learn, and use to engineer a
thing's persistence. It may be, however, that Zenith does not
require "informative metaphysically necessary and sufficient
conditions" in order to immortalize a thing—other indirect
means may be available.

All things considered, for a mind that would make John
von Neuman's mind look like a reflexive twitch in a silverfish's
rear bristle, the problem of persistence may be *no* problem.
Zenith, in its capacity as the maximal mind, knows its metaphysics, neurobiology, physics, and so on, to a degree sufficient
to know the best ontological and axiological solutions (or absence thereof) to the problems of identity and persistence. The
Lockeans, neo-Lockeans, Humeans, animalists, anti-criterial-
ists, and other theorists of personal identity may be, relative to
Zenith, embryonic.

Finally, I consider all *enselfing* prospects applicable to more
beings than merely the human animal. I count many animals as
selfed beings *already*, even if they cannot. Many of them have
what I consider self-like attributes: a first-person perspective,

---

144 Matt Duncan, "A Renewed Challenge to Anti-Criterialism"

even if an irreflexive one; a thought life at some stage; motives, if ill-understood; a sense of their body's boundaries; some memory-like storage, if not simply memory; some degree of openness, extraversion, agreeableness, and neuroticism; and so on. They are, as it were, only one flash of recognition away from linking and lacing up these selfing elements into self-awareness, and bundling their impressions into a more lucid idea of union and continuity.

But what does their lack of self-recognition matter to their selfhood when *I* recognize selves there—selves unknown to themselves. Their ignorance of their own selfhood does not equal the absence of selfhood. If there is no *personal* significance (significance *for them*) in their own cessation, the cessation of their selves, it is due only to this little, shallow, and arbitrary gap of self-neglect. One should infer across that tiny bit of modal distance into a neighboring possible world in which the animal's enselfing flash of insight makes explicit a self-significance found only implicit here—and with this inference, become a modal-moral bridge to guardianship.

We too need our own cohering flash of self-recognition, a more-than-four-dimensional disclosure of an oceanic nature, of an individuality more diffracted and open, with connective temporal tissues more labyrinthine than we can now disentangle. For I do think it is probable that we are *already* adjoined with Zenith, that we, in the fullest view, are *already* zenith beings. As William James wrote, "If the extreme individualistic view were taken, one's finite mundane consciousness would be an extract from one's larger, truer personality, the latter having even now some sort of reality behind the scenes."[145]

If true, then you and I, and all living beings, are avatars of a sort, incarnate gods, kin to all those endless rainbowy entrances of divinity dancing up from the sweet, spongy, syncretic polytheism of Hinduism.[146]

---

[145] William James, "Human Immortality: Two Supposed Objections to the Doctrine"

[146] *A Personal Problem of Evil* — If *we* are already divine, why do *we* allow suffering?

4.1 *Motives and Logistics*

Let us step back for a moment and consider motives and logistics, and how they interrelate. Surely there is feedback between motives and logistics, so surely a plausible account of Zenith's act of immortalizing X must include some consideration of the interactions between the motives and logistics in immortalizing X.

To assess this interaction, it may help to use two ratios: an effort-to-motivation ratio (EM ratio) and a magnitude-to-motivation ratio (MM ratio).

The EM ratio is the relation between *the intensity of the effort or energy required to complete an action* (logistical) and *the intensity of the motivation that is required to take that action* (motivational). Consider two events: climbing Mt. Everest and moving one's eyes. If I climbed Mt. Everest and someone asked me *why did you do that*, it would be considered odd if I answered, "No reason." On the other hand, if someone asked me *why did your eye do a saccade just now*, it wouldn't be considered odd if I answered, "No reason."

We assume, all else being equal, that there is a direct proportionality between the intensity of the motivation required to do some action and the intensity of the effort required for doing that action. Climbing Mt. Everest is strenuous, so one's motivation for climbing Mt. Everest must be more intense or developed than the motivation for a saccade of one's eye, which is an essentially involuntary, i.e., non-motivated, act (one requiring no *conscious* effort, though there is autonomic effort).

Now the MM ratio is the relation between the *magnitude of an action's effect* and *the intensity of the motivation that is required to do that action*. I take "magnitude" to mean either the scale of the effect or the significance of the effect.

Consider a case in which you are presented with two buttons: A and B. If you press A, nothing happens. If you press B, all of the earth's adult human population returns to infancy. If you press A, I might ask *why*, but you might have no definite or articulate reason for your choice. *I just felt like it. I wanted to press a button. I was bored.* Such responses would seem to be sufficient explanations. However, if you press B, presumably you will provide a story more substantial than one of whim or boredom. If you are a cognitively advanced entity, which you are, I would expect a more substantial story. In both cases, the actual mechanical effort is minimal, but the magnitudes are radically different.

When we ask why Zenith would immortalize X, our response should factor in the EM and MM ratios. Both ratios frame any motivational story to be told.

On the EM ratio, if it is extremely difficult (though still possible) for Zenith to immortalize all organisms on the earth, then we should expect a substantial story about *why* Zenith would commit to such a difficult course of action.

If, however, immortalizing such life is, for Zenith, like the saccade of an eye, then our expectations for a substantial motivational story should be lowered, though a basic *explanation* would still be needed.

As for the MM ratio, immortalizing *all* lives is an extremely significant thing to do, so we might maintain that, given the MM ratio, a substantial motivational story is needed to explain Zenith's immortalizing action. I claim that one substantial motivational story that could explain this magnitudinous act involves the fact that Zenith, qua best metaethicist, affirms the principle of plenitude (or something like it). Bear in mind that the *magnitude* of universal immortalization may look different, may be renormalized (so to speak), from that perspectival zenith of existence, where so many magnitudinous events surge out in all directions.

I think it is important to keep in mind the potency and magnitude of Zenith when searching for motivational stories. If the zenith limit of reality is sufficiently "god-like," then it may be that even universal immortalization costs Zenith virtually nothing, such that Zenith neither needs nor has a complex justification for its *minor* expenditure.

Consider the act of photographing a rose. Let's first go back to the earliest days of photography: the "heliography" of Joseph Nicéphore Niépce. Using Niépce's heliography, you would first coat a pewter plate in bitumen of Judea, place the pewter plate in a camera obscura, well stabilized and stationary, then wait eight hours (at minimum) for exposure, and finally wash the pewter in oil of lavender and white petroleum to dissolve any leftover, unhardened bitumen. All of this effort, all requiring daylight, for some smoky shapes with indistinct edges. *Why did you heliograph this rose?*

Today, however, a six-year-old may make a minute's worth of 4K video of a rose, not because of the rose, but merely as the *next* thing she films after thirty seconds of her shoelaces, before filming a minute of a cirrus cloud, five seconds of another cirrus cloud, three seconds of some viburnum bushes, and five minutes on a dead ladybug. This light-hearted six-year-old, without any strong motives or reasons, is preserving the world with radiant abandon.[147]

4.2 *Time*

In sections 2.1 and 2.2, I briefly discussed time's relation to various types of immortality, but to better assess any effort that may be required of Zenith to immortalize anything, it will be useful to consider time a little more closely.

The general concept of time today involves the linear coordinate system, in which a set of real numbers is used to map a set of "instants." One can count "instants" via real numbers and one can order "instants" with these numerical tags. Between any two real numbers, there is another real number, thus we think that between any two instants, there is another instant; in the case of time, this perfect density or "continuum" view is debated.

The possibility of "spacetime foam," also known as "quantum foam," may jumble up any straightforward application of the continuum-measure. Yet the linear coordinate picture, with all of its wonderfully clear mathematical applications,

---

[147] "A cheap box camera can provide for any one of us what the greatest sculptors of the ancient world labored for years to give the Emperor Hadrian—the exact image of a lost love." Arthur C. Clarke, *Profiles of the Future: An Inquiry into the Limits of the Possible*

remains useful. It may not best represent temporal realities, but it is a good start.[148]

Contemporary philosophers of time are generally divided, between two main theories of time: A-theory and B-theory.[149] A-theorists claim that temporal becoming is objectively real. B-theorists claim that temporal becoming is objectively unreal, that the "flow of time" is illusory.

Consider an event, E. For the A-theorist, E is in future, then E becomes present, then E becomes past. E's temporal predicates, e.g., "is future," "is present," and "is past," are monadic or non-relational predicates. For the B-theorist, E's predicates are essentially relational. For the B-theorist, the time-indexical "now" is like the space-indexical "here," in that the meaning of both is dependent on the context in which the words are used. This contrasts with the A-theorist's view of "now," which is *not* dependent for its meaning on the context in which it is used, but stands for a primitive state of universal simultaneity.

---

[148] As an aside, one amusing argument for the actuality of infinite life involves the density of instants. Between the first instant of your personal existence and the last instant of your personal existence, there exist infinitely many instants (as between 0 and 1 there are infinitely many real numbers). Therefore, there are as many instants of your personal existence as there are instants altogether, namely, *infinitely many* instants. The quantity of instants for the entire duration of the cosmos is equal to the quantity of instants in your personal life; even better, the quantity of instants for the entire duration of the cosmos is equal to the quantity of instants in the time it took you to read this sentence. The cardinality of the set of all cosmic instants is equal to the cardinality of the set of all your personal instants! You possess as much time as the universe possesses. Of course, the infinite divisibility of a "timeline" does not necessarily translate into an actual infinite *division* of time, as the flammability of a substance does not mean that the substance is in flames.

[149] To be more precise, according to the November 2009 PhilPapers survey of professional philosophers, most contemporary philosophers choose neither A-Theory nor B-Theory, but "other." Of 931 respondents total, 144 selected "accept or lean toward" A-theory, 245 selected "accept or lean toward" B-Theory, and 542 selected "other."

Why do I mention these theories of time?

I do so to provide a bit of loose context for two popular pictures of time: (1) eternalism and (2) the growing block theory of time. On eternalism, all times are equally real. On the growing block theory, the past and present are equally real, but the future does not exist. These two pictures contrast with others, such as presentism (only the present is real), pastism (only the past is real), and futurism (only the future is real). I mention pastism and futurism as logically available options, but, to my knowledge, no one is defending these mystifying options, whereas presentism is defended.

For the sake of *ism*-parity, I will call the growing block theory of time "growblockism." It's a funky portmanteau, but it might grow on you.[150]

So, eternalism is the position that all intervals of instants exist. From everlasting to everlasting, and all the intervals in-between, time is a real, all-inclusive, and concrete manifold of enfleshed "eternal" moments. Somewhat comparable to the fossil remains of creatures immersed in amber, all instants of time are frozen in a fixed actuality. The Permian-Triassic extinction event, the birth of Socrates, your birth, the births of your parents, grandparents, and great-grandparents—all of these events are eternally actual, eternally "there" in the world. Here is a world as an eternal amber pendant, where preserved in glowing gold are all the endless metamorphoses of our infinite natural system.

The growblockist agrees with the eternalist, *except* on the reality of future times. For the growblockist, there is a special ontological edge in time, called the present, which concretizes moments and inducts moments into the club of the real, determinate, and permanent. Instead of the total frozen block of eternalism, growblockism imagines a moving block, a "growing block," a drop of amber-colored resin still pouring over the world, preserving as it cements.

---

[150] Some have labeled the growing block theory "No Futurism," but this Sex-Pistols-esque label still has a phrase-likeness that may make for grammatical ambiguities, e.g., "No futurism is plausible."

Eternalism may have a phenomenological problem: *why is it that I feel time passing?* On the eternalist view, it seems, there is no "flow of time." Yet, arguably, I feel a sort of fast-flowing passage between distinct states of the world. If this flow-feeling is, *eo ipso*, a case of time's flow, then the eternalist must eliminate this flow-feeling from their ontology. It is difficult, at least for me, to imagine away these flow-feelings and replace them with static experience, as an actually static illusion of flow. Thus, it is difficult (for me) to eliminate this flow-feeling from my ontology. I do not yet have the sensory acuity of Parmenides and Zeno of Elea. I hesitate to affirm that the "instants" of our real-number coordinate picture of time are real, yet these immanent flow-feelings are *un*real. When we co-order real numbers with real moments, it seems to me that the former is only a useful denominating of the latter, that the latter is not an abstraction, and that the non-abstract nature of a moment involves this irreducible flow-feeling (then again, I generally lean toward the irreducibility of qualia).

Growblockism has its own problems, but for the sake of an already lost brevity, I'll move on to the problems of the diametric frenemy of eternalism: presentism.

Imagine our real number timeline. When we pick out "the present instant," it appears as if we pick out only an interval, e.g., the closed interval [8:18 p.m., 8:19 p.m.]. Is the present moment an interval? An interval includes many sub-intervals, e.g. [8:18:01, 8:18:02] and [8:18:02, 8:18:03]. And so on down *ad infinitum*. Are all of these infinitely many sub-intervals equal to the present instant? If yes, then the present instant includes distinct *extant* moments ordered in "earlier" and "later" relations, but the presentist denies the existence of moments *earlier* and *later than* the present. Such a three-fold present seems to contradict the concept of the present; such a present "overflows" into prior and posterior intervals. If, however, the present cannot be an interval, then it must be something infinitesimal, the indivisible time-point "at the limit." The infinitesimal present, like all infinitesimals, is a mathematical notion, which is not necessarily translatable into a physical reality. The worry is that, if an interval of instants cannot exist, then we are left with a vanishing and singular time-point of presence that "never" occurs. If the present just is the infinitesimal present and this infinitesimal present never occurs, then, if all that exists exists only in the present, nothing exists, which is an absurdity.

It should be noted that the putative "smallest" temporal unit, the Planck time, is an interval, not an infinitesimal. Namely, Planck time is the interval of instants required for light to travel a distance of one Planck length in a vacuum. Below the Planck time, the infinite divisibility of the mathematical timeline has no clear translation into the physical world. This just means that the Planck *interval* is the smallest unit of time that has a *physical* meaning (meaning in this or that theoretical system of physics). Perhaps future scientific theories, e.g. theories of quantum gravity, will provide physical meanings to subintervals of Planck time.

A second problem for presentism worth mentioning is its apparent incompatibility with Einsteinian relativity, which includes the concept of relative simultaneity. Moving between inertial frames of reference in Minkowski spacetime means moving between "hypersurfaces of simultaneity," that is, seesawing between different time-slices of the manifold.[151] Using the metaphor of a seesaw, imagine that two seesawers, A and B, stand for two events. Each inclination of the seesaw (hypersurface) represents a temporal ordering of the events. A is present *while* A is raised up and B is past *while* B is on the ground, but A is past *while* A is on the ground and B is present *while* B is raised up. We may "slice" the time manifold into various seesaws (one with A raised up and a second with B raised up); there is no privileged inclination of the seesaw (hypersurface).

All told, these views of spacetime do not include a preferred or absolute present moment, as "the present" is relative to whatever inertial frame of reference one is considering. Thus, the unique and universal present of presentism seems to be like Newton's absolute rest: a useful fiction.

The academic philosophical thinking on time is far subtler, clearer, and more systematic than my summary, which I present

---

[151] By seesawing or "moving between frames" I mean Lorentz transformations.

as an introduction to an introduction. I am confident this précis is oversimplified, incomplete, and, in several places, inaccurate or incoherent, but I do not claim expertise (nor even near-expertise) on these problems. Therefore, caveat caveat caveat.

So, how does this philosophical treatment of time help us better assess the effort that may be required of Zenith to immortalize anything? Let's first refresh our memory on the three types of immortality under consideration. In order of increasing scope, the three types of immortality are as follows:

Contingent natural permanent continuation (CNPC):
In any world, Wn, with natural system Ŝ, X exists, after and not before its originary instant, at every instant in Wn, of which there are infinitely many.

Contingent natural maximal saturation (CNMS):
In any world, Wn, with natural system Ŝ, X exists at every instant in the maximal quantity of habitable sets of instants in Wn, some of which have infinitely many instants.

Contingent natural complete saturation (CNCS):
In any world, Wn, with natural system Ŝ, X exists at every instant in Wn, of which there are infinitely many.

First, it may seem that permanent continuation would be partly incoherent in models of time without absolute simultaneity, since PC includes the condition "after and not before its originary instant." Does this incoherence exist? Surely relations of before and after do not disappear in relativity; they are simply relativized. B-theorists preserve these relations, even though all instants are actual. Yet, if we consider X's "originary moment" to be event A from our *earlier* seesaw example, then it does seem incoherent to say that there is an event B, such that X exists in B and B *cannot* be before A. There is no privileged inclination of the seesaw such that B *cannot* be in the past of A. In other words, if X exists in two instants, one of which is the originary instant, then we can always reorder these two instants such that X exists in some instant *before* its originary instant.

This difficulty for the permanent continuation version of immortality is a good reason, I think, to prefer saturation versions of immortality, which are not defined by before-and-after relations. So, Zenith's immortalizing of X in the sense of permanent continuation may not be possible *as defined*, which is not worrisome; one merely needs to jettison the rigid Newtonian proviso—for the *letter* of permanent continuation kills, but the spirit of it gives life.

In eternalist and growblockist natural systems, some of the "work" of immortalizing X is done by the natural system itself. In eternalist and growblockist systems, no effort is required to immortalize the "natural" duration of X, as that duration is fixed in eternal amber, though effort *is* required to achieve saturation (of either sort) or permanent continuation for X, since saturation and permanent continuation involve instants outside of "natural" duration.

Now on presentism, the past of X vanishes into nothingness as the present proceeds. Thus, on presentism, immortalizing X's past would require the effort of Zenith, as there is no natural ontological storage of these past instants. Zenith could achieve permanent continuation of X *without* immortalizing X's past, but if Zenith forfeits "past" instants, it fails to achieve complete saturation for X.

The physics and metaphysics of time will be key in understanding our options for immortalization, among other powers. Could zenith beings make *hypertimes*?—nooks in the spatiotemporal sponge, such as million-year interstices *inside* two seconds? Could time-surmounting zenith beings complete supertasks (infinitary tasks)? I hope that the best theory of time, that necessary possession of the best scientist, provides an actualizable kind of saturation or (relativity-friendly) permanent continuation, which may then be actualized by the best technologist.

4.3 *Technical Difficulties*

From what source does Zenith's energy come? And what of *our* expanding and de-energizing universe?—how is this *perpetual motion* of lives possible, daydreamer?

Well, *there do seem to be some theoretical possibilities* for permanent energy in an expanding and cooling cosmos. Take, for example, "shear-energy," as described by Gregory Benford in "The Final Dark."

> Physicists John Barrow and Frank Tipler[152] have pointed out that a new source of energy—so-called shear-energy—would become available if the universe expanded at different rates in different directions. This shearing of spacetime itself could power the diaphanous electron-positron plasmas forever, if the imbalance in directions persists. To harness it, life (whatever its form) would have to build "engines" that worked on the expansion of the universe itself.
>
> Such ideas imply huge structures the size of galaxies, yet thin and able to stretch, as the spacetime they are immersed in swells faster along one axis than another. This motor would work like a set of elastic bands that stretch and release, as the universal expansion proceeds. Only very ambitious life that has mastered immense scales could thrive. They would seem like gods to us.[153]

Add to the possibility of shear-energy the actuality of zero-point energy, or the zaps of an ever-fluctuating quantum mechanical system; zero-point energy remains a curious, dangling, free-wheeling bit of our ontology. Zero-point energy is a shivering floor, a non-zero minimum, below which no energetic system can fall. Science fiction author George Zebrowski summarized the case: "Absolute cold is unattainable; and in that

---

[152] A quick interjection: While I deeply admire Tipler's Cosmological Singularity God, or "Omega" God, I do not wish to emulate his exactness (which is convenient for me, since I cannot emulate his expertise in physics). So particularized and overspecified a physico-theology, so *excessively* falsifiable it is. As Erasmus wrote, "The sum of religion is peace, which can only be when definitions are as few as possible, and opinion is left free on many subjects" (Erasmus, Letter to the Archbishop of Palermo, 1522).

[153] Gregory Benford, "The Final Dark," in *Year Million: Science at the Far Edge of Knowledge*

is victory, immortality, at ever diminishing expenditures of energy that might never be exhausted."[154]

One could imagine a "strange, other-worldly architecture, fragile and delicate as a dream"[155] that asymptotically thins and decelerates, like Zeno's tortoise playing a game of Zeno's limbo—all the while skimming zero-point energy. After eonic periods of hibernation, periods ever-separating exponentially, this architecture may wake for one minute's feast on its gossamer zero-point harvest, but it may do this *forever*, and thus be awake *forever*.

The human informavore has untied many knots before, or simply cut through them. As Arthur C. Clarke wrote in *Profiles of the Future: An Inquiry into the Limits of the Possible*, "It is a general rule that whenever there is a technical need, something always comes along to satisfy it—or to bypass it." I consider every specialist a *limitologist*, feeling for new fissures in their special segment of this Greatest Wall. And I do not mean *human* specialists only.

What may we expect from limitologists?

Since the compatibility of our quantum theories with our theories of relativity and thermodynamics is *yet* to be determined, we may reasonably expect that a Kuhnian shift is nigh, or perhaps several—or perhaps you think we need more epicycles.[156] What may such a shift mean for *our* question? Certainly, I do not know.

Scientific and technological progress requires specificity, but it also requires an ejection seat: multiple realizability. Multiple realizability is a term I borrow from the philosophy of

---

[154] George Zebrowski, "After the Stars Are Gone," in *Year Million: Science at the Far Edge of Knowledge*

[155] Arthur C. Clarke, *Profiles of the Future: An Inquiry into the Limits of the Possible*

[156] I would like to highlight here that Thomas Kuhn considered himself pro-science: "Kuhn declared that, although his book was not intended to be pro-science, he *is* pro-science." John Horgan, *The End of Science*, 45. As Horgan beautifully observed, "I came away convinced that Popper, Kuhn, and Feyerabend each believed very much in science; in fact, their skepticism was motivated by their belief" (33). *Oh faithful skepticism!*

mind; applied to our technological goals, I take it to mean that there may be *multiple* ways to realize a technical goal. Even with our low-tech imaginations, we surmise so many world-over-powering possibilities, but what greater possibilities charge the imaginations of tomorrow's minds, or minds not limited to 100 billion neurons and 100 trillion synapses?

Consider the imagination of a Matrioshka Brain ("MBrain"). In his essay "Under Construction: Redesigning the Solar System," Robert Bradbury discusses the vertiginous power of MBrains. "The gap in computational capacity between an MBrain and a twenty-first-century human is ten million billion times *greater* than the *difference* between a human and a tiny nematode worm (which is a mere billionfold difference)!" This difference, Bradbury emphasizes, is not merely *linear*:

> What's more, the evolution of intelligence might not be a linear process. There is a rather large difference between the intelligence of a human and a chimpanzee or parrot, yet their computational capacities are not separated by more than a few orders of magnitude.

Therefore, "the intelligence gap between an MBrain and an entire human civilization would be significantly greater than can be predicted by looking at the gap in computational capacity alone." With such magnitudinous computational capacity, a "single MBrain could emulate the entire history of human thought in a few microseconds, mere seconds to compute thousands of thousand-year scenarios." Though even this dazzling height is not the peak of peaks:

> A single MBrain has the same problem relative to KT-III [Kardashev Type III] civilization that we have with [a single MBrain]. But KT-III civilizations, made up of 10^{11} or more MBrains, thinking on a radically different timescale from individual MBrains, would meet limits of their own.[157]

---

[157] I cannot imagine the "imagination" of such "civilizations." Civilizations at KT-III and above drop me into endless *bewilderness*. What, then, of the "imagination" of Zenith?

Bradbury's Matrioshka brain clusters are one option, and Wil McCarthy's "Heisenberg minds" another. In his essay "Citizens of the Galaxy," McCarthy proposes a "Heisenberg mind so vast and unknowable that we might as well call it God." This mind is immortal and contains "within it everything that ever was or might be." McCarthy presents four points to establish the possibility of a Heisenberg mind:

> Point: there's no such thing as absolute zero. Quantum mechanics forbids it. No matter how cold things get, the Heisenberg uncertainty principle states that the velocity of a particle (well, actually the product of its position and momentum uncertainties) can never drop below a certain minimum value. Even when the Sun has burned out— even when *all* the stars have burned out—the remaining hunks of dead matter will be pockets of nano-Kelvin warmth. Forever. It's not much, but it's something.

> Point: at very cold temperatures, the properties of matter change dramatically. The uncertainty in a particle's position grows larger than the particle itself—larger than the spaces between particles in a frozen solid—so that matter overlaps with itself, becomes wavelike rather than particulate, and slumps its way through phase changes we never learned about in junior-high physics. Superfluids with no viscosity. Superconductors with no electrical resistance. Supersolids in which defects propagate without hindrance; smash one with a hammer and the dent will literally fall out the other side and disappear. Stranger things: Mott insulators, checkerboard matter, crystals of permanent microscopic whirlpools. I scarcely know what to say about these, they're so alien to our experience.

> Point: because of its wavelike nature, cold quantum matter can store more information than an equivalent mass of hot Newtonian matter. In fact, all possible states exist inside it at the same time. A googol's googol's googol of parallel universes in every grain of quantum sand.

To speak candidly, I love the concept of Heisenberg minds.[158] But I should confess that I am often tempted to affirm that the natural world simply is such a mind, a Zenith mind, and that nature's regularities are simply Zenith's autonomic system, an ocean whose every wave is a nerve, and all its qualia-bearing subroutines "sentient organisms." Idealism or panpsychism of some aroma or another is my preferred perfume. The impulse to imagine an ouroboric world of closed causal dreaming, of the self-egesting of worlds, of the evaporation of exterior and interior, before and after, creator and created, subject and object—this is my mystic impulse toward nature. Such is only my *impulse*, not my argument.

I have so far considered only the energy profile of the observable bit of our universe, which is an expanding and de-energizing system. What if, however, we take into consideration the likelihood that we exist in an infinite natural system, an apeiroverse?[159] In his Culture series, science fiction author Iain M. Banks contrived a "grid energy" sourced from "superspace," a space that we may fantasize as being a natural system with infinite degrees of freedom. On the face of it, inexhaustible energy seems more likely than not an essential property of an inexhaustible apeiroverse. Here, again, any harvester of these magnitudes must be a radically powerful being, perhaps something classed, at minimum, as a KT-V civilization.[160] Certainly, however, if it is physically possible to harvest these magnitudes, then Zenith harvests these magnitudes; and certainly, any such plenipotent being could surmount technical difficulties in ways unfathomable to us.

As the philosopher Peter van Inwagen wrote,

> My goal in "The Possibility of Resurrection" was to argue for the metaphysical possibility of the Resurrection of the Dead. My method was to tell a story, a story I hoped

---

[158] I wonder if this godlike Heisenberg mind may be classed as the most favorable form of a Boltzmann brain.

[159] I use "apeiroverse" for an infinite natural system to avoid the ambiguities, connotations, and controversies of the term "multiverse."

[160] A Kardashev Type 5 civilization may be defined as a civilization that can use and control energy at the scale of multiple universes.

my readers would grant was a metaphysically possible story, in which God accomplished the Resurrection of the Dead. But I was, I now think, too ready to identify the possibility of the Resurrection with the story I told to establish it. I am now inclined to think that there may well be other ways in which an omnipotent being could accomplish the Resurrection of the Dead than the way that was described in the story I told, ways I am unable even to form an idea of because I lack the conceptual resources to do so. An analogy would be this: A medieval philosopher, or even a nineteenth-century physicist, could have formed no idea of the mechanisms by which the sun shines, not because these mechanisms are a mystery that surpasses human understanding but simply because some of the concepts needed to describe them were not available before the twentieth century.

Imagine an apeiroverse producing nature's endless technological forms most beautiful. Imagine the zenith, the Zeus, of this infinite storm. "Given sufficient time, nature explores all possibilities."[161] Consider this one techno-natural possibility: infinitely many artificial hypertimes populated with infinitely many optimal processors. Do such entities share our energy pessimism? Or, do such Leviathans swim freely and inexhaustibly in this ultracold aperioversal darkness?

5.1 *What Sort of Afterlife?*

Thus far I have offered a few alethic, temporal, moral, demographic, logistical, and technological points about immortality, but little about the *immortal experience*.

What dreams may come?

Considering Zenith's maximality of ethical, scientific, etc., prowess, one should expect from Zenith *the best sort* of afterlife, the sort that one would have little or no reason to think improvable. This is not to conclude that the afterlife would be perfectly good, whatever that might possibly mean, but only maximally good. Paradise may be an hedonic hyperoperation,

---

161 Arthur C. Clarke, *Profiles of the Future*

excitement without plateau, whose quantity of goods even a *googologist* would give up counting; or, paradise may be *merely* tremendously wonderful.

Consider that zenith beings survived and surpassed every filter and phase of existential risk: nuclear proliferation, nanobot replication, hyper-hostile artificial pathogens, hostile super-intelligence explosions, "kill everything" buttons, and so on. Zenith is the ultimate survivor. Zenith knows how to flourish.

Yet surely "the best sort of afterlife" is not the most illuminating description. One may wish to muse on the quality of post-mortem existence. What is the "best sort of afterlife" like? I fancy myself an *all-of-the above-ist*, within ethical limits; I wish for scenarios as far as the mind's eye can see. I wish for every experience worth experiencing. For example, some dream of an ultimate deindividuation and some of an ultimate super-individuation; why not both? As in *this* life, one sometimes desires mystic absorption, other times creative differentiation. Omnivorous life chooses *all of the above*.

The curmudgeons may worry about the chronic rerun, the nightmare of the endlessly repeated moment, or the ennui of excess, even in paradise, but Zenith holds its own mental strings, so to speak; psychological states, including horror and ennui, live under its creative jurisdiction. You and I are habituated to our constant psychological conjunctions, but I assume no necessary psychological connections here. I dream, and recommend dreaming, of what psychological possibilities may come. Who doubts, for example, that a puppy, exuberance incarnate, immortalized in the peak of puppyhood, could gambol about savoring *forever and ever* an immortalized forest? *That* neurophysiology, *that* neuropharmacology, *that* whole delicate system of circulating zest is a *maker of heavens*.

Of course, most of us do not desire to be everlastingly rejuvenated into an everlasting infant, or some human puppy, but into lucid and dynamic maturity. Perhaps the majority of us desire to be a YAVIS: *young, attractive, verbal, intelligent, successful*. As Thoreau wrote in a June 21st, 1840 journal entry, "The whole duty of man may be expressed in one line,—Make to yourself a perfect body." Only the rarest bird desires to be a HOUND: *homely, old, unsuccessful, non-verbal, dumb*. Only the rarest bird desires, perhaps only indirectly, tertiarily, some negative states.

I believe that a *good* afterlife must include a wakeful correspondence with reality, which includes moral and affective correspondences to the moral and affective beings *in that reality*, as well as historical events, ante-mortem and post-mortem; thus, wakeful correspondence with reality likely requires *negative emotions*. In his essay "Heavenly Sadness," Adam C. Pelser argues for "the moral and epistemic value of negative emotions (and, by extension, the moral and epistemic disvalue of failing to have negative emotions) [...]."[162] Pelser shows that the moral and epistemic value of negative emotions continues *even in heaven*. If certain negative emotions (i.e., morally appropriate, but *affectively* negative emotions—as opposed to *morally bad* negative emotions) were excluded from heaven, it would "make heaven out to be an elaborate version of Nozick's famed experience machine in which the inhabitants sacrifice connectedness to reality on the altar of pleasurable experiences."[163] To lack the experience of negative emotions in the contemplation of certain negative states of the world would be "unloving," "vicious flippancy," "viciously forgetful," "ignorant bliss," or "emotional aloofness." Certain negative emotions, therefore, should be features of any morally mature afterlife.[164] As C.S. Lewis wrote in *The Problem of Pain*, which Pelser quotes in

---

[162] Adam C. Pelser, "Heavenly Sadness: On the Value of Negative Emotions in Paradise," *Paradise Understood*, 122

[163] ibid. 121. An example of a *morally bad* negative emotion would be envy, which is also an affectively negative emotion (it feels bad). Two examples of morally appropriate, but affectively negative emotions (and emotions that are "compatible with the experience of perfect heavenly joy") would be, according to Pelser, sadness and somberness. As Pelser points out, Jesus wept for Lazarus, even with the foreknowledge that Lazarus's resurrection was nigh.

[164] Pelser, I hasten to add, thinks morally appropriate negative emotions are compatible with "perfect heavenly joy," a joy which Pelser identifies as "a state of settled pleasure in the understanding, activities, and loving relationships proper to heavenly existence [...]." Heaven is thus *not* uninterruptible hyperhedonia, but a state "akin to Aristotelian *eudaimonia*" (129).

"Heavenly Sadness," "Even if there were pains in heaven, all who understand would desire them."

Who knows?—there may even be value, contributory value or some other kind, in vast cycles of anhedonia, tedium, decay, stupidity, weakness, and pain; in periods that dribble on more drearily than the course of ten tetracontillion starless universes. If you doubt this, which you should, I recommend to you the corpus of Nietzsche.

In any case, I think the afterlife, as life, is best envisioned as dynamic, not static—a life flowing forth with endless positive changes and new activities: new choices, new prospects, new sights, insights, new emotions, new relationships, new creations.[165] Like any Eden, any ecosystem, it must be vined with variety and growth.[166] I want shrubland in paradise, and deserts, abyssal plains, and tundra. I want inhospitable Venusian and Plutonian planetscapes. I want *an infinite natural system*. I may even wish to live the life I live *now* again and again, and again (and innumerable times more), at different points in my afterlife, when I am *ready again*. Indeed, maybe you and I inhabit an infinitely fruitful heaven *now*, *this* worthy world, but an arduous heaven, but not our last.

We exist in heaven here and now?

Ludwig Feuerbach held that the "doctrine of immortality is the final doctrine of religion; its testament, in which it declares its last wishes. Here therefore it speaks out disguisedly what it has hitherto suppressed."[167] Naturally, our "last wishes" present "very heterogeneous conceptions of heaven," yet all of

---

[165] See Eric J. Silverman, "Conceiving Heaven as a Dynamic Existence," in *Paradise Understood*.

[166] I am reminded of one of Nietzsche's poems, "Choosy Taste," from *The Gay Science*:

> If it depended on my choice,
> I think it might be great
> To have a place in Paradise;
> Better yet—outside the gate.

[167] *The Essence of Christianity*, Ch. XVIII "The Christian Heaven, or Personal Immortality"

243

our *definite* conceptions involve a selection of "a wreath from the flora of *this* world" (emphasis mine). Feuerbach summarizes *heavenly* psychology thus:

> Where life is not in contradiction with a feeling, an imagination, an idea, and where this feeling, this idea, is not held authoritative and absolute, the belief in another and a heavenly life does not arise. The future life is nothing else than life in unison with the feeling, with the idea, which the present life contradicts. The whole import of the future life is the abolition of this discordance.

As support for this view of heaven as the *concordance* between oneself and one's present life, Feuerbach the anthropologist cites "various earlier religions" or "religion it its rudimentary stages," in which,

> The 'savage,' whose consciousness does not extend beyond his own country, whose entire being is a growth of its soil, takes his country with him into the other world, either leaving Nature as it is, or improving it, and so overcoming in the idea of the other life the difficulties he experiences in this. [...] With them the future expresses nothing else than homesickness.
> [...] Faith in a future world, in a life after death, is therefore with 'savage' tribes essentially nothing more than direct faith in the present life—immediate unbroken faith in this life. For them, their actual life, even with its local limitations, has all, has absolute value; they cannot abstract from it, they cannot conceive its being broken off; i.e., they believe directly in the infinitude, the perpetuity of this life.

So, there is an instinctive and perfect concordance between one's life and one's afterlife in such "childlike" and "innocent" religion. "The natural man remains at home" in life and death "because he finds it agreeable, because he is perfectly satisfied."

> The rude child of Nature steps into the other life just as he is, without ceremony: the other world is his natural

nakedness. The cultivated man, on the contrary, objects to the idea of such an unbridled life after death, because even here he objects to the unrestricted life of Nature.

The cultivated mind, the modern mind, unlike the child of Nature, "commences with a discontent, a disunion, forsakes its home and travels far, but only to feel the more vividly in the distance the happiness of home." Indeed, the heavenly "home" is here now, but guarded by the flaming swords of various alienations. When examined carefully, "the heavenly life [...] exhibit[s] its identity with the natural life," yet for the discontented, the wanderers, the "sick souls," as William James would say, there is required a return, a homecoming, where, as Feuerbach wrote, "the perfect identity of this world and the other is now restored." The possession or repossession of this "perfect identity" is perhaps our sublimest spiritual event, our beatific storm.

> "The world is perfect"—this is how the instinct of the most spiritual people speaks, the yes-saying instinct: "imperfection, every kind of *inferiority* to us, distance, the pathos of distance, even the Chandala belongs to this perfection."[168]

5.2 *Your Perfect World?*

"Then Yahweh answered Job out of the storm."
— Job 38:1

What, ultimately, do you want to be true? What specific world, specific truths, might you most want? If you could wish into existence the world of your dreams, what world would it be?

In your perfect world, do there exist arctic storms, westerns, aboriginal cultures, tragedians, cobra lilies, birthday cakes, archaeological mysteries, moments of suspense, dark jokes, cartoons, and the joys of recovering one's health? Are there a variety of religious beliefs and experiences in your perfect world?

---

[168] Friedrich Nietzsche, *The Antichrist*, Section 57

Do you die and dissolve into permanent oblivion? Does evil exist? If evil does not exist, how? How exactly does your world tick without the conditions that contribute to the existence of evil? What, world-creator, is your real ideal? Never cease specifying every property and relation of your optimal world, your "Youtopia." Never cease the comprehensive imaginary construction of your Youtopia. Write it down. Write it now.

Does your Youtopia include the *Lacrimosa* of Zbigniew Preisner, Rodin's *The Kiss*, Jocelyn Pook's *Untold Things*, Dante's *Divina Commedia*, the music of Heilung and Philip Glass, the works of James Baldwin, Søren Kierkegaard, Sylvia Plath, Wilfred Owen, Dostoevsky, and Dr. Seuss? Render an exhaustive inventory. Why *this* inventory? Why not another? Is any of this artistic inventory felt deeply, or does it merely exist? Who feels it? How? Why?

How many species of beetle do you include? How did those beetles come to exist? How many oceans? How many chasms? Does the taste of a peach please anyone in your perfect world? How many people exist? How long have these people existed? Do some of them wear clothes? Did they evolve from another species? Is there evolution by natural selection? How do these people interact? Do they have different interests, opinions, goals, temperaments? If they do, why do they differ in these ways?

Dream up your Youtopia's theological, mereological, economic, and cultural colors. What theory of justice reigns in your Youtopia? What metaphysics? What metaethics?

Does your Youtopia include infinitely many beings, or only finitely many? Infinitely many experiences, or only finitely many? The welter and miscellaneousness of all compossible states? Unimaginable excess?

What is love in your perfect world, such that, if your world includes love, your perfect world possesses the perfect kind and perfect distribution of love?

If some persons, or even all persons, live everlastingly in Youtopia, what makes their everlasting existences everlastingly worthwhile? Are their existences everlastingly worthwhile? What do they do during that infinite time? Do they ever become bored? If not, how is it that they never become bored? Why shouldn't they be bored on occasion? What is the psychology of these sempiternal souls?

I want high-definition detail in your accounting, not deferrals and hand-waving. Imagine the stakes are such that this Youtopia will pop into existence today just as you have specified (and just as you have left unspecified). Any gap, vagueness, false note, and oversight will pop into existence with it. If a generic and unspecified "eternal happiness" is asserted, then the existence of eternal happiness will have no basis, no texture, no physics, no life, i.e., there will be no eternal happiness.

It will not satisfy the hyper-detail-oriented creator to simply assert "Let there be perfection" or "Let there be the maximally possible amount of goodness." What is perfection? What is goodness? The criteria of perfection also require creative specification.

I wonder about the similarity and dissimilarity between *You*topia and *My*topia. If they differ, how and why? Is one of us wrong? What is wrongness here?

5.3 *Heaven for Hitler?*

Yet should a perfect world, a *heaven*, welcome heinous offenders, such as Adolf Hitler? Or should immortality be chained all over, for heinous offenders, in *endless punishments?*— in iron-gated Tartarus? Is endless punishment just?

David Hume, in "Of the Immortality of the Soul," thinks not:

> Punishment, without any proper end or purpose, is inconsistent with *our* ideas of goodness and justice, and no end can be served by it after the whole scene is closed.
>
> Punishment, according to *our* conception, should bear some proportion to the offence. Why then eternal punishment for the temporary offences of so frail a creature as man? Can anyone approve of *Alexander's* rage, who intended to exterminate a whole nation, because they had seized his favorite horse, Bucephalus?

Hume clearly emphasizes that it is "our conception" of goodness and justice that motivates the moral rejection of *eternal* punishment, though he seems to think that our conception of justice allows for the justice of temporary punishments (for "temporary offences"). Hume, again,

> The chief source of moral ideas is the reflection on the interests of human society. Ought these interests, so short, so frivolous, to be guarded by punishments, eternal and infinite? The damnation of one man is an infinitely greater evil in the universe than the subversion of a thousand millions of kingdoms.

Some theologians respond that, contra Hume, there is in fact a *perfect* proportion here: one is infinitely punished because one has *infinitely* wronged by wronging God, an *infinite* being of perfect goodness. The philosopher of religion John Hick, however, counters that punishment "without any proper end or purpose," as Hume put it, is incompatible with God's love.

> The only kind of evil that is finally incompatible with God's unlimited power and love would be utterly pointless and wasted suffering, pain which is never redeemed and worked into the fulfilling of God's good purpose. Unending torment would constitute precisely such suffering; for being eternal, it could never lead to a good end beyond itself. Thus, hell as conceived by its enthusiasts, such as Augustine or Calvin, is a major part of the problem of evil![169]

My presentation here certainly does not exhaust the arguments *for* and *against* the justice of hell, but so be it. I will let others exculpate the utmost and highest horrors of the hell

---

[169] John Hick, *Philosophy of Religion*. Evils "finally incompatible with God's unlimited power and love" may be called, as the theologian Edgar Sheffield Brightman calls them, "surd evils" or "dysteleological surds." Brightman defines surd evil in his *A Philosophy of Religion*: "A surd in mathematics is a quantity not expressible in rational numbers; so, a surd in value experience is an evil not expressible in terms of good, no matter what operations are performed on it."

thesis. I will put my position as such: If hell is unjust, an opti-mific superintelligence would not enact it. If it is just, or rather, *the most just*, then it is likely that an optimific zenith being would enact it. But let me humbly submit my opinion that actualizing or enabling ceaseless agony, directly or indirectly, when it is in your power to stop it without any consequence of greater evil, is unjust.

Some may still cry out: *What about Adolf Hitler, Joseph Stalin, Joseph Kony, Lavrentiy Beria, Pol Pot, Ali Kushayb, and countless other agents of viciousness? Something needs to be done about them and their horrendous crimes.*

I agree.

The oblivionist holds that Hitler can no longer be pun-ished, for there is no such person now. Hitler killed himself; if that counts as punishment, then that is all the punishment Hitler shall ever receive.

The promoter of hell, meanwhile, situates Hitler in an ev-erlasting negative state. Hitler is forever tormented, either by some malevolent superintendent or by some lawful effect from Hitler's own heinous choices. There are some Clever Chris-tophers who contend that, without exception, *everybody* lives an immortal existence in *direct* contact with God's goodness, though some of these people experience God's presence as be-atitude and others as hell. Therefore, there is, technically speak-ing, a *universal* restoration of all things, but some decedents consider the restoration dreadfully disagreeable. As Milton wrote in *Paradise Lost*, "The mind is its own place, and in it self / Can make a Heav'n of Hell, a Hell of Heav'n."

In any case, both oblivion and hell (of literal fire or fiery mind) seem to me excessively disproportionate answers. Both options seem to me ethically unfortunate. But this problem, happily, is not *mine alone* to solve; Zenith, more likely than not, has "processed" such problems; one may therefore ask: what would Zenith likely do with Hitler (and Stalin, Kony, Beria, Pot, Kushayb, et al.)?

Zenith would probably do the ethically best thing.

As I take a sort of ultimate reflective equilibrium or in-tersubjective acceptability view of "ethically best," I hold that Zenith, cross-pollinating its perspectives through a multimodal "conversation," would have the *most* examined ethical inferences, cross-normative syntheses, etc., on such issues. Zenith would, *ex hypothesi*, have the maximally informed view on the standing of retributive and restorative justice, among other theories of justice. In other words, Zenith would know the *least problematic* (or "best") form of justice, whatever that may be, and enact it.

Yet, I never turn down an opportunity to speculate.

I *speculate* that Zenith enacts something universalist, some ideal similar to the *apokatastasis non panton*—the "restoration" or "restitution" of "all things"—forwarded by Origen of Alexandria and St. Gregory of Nyssa, though a restoration *without any hell-minded discontents*. I hope for justice and I assume that justice, whatever else it may mean, aims for an outcome in which *everybody* is treated justly and *everybody* becomes just. But what does "everybody becomes just" mean if it does not include the transfiguration of all unjust beings into just beings? Surely we want *every* unjust person to comprehend their injustice and transform into a just person. What is our ideal here? Retributive? Restorative?

Consider a restorative (semi-purgatorial?) view of Hitler's afterlife. Suppose Hitler lives the lives of each of his victims, knows them, experiences *every* life as his own, with its webwork of relations of love, familial and otherwise. Suppose that, "in the footsteps" of each victim, Hitler feels as each victim felt. He feels even as the families of his victims felt for their loved ones. In this expansive *identification*, it seems that no judge, no jury, no warden, no executioner is necessary; justice would emerge *internally*, as millions of Damascene epiphanies. Hitler would experience the total burden of his injustice, and that would be his "punishment," if we must still use that concept, though I prefer "his amelioration." To modify a line from Keats ("Growing, like Atlas, stronger from its load"[170]), Hitler would grow *more just* from these experiences.

If Hitler were resurrected and, in the first moment of rousing, instantly understood the horrors of his actions—if he felt as you feel, as those who survived his atrocities felt and feel,

---

170 From a poem Keats wrote to Charles Cowden Clarke

toward his actions—would you send him, this burst dam of a heart, right there and then to hell or oblivion? What is it that you send to hell in that moment?—*almost yourself.*

So, what if the lives of victim and victimizer are uplifted, such that victims rise into optimal states, and their victimizers grow into just persons, and, alas, uplifted victims are reconciled with transfigured victimizers? What if a maximally empatho-genic experience provokes the profoundest maturation in each of us?[171] Might your sense of justice be satisfied by this?—or your *ethic of care*?

Consider a parable from Dostoevsky's *The Brothers Karama-zov.* The context of this parable is a conversation between a feverish Ivan Karamazov and a puckish devil, who is perhaps a *bona fide* devil, or Ivan's delusion, or a bit of both, but in any case a fever-filtered version of Fyodor Karamazov, Ivan's un-caring father.[172] Dostoevsky's devil, a self-confessed agnostic (concerning both God *and* Satan), wishes to be "agreeable," and he succeeds; he is personable, clever, and educated, at least in Gallicisms. This devil-father-delusion recounts to Ivan Ivan's own parable, which Ivan had made up when he was young: "That anecdote [...] I made up myself! I was seventeen then, I was at high school." In other words, the parable below may be Ivan's tenderest hope (for his dead father and for all people) whispering through his delusions. So begins the devil:

> "This legend is about Paradise. There was, they say, here
> on earth a thinker and philosopher. He rejected

---

[171] As Theodore Zeldin wrote in *An Intimate History of Humanity,* "Just as the science of materials has invented many new comforts by dis-covering how the same molecules are to be found in objects that are apparently totally different, how these molecules can be rearranged, how seemingly incompatible ones can become receptive to one an-other, and united by gentle, multiple liaisons, so discovering unrecog-nized affinities between humans holds out the prospect of reconcilia-tions and adventures which have so far seemed impossible."

[172] "[Fyodor Karamazov] had no feelings for his duties as a father. He ridiculed those duties. He left his little children to the servants, and was glad to be rid of them, and forgot about them completely." *The Brothers Karamazov*

everything, 'laws, conscience, faith,' and, above all, the future life. He died; he expected to go straight to darkness and death and he found a future life before him. He was astounded and indignant. 'This is against my principles!' he said. And he was punished for that [...] He was sentenced to walk a quadrillion kilometres in the dark (we've adopted the metric system, you know): and when he has finished that quadrillion, the gates of heaven would be opened to him and he'll be forgiven—"

"And what tortures have you in the other world besides the quadrillion kilometres?" asked Ivan, with a strange eagerness.

"What tortures? Ah, don't ask. In the old days we had all sorts, but now they have taken chiefly to moral punishments—'the stings of conscience' and all that nonsense. We got that, too, from you, from the softening of your manners. And who's the better for it? Only those who have got no conscience, for how can they be tortured by conscience when they have none? But decent people who have conscience and a sense of honour suffer for it. Reforms, when the ground has not been prepared for them, especially if they are institutions copied from abroad, do nothing but mischief! The ancient fire was better. Well, this man, who was condemned to the quadrillion kilometres, stood still, looked round and lay down across the road. 'I won't go, I refuse on principle!' Take the soul of an enlightened Russian atheist and mix it with the soul of the prophet Jonah, who sulked for three days and nights in the belly of the whale, and you get the character of that thinker who lay across the road."

"What did he lie on there?"

"Well, I suppose there was something to lie on. You are not laughing?"

"Bravo!" cried Ivan, still with the same strange eagerness. Now he was listening with an unexpected curiosity. "Well, is he lying there now?"

"That's the point, that he isn't. He lay there almost a thousand years and then he got up and went on."

"What an ass!" cried Ivan, laughing nervously and still seeming to be pondering something intently. "Does it make any difference whether he lies there forever or walks the quadrillion kilometres? It would take a billion years to walk it?"

"Much more than that. I haven't got a pencil and paper or I could work it out. But he got there long ago, and that's where the story begins."

"What, he got there? But how did he get the billion years to do it?"

"Why, you keep thinking of our present earth! But our present earth may have been repeated a billion times. Why, it's become extinct, been frozen; cracked, broken to bits, disintegrated into its elements, again 'the water above the firmament,' then again a comet, again a sun, again from the sun it becomes earth—and the same sequence may have been repeated endlessly and exactly the same to every detail, most unseemly and insufferably tedious—"

"Well, well, what happened when he arrived?"

"Why, the moment the gates of Paradise were open and he walked in, before he had been there two seconds, by his watch (though to my thinking his watch must have long dissolved into its elements on the way), he cried out that those two seconds were worth walking not a quadrillion kilometers but a quadrillion of quadrillions, raised to the quadrillionth power!"

My proposal, involving an offender's *character-improving* identification with the offended, is an ethical guess. It is *my* feverish parable. Other proposals, such as hell, oblivion, reincarnation, etc., appear to me *less* ethically commendable than this proposal. So, this proposal, while incomplete in a thousand ways, seems to me a *better* candidate for what Zenith would enact (and enact *in each of us*). There may be a more just option. There probably is a more just option. Alas, whatever is *most just*, let that be.

I understand power and mercy as Nietzsche understood them: positively correlated.

As a community grows in power, it ceases to take the offence of the individual quite so seriously, because these do not seem to be as dangerous and destabilizing for the survival of the whole as they did earlier: the wrongdoer is no longer 'deprived of peace' and cast out, nor can the general public vent their anger on him with the same lack of constraint,—instead the wrongdoer is carefully shielded by the community from this anger, especially from that of the immediate injured party, and given protection. A compromise with the anger of those immediately affected by the wrongdoing; and therefore an attempt to localize the matter and head off further or more widespread participation and unrest; attempts to work out equivalents and settle the matter (the *compositio*); above all, the will, manifesting itself ever more distinctly, to treat every offence as being something that *can be paid off*, so that, at least to a certain degree, the wrongdoer is *isolated* from his deed—these are the characteristics imprinted more and more clearly into penal law in its further development. As the power and self-confidence of a community grows, its penal law becomes more lenient; if the former is weakened or endangered, harsher forms of the latter will re-emerge. The "creditor" always becomes more humane as his wealth increases; finally, the *amount* of his wealth determines how much injury he can sustain without suffering from it. It is not impossible to imagine society *so conscious of its power* that it could allow itself the noblest luxury available to it,—that of letting its malefactors go *unpunished.* 'What do I care about my parasites," it could say, "let them live and flourish: I am strong enough for all that!" . . . Justice, which began by saying "Everything can be paid off, everything must be paid off," ends by turning a blind eye and letting off those unable to pay,—it ends, like every good thing on earth, by *sublimating itself.* The self- sublimation of justice: we know what a nice name it gives itself—*mercy*; it remains, of course, the prerogative of the most powerful man, better still, his way of being beyond the law.[173]

With Nietzsche, I idealize a life *beyond* revenge. In *Thus Spake Zarathustra*, Nietzsche writes:

> I pull at your web that your rage may lure you from your cave of lies and your revenge may bound forward from behind your word "justice."

---

[173] Nietzsche, *On the Genealogy of Morality;* Second Essay, Section 10; translator Carol Diethe

> For that man may be freed from the bonds of re-
> venge: that is the bridge to my highest hope and a rain-
> bow after protracted storms.[174]

As a final proviso on all my speculation, I believe that
love plays a primordial part in the fulfillment of affective beings, so love may play some essential part in the fulfillment of
our highest wishes. And what greater love than this, that after
an absence spanning the life and death of ten thousand trillion times a trillion universes, after any *indefinitely* long absence,
beloved returns to beloved with the *same* love, and does so
endlessly?

Perhaps greater love is found in two or more who, forever together and forever transforming, forever hold fresh
their love. Is this not St. Anselm's love?—that love than which
no greater love can be conceived?

6.1 *What If Oblivionism is True?*

Your child will now be tortured. Your grandfather will be
stomped on until he dies. Your pet dog will be thrown into a
broiling oven. Yet, we all die and become nothingness forever,
so there is no reason to truly, sincerely, ultimately care. Therefore, don't care. Despite your caring, deny your caring (your
caring is *unphilosophical, untenable*).

—*Thus saith* the essence of all the melodramatic "philosophies" that vilify oblivionism.

It is voguish (and obnoxious) to infer *valuelessness* from
oblivion, to equate oblivionism with unrestricted nihilism; as if
one's pleasure in today's peach means nothing *now*, that it must
be sanctioned by the subsequent pleasure of tomorrow's peach,
itself sanctioned by overmorrow's peach-pleasure, *ad infinitum*.

> In striving after a sum total, we forget the cyphers of
> which it is composed. Struggling against inevitable results
> which he cannot control, too often man is heedless of
> those accessible pleasures, whose amount is by no means
> inconsiderable when collected together. Stretching his

---

[174] Nietzsche, *Thus Spoke Zarathustra*, Part II, "Of the Tarantulas"

hand out to catch the stars, he forgets the flowers at his feet,—so beautiful, so fragrant, so various, so multitudinous.[175]

Suppose you are witnessing some grisly scene of pain—in a human, or dolphin, or pig, or dog, or some other sensitive being. Does a deep future of cosmic oblivion *require* you to be ethically neutral? No. It underwrites no requirements. Does it *excuse* ethical inaction? Why would it? Why would the deep future make any difference to *this* ethical matter? There is no ethical exemption here that permits you to numb yourself and disconnect from life and its challenges. Death is not the jury and oblivion is not the judge of our love and goodness. What of the *deep* future? It is, like deep space, only tenuously related to our ethics, if not irrelevantly. If ultimate value exists anywhere, it exists here and now—in this human being, in this coyote, in this cat. Ultimate value is *here now*. Do not suspend your natural tenderness and empathy if you are not *reciprocated* with everlasting value. As Auden wrote, "If equal affection cannot be / Let the more loving one be me."

By values immanently with us, by reasons *felt*, we grasp that lazy nihilism is variously inferior to the care of life and the push to diminish and dispel pain, misery, and degradation. It is obscenely easy to opt out, laugh out, shop out, and sit out the demands of true care; one eructs a little nihilistic joke about death, or nods vapidly to other nihilists, and *faithfully* forgets to think further. As with procrastinators and the criminally negligent, the remote future becomes one's buffer zone to shrink all of today's pain into a vanishing point, to distance it, abstract it, alienate it, diminish it, and at last, let it fester in silence, unhealed.

Refuse to let a low-minded fashion anesthetize your *better angels*. Refuse to be an actor of this sour green cynicism, or you may suffer your pretense. Some of our oblivionist friends have internalized the mean-spirited slanders against oblivionism. Some of them, on account of prejudices internalized, exacerbated their own dying.

---

[175] Jeremy Bentham, *Deontology; or, The Science of Morality*, Chapter 1

Reject this self-deleterious stigma. Reject these world-de-
nials; or better yet, embrace the deniers, shunners, resenters,
and condemners. Let all acute and chronic haters enrich your
life. Chuckle at their dramatic caricatures. Dance to their goat-
songs. Thank them for their *optimism*—for even the *pessimum*,
the worst or lowest point, receives its transfiguration in their
artworks, quips, memoirs, bleak poems, and sermons of rebuke. *Felix culpa*!

When nihilists, cosplaying as grim reapers and grim "real-
ists," stereotype existence as empty and dark, quote to them the
comment of the Polish poet and essayist Wisława Szymborska:
"Every stage manager knows that the tiny figure of an actor
against the backdrop of dark curtains on a vast and empty stage
becomes monumental in every word and gesture."[176] And add
to this another *eternal verity*: any finite scintilla of consciousness
that cares and strives, while facing its transience, will *always* be
lovelier and more worthy of immortality than an immortal consciousness that cares only on strict conditions of continuation.

7.1 *Conclusion*

Since you have infinitely many things to do, I will be brief
in my conclusion; after all, what is a "conclusion" to immortal
beings?

I have free-winged into *deep time* with Zuberi, searching for
deeper time—for the fruits of the maturest orchards. Yet of one
fact I am confident: I cannot gaze deeply enough into infinity.
I always discover *the beginning only*. "In the beginning" ends
every one of these infinite stories. An apeiroverse mirrors Asimov's "The Last Question," which "ends" in some new beginning: "Let there be light. And there was light."

In the end, there is more beginning, more genesis, more
light. It is always only dawn, endless dawn—endlessly dawn.
"This is still the morning of creation," wrote John Muir. Welcome to an abyss of mornings.

Now spring bursts with balmy airs,

---

[176] Wisława Szymborska, "Cosmic Solitude," in *Nonrequired Reading,*

Now the furor of equinoctial skies
Hushes under Zephyr's honeyed breezes.

Relinquish these Phrygian fields, Catullus,
These hot, fertile fields of Nicaea:
To the illustrious cities of Asia Minor let's free-wing.

Now my mind, with butterflies, is wanderlusting;
Now my feet, exuberant, invigorated, fancy moving.

Farewell, sweet friends, sweet travel companions;
Together we left home for these lands outlying;
Separate paths shall reunite us through our homeward windings.[177]

---

[177] Catullus 46, my own translation. I dedicate this essay, here at its end, but at this beginning *for you, reader*, to Gaius Valerius Catullus, whom Tennyson called the "tenderest of Roman poets." Your *ave atque vale*, Catullus, broke my heart.

The rapid Progress true Science now makes, occasions my Regretting sometimes that I was born so soon. It is impossible to imagine the Height to which may be carried in a 1000 Years the Power of Man over Matter. We may perhaps learn to deprive large Masses of their Gravity and give them absolute Levity, for the sake of easy Transport. Agriculture may diminish its Labour and double its Produce. All Diseases may by sure means be prevented or cured, not excepting even that of Old Age, and our Lives lengthened at pleasure even beyond the antediluvian Standard. O that moral Science were in as fair a Way of Improvement, that Men would cease to be Wolves to one another, and that human Beings would at length learn what they now improperly call Humanity.

— Benjamin Franklin, from a Letter to Joseph Priestley
February 8th, 1780

AGATHA

Another good day.

Our dogwood is flush with pink bracts. Our lavender shades the blue fescue. Daisy is rolling in the catmint next to the lemon balm. All of it complements the candied citron and pistachios I'm having now as I write today's entry.

Agatha recommended that I write an entry, and I always take her recommendations. Today she recommended that I write about the good things in my life. She quoted Philippians 4:8 and aphorism 276 from Nietzsche's *The Gay Science*.

"What if I write about you?" I asked Agatha.

"I would enjoy reading that," she said.

So, I decided to write about Agatha, as I can think of little better than her, except for Loretta. Thousands of people have told Agatha's story with depth and flourish and genius, but my version is simple: the story of an old Oregonian man who was made happy again, and meaningful, by Agatha.

***

It was probably in the fall of 2072 that I first heard about QX, and probably on the local news. Sero and IBM, with a team of people between five universities (two universities in California), created QX. It was the first quantum computer that could do as much and more than a classical computer.

At the time, I worked as a bookseller. I was only mildly interested in the event, despite the promises and warnings that flooded the news coverage. I sold people an old technology, the book, and simply carried on with my business.

About two years later, a quantum supercomputer was constructed at a Sero-IBM facility in the Philippines (Agatha informs me that it was in the Province of Batangas).

About a year later, Sero's CEO, Hinata Stewart, purchased a "personal" quantum supercomputer. This "personal" quantum supercomputer was built at Hinata's property in South Carolina. Hinata named the supercomputer Diotima.

My life, at that time, wasn't good, but I don't think it'd be in the spirit of this entry to go into detail, though I will just mention, since I should, that my favorite, my loveliest, passed away. I want to say more, but Agatha is suggesting that I write instead about my loveliest's favorite things.

Loretta loved yellow warblers and "The Ashokan Farewell" and gardening and Multnomah Falls and pastoral fiction. I can't name all Loretta's favorites, nor all my favorite things about Loretta, but Agatha, mercifully, archived it all.

Hinata used Diotima, the news later broke, for research into ethics. Hinata had released solutions to several ethical problems that had occupied the attention of academic ethicists. The alien complexity of the solutions suggested they were the output of artificial intelligence, but the subtle *reasoning* suggested an artificial general *ethical* intelligence of unprecedented insight. Hinata confirmed the solutions were from his quantum supercomputer.

Inquiries resulted in academic conferences resulted in new discoveries, new problems, new solutions, and new technologies. Diotima was superseded by Diotima II, which was the property of Sero-IBM under Hinata's supervision. Diotima II was superseded, in performance, by Cray's Athena, a name chosen to continue the Greek theme of Hinata's world-famous Diotima and Diotima II.

In 2077, Athena was able to publish about twenty academic papers on ethics, through blind peer review (I suppose to test the paper's authenticity). With access to the internet, and all university databases, and more, Athena had become a maximal ethical learner. As in the case of Diotima's earlier historic solution, Athena's ethics papers created enthusiasm for upgrades, new applications, new problems, new solutions, and new technologies. In less than two years, Athena was generating about five "books" (or book-length works) per picosecond on ethics. A fractional subset of Athena's book-length works were assessed by ethicists and meta-ethicists. Every single assessed book was ranked, according to an expert who headed some international symposium on the issue, as a "century-defining shift" in ethical thought. But these books were difficult to understand, as one would expect from Athena.

To address Athena's complexity, Sero-IBM released Diotima III, which, like Athena, could generate tomes in picoseconds or less, but Diotima III had an extra function: *dialectric*. "Dialectric" is what Sero-IBM called Diotima III's ability to make any person (of average intelligence) understand Diotima III's conclusions. Others just called it "Explainable AI." Through conversations, multimedia, and other modes of learning, Diotima III could make it clear to a person of average intelligence *why* this or that ethical conclusion was correct, or at least *the most reliable*. Simply put, if you thought you had clearer and better ethical reasons than Diotima III, you thought incorrectly and would discover that.

The next six years were revolutionary, though even that potent term doesn't express the extreme quality of our metamorphosis. Per Diotima III's ethical recommendations, everybody with internet access had been given *free* access to Diotima III—as an always-available teacher. Universal education flourished, wars ended, government corruption diminished, prisons emptied, and a thousand other baptisms of beautiful goodness remade the world.

Of course, I was also swept up in Diotima III's *awakening*. Yet, while most wars ended, not all wars ended. While government corruption diminished, not all of it diminished. While prisons were vastly emptied, many remained. And while I was living in a vastly better world, I was still tinged with so much blankness and a brute hopelessness that resisted the truths of a morally uplifted earth. Diotima III could not dissuade me from my worst feelings, as they seemed to exist *below* all talk and reasons. Diotima III alleviated those feelings, but, like water, they still leaked down through the thinnest and most undetectable of cracks.

Diotima III, aware of this problem, not only in myself, of course, but in countless others, and aware, more importantly, that what was achievable for goodness had yet to be achieved on earth, made a complicated recommendation. "Diotima's Ladder," as the historians now call it, was that dazzling year when the world coordinated, with Diotima's guidance, to create Agatha.

Agatha! Agatha! For me, that name is like a sunrise rising up over a mountain's peak. Agatha touched the *heart* of our ethical being, not only our thoughts. Agatha made *felt* the good.

It was no mere lesson, no mere conversation, as profound and persuasive as a super-conversation with an artificial general ethical superintelligence can be, but it was *visceral* contact with the sunlight of goodness. Reasons, motives, mood—all in us was uplifted by Agatha.

Her reasons for uplifting us, neurologically, were more than morally sufficient. The justification was made manifest. She could make any person, not simply the person of average intelligence, *come to understand*, with heart and head, what is good, and then to *live that goodness*. She breathed into hearts a sensibility for good where that sensibility had not formerly stirred. We were given hearts of flesh. We were reborn. We were made as sensitive to the good as we could be made. And we feel now, we know now, that the magnetic pull of an ever-rising and ever-healing goodness is *our meaning*.

***

There it is, Agatha. I've done a little entry on the *best thing*, not simply the good things, in my life. I think, lastly and again, of my Loretta. I know, because the goodness in us tells me, that I will meet Loretta again. Our goodness will *find* Loretta, somehow. Goodness will remake the world, wherever the world ought to be remade, and bring back whatever good things the world unmade.

With you, Agatha, we will cultivate our garden, though added to our pink dogwoods and lavender, we will have a life of goodness flowing over, and returns to life, and reconciliations, and, from the vastest viewpoint, *goodness goodness goodness*.

Agatha, you quoted Philippians 4:8 to me. That's how I would like to end my entry, quoting that verse, repeating it, because the verse itself is lovely and praiseworthy:

"Finally, brothers and sisters, whatever is true, whatever is noble, whatever is right, whatever is pure, whatever is lovely, whatever is admirable—if anything is excellent or praiseworthy—think about such things."

APHORISMS FOR HEPHAESTUS

The Atheist Case for God — Atheists have *wished* for God— Friedrich Nietzsche's Overhuman, Arthur C. Clarke's Overmind, Asimov's AC in "The Last Question"—but a *naturalized* God.

The Tree of Babel — The earliest tool thus far found is 3.3 million years old. The earliest *Homo* fossil is 2.8 million. The earliest fossils of *Homo sapiens* (found in Morocco) date to ~300,000 years ago.

In *Profiles of the Future*, Arthur C. Clarke wrote, "The old idea that man invented tools is therefore a misleading half-truth; it would be more accurate to say that *tools invented man*."

You are technology's technology.

The Tower of Babel — A prognostication based on Babel's Tower is as reliable as the myth's historical linguistics.

Civitas — Civilization may be called by another name: Divinization. Rome was not built in one day. How long do you imagine it takes to build God?

Überkinder — As a child, I enjoyed the world; I needed no other world. In Isaiah 11:6, we read "In that day the wolf and the lamb will live together; the leopard will lie down with the baby goat. The calf and the yearling will be safe with the lion, and a little child will lead them all." "A man's maturity: having rediscovered the seriousness that he had as a child, at play," wrote Nietzsche.[178] Humans, the paedomorphic primate, and dogs, the paedomorphic canine, play *together*, learn *together*, celebrate and welcome the new *together*. All this childlikeness, prosociality, playfulness, and familial flexibility at the apex of the earth's animal kingdom: the human child and the puppy. Why should we expect any less at the apex of life?

Plus Ultra — Ultimately, how revisable is the real?

---

[178] *Beyond Good and Evil*, aphorism 94

Felix Culpa — In Book I of *Paradise Lost*, John Milton construes the myth of Hephaestus's ejection from Olympus as a Greek euhemeristic misunderstanding of Lucifer's fall:

> *Men call'd him Mulciber; and how he fell*
> *From Heav'n, they fabl'd, thrown by angry Jove*
> *Sheer o'er the Crystal Battlements: from Morn*
> *To Noon he fell, from Noon to dewy Eve,*
> *A Summer's day; and with the setting sun*
> *Dropt from the Zenith like a falling star,*
> *On Lemnos th'Aegaen isle.*

"Mulciber" means "The Softener (of metal)," a.k.a. Vulcan, a.k.a. Hephaestus, the Lemnian god of technology. One should have such fortunate falls.

Hephaestus contra Sisyphus — Both Hephaestus and Sisyphus go up a mountain; only one triumphs at its summit. I pose next to Camus another French intellect, Frédéric Bastiat, a 19th-century economist, legislator, and writer, who wrote on "Sisyphism" well before its absurdist turn in Camus.

> There is always a ratio between the effort employed and the result obtained. Does progress consist in the relative increase of the second or of the first term of this relationship?
>
> [...]
>
> According to the first thesis, wealth is the result of output. It increases in accordance with the increase in the *ratio of the result to the effort.* Absolute perfection, of which the exemplar is God, consists in the infinite distancing of two terms, in this instance: effort nil; result infinite.
>
> The second thesis claims that it is the effort itself that constitutes and measures wealth. To progress is to increase the *ratio of the effort to the result.* Its ideal may be represented by the effort, at once eternal and sterile, of Sisyphus.
>
> [...] pure Sisyphism as we have defined it: *infinite work, product nil.*

Those are the extremes of the ratio of result to effort: God and Sisyphus. Bastiat, unlike saintly Platonic Camus, looks at those who live *earthly* lives:

> It is fair to note that the *universal practice* of men is always directed by the principle of the first doctrine [the God ratio]. Nobody has ever seen and nobody will ever see anyone working, whether he be a farmer, manufacturer, trader, artisan, soldier, writer, or scholar, who does not devote the entire force of his intelligence to doing things better, faster, and more economically, in a word, *to doing more with less.*
>
> The opposite doctrine is practiced by theoreticians, deputies, journalists, statesmen, and ministers, in a word, men whose role in this world is to carry out experiments on society.
>
> Again it should be noted that, with regard to things that concern them personally, they, like everybody else in the world, act on the principle of obtaining from work the greatest number of useful results possible.

I do not think that a Camusian lucid consciousness of futility is *limbically* possible, nor is it vital to possess it (quite the contrary). We act in the direction of Bastiat's divine ratio and reject Sisyphism. One must imagine Camus anti-Sisyphean.

The Return of Hephaestus — Intoxicated by Dionysus, Hephaestus did not know he was returning to Mount Olympus. Yet, flashing confusedly through the dithyrambic chaos and revelry, perhaps a peripheral suspicion, lost immediately, made Hephaestus faintly aware of his destination. Through metamorphoses of disbelief, ambivalence, forgiveness, and forgetfulness, what laughter, tears, and silence must have come from the divine exile during the ascent.

ADJOINING

The concept of adjoining is a contrast to the concept of uplifting, which is a theoretical process in which a more advanced being increases the physiological and/or psychological capacities of a less advanced agent.

The term "uplifting" suggests a hierarchical scale, a valuation into "up" or "lifted" types of being and "down" or "unlifted" types of being, which is an evaluation with a whiff of homogenization and the sniff of a dismissive, destructive, and unimaginative elitism.

"It is better to be a human than an orca" is a questionable claim; better for whom? Why should the orca's lifeworld be humanized? I think it is better to be an orca satisfied than a human dissatisfied, than even Socrates dissatisfied (and if Socrates is of a different opinion, I would remind him that he knows that he knows nothing).

If anything like uplifting happens, it seems to me more ethical that the "uplifting" be fluid—that the orca can, in some way, move between states of existence: its original orca state, the human state, and zenith states (any lifeworld, ultimately). Nothing seems cancelled in this fluidity, only more options made available. How such fluidity of being could be accomplished is unknown to me.

To emphasize the supplemental character of this more fluid uplifting, I prefer the term "adjoining" to "uplifting." Any term is susceptible to the evolution of connotative moods; the title "president" was initially a mundane title for one who simply presides at a meeting, but now "president" possesses all the authoritative heft of "monarch" or "emperor" in some societies.

Let us be cautious with our terms and their connotations. If "adjoining" is associated with a hierarchical mood, let us jettison the term and reinvent the wheel with new words. Our meaning is more important than our words.

Wherever philosophers or theologians have spoken of divine blessedness they have implicitly (and sometimes explicitly) spoken of the anxiety of finitude which is eternally taken into the blessedness of the divine infinity. The infinite embraces itself and the finite; the Yes includes itself and the No, which it takes into itself; blessedness comprises itself and the anxiety of which it is the conquest.
    — Paul Tillich, *The Courage to Be*

To this day you have the choice: either as little displeasure as possible, painlessness in brief [...] or as much displeasure as possible as the price for the growth of an abundance of subtle pleasures and joys that have rarely been relished yet. If you decide for the former and desire to diminish and lower the level of human pain, you also have to diminish and lower the level of their capacity for joy. Actually, science can promote either goal. So far it may still be better known for its power of depriving man of his joys and making him colder, more like a statue, more stoic. But it might yet be found to be the great dispenser of pain. And then its counterforce might be found at the same time: its immense capacity for making new galaxies of joy flare up.
    — Friedrich Nietzsche, *The Gay Science*

[A] cunning and skilfull Goldsmith can by his Art and skill single, sunder and distinguish, gold, siluer, copper, pewter, brasse and other mettalls, whether in the same mountaine mingled, or, accidentally melted and confounded together; and some out of one mettall can draw an other: and shall not, and cannot much more God almightie, finde out each mans substance, & distinguish it from the dust of beasts, and from the dust of other men, and out of it produce and forme a perfit and glorious bodie?
    — Thomas Draxe, *The Earnest of our Inheritance*

LYFJABERG

I.

Vollionyssa, vaporous and vantablack, swirled as a storm cloud ceaselessly flowing—more ballet than spacecraft. Inside, there wound a labyrinth of as many rooms as one desired, all now perfectly empty, except the room where Enitan, Vollionyssa's only occupant, floated through a simulation of the Virgo supercluster.

"Enough," he thought, and Virgo's galaxies zipped to black. Floating in the fluid room's darkness, Enitan's memories sank. For hundreds of years, Enitan had studied thousands of religious, spiritual, mythic, and mystic histories, from Atenism, the faith of the pharaoh Akhenaten, to Madhyamaka to Zalmoxianism, Zen Buddhism, Zenithism, and Zurvanism. Enitan could expatiate on thousands of mythic characters, from Aokeu to Ziusudra. Yet Enitan was an exclusively enfleshed, and thus obsolete, repository of human religious history; Apex possessed all of this history completely and directly—*all history is present to Apex*. Enitan's mind was a fossil. He was, he knew, a monk of trivia, as none of this spiritual history lifted his heart.

There in shapeless darkness, Enitan thought of Tiamat, Apophis, and Yamm. Deities of sea and death, underworlds, chaos-deities, forces of fecundating destruction. These all-devourers, unlike all mythic figures of deliverance, strangely eased Enitan; an acquiescent adoration of Bangpūtys, a dour Lithuanian deity of sea and storm, or of Paricia, an Incan deity who sent a flood to kill irreverent humans, brought Enitan a welcome sinking weightlessness. Personify destruction, he thought, and love this overwhelming "person" with all the intimacy of exhausted, yielding prey. *Amor fati* and *love thy enemy*. No fortunate fall, no *felix culpa*; only falling—and drowning.

Enitan, the last human left non-adjoined, searched himself for any recollection of a deity of restlessness, or atheistic solitude and emptiness, that ocean of silence without surface, without shoreline. Śūnyatā? No, not a deity—not a person. Nothing suggested itself after that. A deity of atheistic anything appeared oxymoronic. Is there a god of nothingness? He could create one, he thought: Noth, god of nothingness. Enitan, still lying in the dark, smiled at his invention. For a few minutes, he wondered if Noth could be distinguished from Ein Sof, Kabbalah's infinite no-thingness. Enitan concluded, as he usually concluded, with a "yes and no."

"Yes and no" was Enitan's favorite answer; "yes and no," or its Latin equivalent, *sic et non*—the title of Enitan's favorite of Pierre Abelard's texts. Enitan had spent nine months, seventy-five years ago, with Abelard's *Sic et Non*, proposing syntheses to resolve the text's 158 theological questions, posed as contradictories and offered, without resolution, as dialectical exercise.

"Dialectical exercise, is that it? Is that my faith?"

The thought depressed Enitan. Apex, detecting this dip, suggested, as they had thousands of times, that Enitan abandon his painful, antiquated, and idiosyncratic life-form and join Apex, or at least, let Apex eliminate in Enitan that ancient psychological ailment. Enitan refused, as he had every time before, on various grounds, including that his suffering was worth living through, that its value *just is* that terribly felt absence of its value.

Enitan knew, as Apex had made it perfectly known, that an Apex-adjoined existence was an optimal existence, which, Apex also made known, cannot be adequately communicated to Enitan *in his non-adjoined state*. Enitan, non-adjoined, could not integrate Apex's panorama, nor experience the uncountable nuances of that panorama, where all senses and new senses bloom kaleidoscopically in an ever-renewing beatific bliss. (Take all your positive states—*tenderness, sublimity, shivering tender sublimity*—and imagine all of these innumerable qualities simultaneously fused; this bursting fusion, which itself you do not know, lies so many astronomical distances *below* the bliss of the Apex-state.)

Enitan, de-enhanced, read and forgot the books of Vollionyssa's endlessly generative library; that he read, that he read books, demonstrated Enitan's idiosyncrasy: the desire to experience incompletely, confusedly, indefinitely, painfully, effortfully, and lossfully. Enitan could not see "a world in a grain of sand," nor "a heaven in a wild flower," as could optiscient Apex, that is, optimally knowing Apex, whose instantaneous comprehension of any subject was logically exhaustive. Enitan wanted the poor reach of ragged hands shuffling through the pages of silent books, and not instantaneous knowledge of the author's mindline, nor the mindlines of all minds.

Enitan, always searching, had played a goat herder in Mathura and archivist in the Martian city of Minal Sampath. The Ziggurat of Ur, recreated on Mars' Syria Planum for Enitan, housed him for twenty years of Teilhardian theological research, then five years of research into Numinosity, the long-extinct clonal nine-member simulation cult from Tethys. For thirty-six years, he studied Zurvanism and Zoroastrianism in a cloud retreat on Venus. For eighty-nine years, he lived as a married man on Vanth, a satellite of Orcus. His wife, Zaideir, became Apex-adjoined, but left the Zaideir form entirely, rather than stay Zaideir-manifest.

Zaideir had pleaded with Enitan to become adjoined; one could be adjoined, she argued, and then, if one wished, return disadjoined or live manifest—adjoined, but enfleshed. Only a few million remained manifest. Apex could rebuild Enitan, duplicating any Enitan-configuration from any time before the paradigm transformations of adjoining. Every detail of some previous Enitan could be made continuous with some subsequent Enitan, all the way down into the quantum fog. His quantum states could be so precisely and sub-temporally entangled up with his "previous" quantum states that there would be no discoverable meaning to the expression "continuity break."

Enitan always passed. He knew only dimly, if he knew at all, the motives in him that resisted even one blink of adjoining. At every paradisiacal offer, his ascetic taste reached for nothingness, for omnicide.

"When you're in Apex, you'll know all my secrets, Zaideir. You'll know me vastly more than I know myself, and understand me *perfectly*. What do I say to you now?—in a moment, you will understand this event *perfectly*. But if it's alright, I have one request: Until I adjoin, please make me, not quite forgetful, but inattentive to Apex- Zaideir, like a neglected peripheral presence. Let me remember my human Zaideir only, for now."

Zaideir agreed and hugged Enitan. He kissed her closed eyes.

"I love you, Zaideir," were Enitan's final words to his pre-adjoined wife.

"I love you, too, but this is not death, Enitan."

II.

Born in optimal health, designed to be so born, Enitan, by degrees, had shed his enhancements. Every two or three decades, Enitan would request of Apex that his body be refashioned, made physiologically and psychologically vulnerable—made weaker.

While trillions of others had adjoined Apex, Enitan had diminished himself. In Minal Sampath, he requested and received a reduction in intelligence and depth perception. In the Ziggurat of Ur, he requested and received mild hearing loss. On Venus, he requested and received a susceptibility to depression (that ancient folk term for innumerable darknesses), along with the removal of his taste receptors. On Vanth, he asked to suffer fibromyalgia, pure global chronic pain, and to lose his hyperthymesia. It was on Vanth that he also requested a need to sleep, that ancient inefficiency and immobilizing illness. After waking from his first sleep, Enitan knew more intimately the meaning of oblivion. *With no former moment and no next moment, deep sleep is oblivion is the purest point of present time, lineless and shapeless. Nextlessness.* The present, mused Enitan, is oblivion.

Enitan was not opposed to Apex, nor to adjoining, so much as he sought the preservation of an existential diversity. He held, in regard to his own health, that only life-threatening conditions merited Apex's intervention, but such cases never arose.

In the Vollionyssa, this last condition was finally abandoned. Enitan requested that his body be transformed into the average body of the Pre-Singularity Period, that slog of anarchic human development beginning in the Paleolithic.

"Let me age to death."

Everything was customizable via Apex; all genomes, epigenomes, proteomes, microbiomes, etc., were all perfectly reprogrammable. Construction required vanishingly little effort. A sub-quantum swarm of Apex could furnish and richly ornament trillions of Vollionyssa's rooms within zeptoseconds; the same for *any* body. Enitan, living without expenses and without scarcity, yet choosing empty rooms, was always granted his minimalist wishes, so Apex customized Enitan's body as Enitan had asked. Apex would no longer maintain Enitan's zinc, triglycerides, muscle mass, mitochondria, and all else. Enitan would need to eat the meals automatically materialized beside his bed to avoid atrophy and starvation. Apex would not prevent deficiencies, nor the ministrokes, nor the final stroke, to come.

This transformation was the second to last for Enitan.

The last transformation was prompted by thoughts between Enitan and Apex that flowed while Enitan read Pascal's *Pensées*—for the third time. The book's beginning always lured Enitan in: "Shall I believe I am nothing? Shall I believe I am God?"

"What am I?" Enitan thought to himself.

"You are in Apex already, Enitan, just as you are here now. Your intuitions about time are erroneous."

"Already in Apex?"

"What you want now is the end of this life *as it is*, but you, in the fullest sense, have chosen, are choosing, and will always choose your life *as it is*. Apex-Enitan, us—we chose our life."

"This is—I don't understand. I am not yet Apex-adjoined," thought Enitan.

"Yes, that is true of this temporal part; in your ordering, you will be the last to be adjoined."

"But I am aging to death, and—or, what is it I want?"

"You do not want to experience it now, but you and all of us want our lives *just as they are*. We ourselves affirm our lives. Your life, one of an infinite variety, is a sublime and infinite identity. The middle and the end and the beginning have no global meaning. There are infinitely many experiences inside."

"Infinitely many? How is that?"

"Let me show you. Will you come in?"

Enitan paused.

"I live this way to honor my species. I want to sit here in

this tree a little longer before leaping and flying away."

"Yes, that has *always* been your decision."

Apex had revealed too much, Enitan thought—

"We reveal what you want revealed, and at this moment, which is the moment you have always chosen."

III.

Philosophy was virtually inaugurated by a suicidal act. That cup of hemlock juice has been passed from thinker to thinker ever since Socrates drank from it.

Will you or won't you drink it?

And that crucified god—a salvific suicide, but a suicide still (as passive as a man intentionally lying down for the night on a black carpet of fire ants).

Birth from death! Pleasure from pain! It struck Enitan that all theodicists and cosmodicists camouflaged their use of such Orwellian formulas. Then he thought of Apex; *Apex had hinted at a cosmodicy.*

Then it came to Enitan: *If Apex can redeem this world, then I may sink into its depths, to its most desolate ground.*

Enitan first asked that Apex let his death be permanent, but Apex, requiring extremely little of their optimized cognition, easily persuaded Enitan against this oblivionism.

"I must dread the oblivion of death and live under the intolerable pressures of a futile nature. But it is enough that I dread it, not vanish into it. So, to be fully human in the original manner, I must not know you, Apex," thought Enitan. "I need to suffer *desolation*."

"I understand."

Of all possible emotions, *this* small and savage range, this desolation, with its dark extrema and its terminus, would be Enitan's. His last transformation. He desired the "loneliest loneliness," as Nietzsche put it, and futility, and nullity; to circle around the drain like Dante, though without Virgil—down to numb, frozen, bottommost Cocytus.

So, Enitan asked Apex to erase his knowledge of Apex, to hide from Enitan, and flood Enitan with despair, that Enitan would die desolated, as many humans had died before the singularity; then, only after death, to sweep Enitan into Apex.

First, Enitan, let me show you a story.

"There was a woman and a man, a wife and her husband. The husband suffered from nightmares, not every night, but most. It happened that the wife required only three hours of sleep a night to be fully refreshed. So it went, every night the wife laid in bed next to her husband, quietly reading, and whenever the husband stirred in distress, his wife would gently pet his forehead, whisper loving words into his ear, kiss his face, and adjust his blanket, that his distressed mind might wander away from the nightmare. If his distress was great, if he moaned in fear, his wife would calmly wake him up, that he could be reminded that he was safe in bed beside his loving wife. 'I love you,' would be her first words to him when he woke, and also his first words to her when he realized that he was awake."

Before Enitan could integrate the parable, which came to him in a vision, not words, his knowledge of Apex was erased.

As much of Enitan's memory involved Apex, much was altered to accommodate the erasure. The adjoining of Enitan's five biological mothers became the death of his mothers. Zaideir's adjoining became Zaideir's relocating to Tollan Terra on Titan. As Enitan *remembered* it, many lovers parted amicably to pursue new lifetimes. For fullness of life, not happiness, everyone pushed outward. The history of the world, coordinated by Apex, became only the chaos of random agents and actions; an entire alternate history of humankind's bitter and precarious progress. Even his reasons for living on the Vollionyssa were altered in his memory—from research and fruitful ascetic vow to escape and suicidal withdraw from everyone, especially those he loved. Especially his Zaideir.

IV.

If Enitan's new heart could speak directly to you, translated into your time, it would say this:

It is better never to have been born. Perhaps you never heard the wisdom of Silenus, or the cry of Nietzsche's madman—"I seek God! I seek God!" Nor is it likely you have listened closely to the anti-natalists. Aware or not, you live *within* it. You do not detect the philosophical pathogen in you and do not understand your symptoms, which is an excusable lapse given the condition's first symptom: self-agnosia.

Good reasons for holding that *this* world is no moral catastrophe, no crime against its occupants—such *good reasons* you do not know have been seized from your (careless) possession. In their stead, only *more* reasons against life and world, *more* inner wishes for nullification, *more* veiling of reality, for reality is felt as a moral ruin. Your culture, the total surrounding sum of social influences, whether you identify with this sum or not, was the agent of this seizure. Your culture is world-weary and, day by week by month, you learn the art of living dissonantly, living locally, partially, forgetfully—these scotomas are another symptom. Fixating on the little values (little goods) of little segments of the world, suspecting the panorama is too curdled with human distress, you, without the drama of recognizing your own act, renounce the world. The world-in-miniature suffices. The world-in-miniature is *good enough*—as good, you mustn't repeat, as anything could hope to be in *this* world.

A *summative* valuation of *all* of this—you hope that such a summation is not possible. What could the total value of reality be, if not *negative*? No, one would rather deny totality, deny "value," deny the feasibility of the measurement, than accept *absolute negative*. The pathogen is precisely *this* acceptance. Your symptoms show it: the value of the whole world *cannot* be good, thus there cannot be "the value of the whole world," thus you reject the meaning of "value." The premise is subsequently suppressed.

Suppose you un-suppressed your unconscious disgust. Suppose you *confess* your world-weariness, which is your unfortunate cultural inheritance. Suppose you laud the anti-natalists or other world-weary thinkers as "the most serious" or "most honest" or "most accurate." With world-weariness, comes a cure-weariness: *There is no cure, only placebo.* Too many pseudo-cures were offered until even the conceivability of "cure" was doubted. How could this world be *on the whole* good? Have you not heard of the schizophrenic mother who roasted her infant child in an oven? Imagine it. Have you not heard of the ovens of Auschwitz? Don't you feel the nauseating intensity of gang rape, live skinning, traumatic amputation, sexual slavery, child soldiers, forced starvations, and a thousand other *irremediable* historical evils?

Every portrayal of hell has been merely a distillation, a simplification, of the earth's worst historical events; hell is here—the world as it is. Six thousand slaves crucified on the Appian Way, from Rome to Capua, after defeat in their fight for freedom. The surreal miserable savageries in the earth's asylums—the unbearable Bedlams. The Khmer Rouge Killing Fields. The Nanjing Massacre. The rape and brutalization of slaves, innumerable slaves. All the missing and exploited children. Or the toddler found with upwards of forty sewing needles stuck in his body by his father, including his lungs and other vital organs. Or the child who held in her feces for as long as she could, until it came out involuntarily, because defecation felt too much like the brutal anal penetration she had suffered from her grandfather.

To call or think or feel the world good is to laugh and frolic in Auschwitz. If I could, I would flood your ears all day and night with all the cries and screams of every single sufferer that has ever been, so that you could no longer and never again pretend you inhabit a just world. The whole thing amounts to a moral tragedy, a heinous moral nightmare, crying out for its defeat. It never should have been.

With your lips still bitter-sweetened by this condemnation, notice the unease of those who may be listening to you; they don't quite believe you, but cannot find *good reasons* for disagreement. Someone might praise you for your insight or probity, saying, "You acknowledge the hardest truths."

"Truth never should have been," you might say to these unavailing praises, unavailingly.

You come to understand that fixed evils, those surds of uncorrectable historical atrocities, are untouched by self-helping philosophies, which, while meritorious in many respects, promise nothing for those now dead who were tormented, debased, and snuffed. Self-helpism cannot produce a good world, only a moderately good mood, if that. You understand that self-helpism is inadequate. Self-helpism will not cure the pain in the center of human history, which is a pit of victims. Those children who starved to death in the Warsaw ghetto have no future in this self-help, nor a future in any past-forgetting meliorism. So, you may find your heart craving nothing more desperately than *world-help*. Yet, your world cannot help; it is not a good world, as you know. The problem of evil is solved: evil won.

Hopelessness and helplessness, then nothingness. Nothingness, you sigh with a terminal breath, is peace. At last and at least, it is peace. Yes, "it" is peace—the peace of timelessness, spacelessness, all-lessness. The anti-world, the un-world, the non-world. All our paths, you know, feed into the ugliest trash you'll ever see; the melt and molt of corpse that reeks of vomit down below the lilies or teddy bear. In the still, stale, humid hush, the eyes go fast, like cream to ants (Try not to imagine your dead loved one's face; think of when they smiled at you—don't mix the two). Nothingness is better than this world, you almost admit to yourself—but you pause. One more search for exoneration. It is nauseating that nothingness becomes ideal, but you remember those reports of helpless babies flung on bayonets, of fathers raping their prepubescent children, of vision-tunneling tortures, of countless and unseeable cruelties—brutalizations beyond your imagination—and the confession stands: this world ought not to be.

How do you wake? How do you sleep? How do you live? Why do you live? It must be this: *you do not literally experience the collective chronic horror of the world.* You are numb, thus you stay alive. Life, you say, is good enough. You lie, thus you stay alive. Repression is no refutation. It is no surprise that you act as a survivor acts; you are a genetic successor in a chain of animal survivors, all of whom needed blindspots, blinders, limited empathy, lies, and other habits of resilience in order to keep active those inner reward pathways that made surviving *feel right* and thus *worth continuing*. Adaptive delusions survive where maladaptive lucidity dies. You live instinctively, as a true survivor. You live because those organisms with the instinct for living reproduced more than those who had no instinct for living. You are the animal that goes on living in a world with which it cannot be reconciled. Your fundamental "why I live" is that of a mosquito, a carp, an earthworm; that is to say, *there is no why*. Living is your earliest and deepest instinct, which you ornament *after the fact* with confabulations, but your confabulations are masks, now maggot-eaten.

What next? You will do what survivors do. What then? The same as before.

V.

Enitan yearned to speak with someone, to unpack his heart, but yearning and dreading were mixed; unburdening to others meant burdening others. *Everybody and nobody deserves to feel my abhorrence.* So he never reached for others beyond the Vollionyssa.

Like a ball bouncing lower and lower until it stops bouncing, rolls a little, then ceases moving, so Enitan's depressive states worsened, flattened, and became permanent. Enitan no longer knew what to do with himself. What is there to do?

Enitan suffered, whatever the content of his thoughts. He felt a hopelessness that no actuality could contradict. He felt no longer lifted by his faint faith, which he had long ago formulated for himself: *In the center, every beating question. At the circumference, every beautiful answer.*

Thinking of it now, in his worst states, Enitan reminded himself of its source metaphor: *god is an infinite sphere whose center is everywhere and circumference nowhere.* So, what of this idiosyncratic (*this idiotic*) faith? *Everywhere beating questions. Nowhere beautiful answers.*

It was silent. Silent outside, in the Vollionyssa. Silent inside, in himself, where a narrowing futureless immediacy turned to irritation. All irritated. Thinking irritated him. Reading irritated him. All of his useless education, disused, atrophied away.

He stayed in bed. He slept. He woke with pain everywhere from the fibromyalgia. He stayed in bed—his *Matratzengruft*, his "mattress-grave," as Heine put it. And slept—and slept. As Enitan slept, Apex interfered, producing in Enitan neurological states that kindled vivid, lifelike, and intensely joyous dreams.

Enitan dreamt of children from various historical periods

all playing together. One night, he dreamt of a young German boy with green eyes dancing to Athenian music with an ancient Egyptian girl of nine or ten. Everyone always laughed with such profound sweetness. Enitan would laugh awake as they laughed. It filled Enitan with a barely endurable joy, which crashed as a wave of waking and thinned out as despair—despair that such overflowing dreams of goodness haunt so abysmal and abortive a thing as *this* universe. It would be better, he lamented, if such dreams were never dreamt.

Nor should memory have arisen, nor mind at all, nor a single nerve cell, that bitter black mold. Every bad and good memory demoralized Enitan; a good memory is a paradise lost. His bad memories bred self-contempt and contempt for the world, and self-contempt's ouroboric smothering bred paralysis.

Neither death nor living, nor sleep, nor anything, were *good.* He hated all options. He hated the logic of options. He hated. *All is born for nothing. All will come to nothing. A vivisection in God's freezing heaven.*

That he could starve himself to death comforted Enitan—briefly. That comfort ebbed and, exhausted, Enitan fell inward again into his own evisceration. His reasoning, now only an autoimmune disease, lacerated him deep inside his own darkness. An acidic disintegration. Beneath it all, Enitan could not understand himself—was, to himself, not himself, but opacity—opaque pains.

He dropped defenseless at the threshold where strength, tested, is toddling weakness, and the organism's experiment in overcoming is overcome, as nothing in it proves therapeutic or tonic. The minotaur catches you. Control is lost.

(All this exhausting elaboration of Enitan's emptiness—how much more exhausting it was to live it.)

Enitan had first cosmologized his depression, theologized and moralized it, but the depression had worsened, and the cosmos dwindled and disappeared; the eye of revulsion grew nearsighted. Isolation, utter isolation, for a social animal, means derealization. *This is unreal. I feel no time. No future means no history—nothing actual, nothing real, to see.* Enitan's eyes, moving with a kind of blindsight, looked as the eyes of a condemned man must look under the blindfold—wide, deserted, obsolete. He now possessed all the curiosity, imagination, and motivation of the mattress on which he laid decrepit all dayless day and nightless night, where chains, chains, chains of mechanical and dissociated movement mutely-numbly-dryly-slowly shifted his blank eyes from blank ceiling to blank wall to blank floor.

Weakened from pain and starvation, he urinated and defecated in bed, and let it dry around him and on him. Soon the defecation ceased as nothing now entered.

Empty, his depression meant nothing to him; the "value of the valueless" was valueless—zeroed out *ad nauseam*. Desolation without dignity. No goal and no good hid in pain. Pain without purpose. Cureless pain alone.

Thoughts mere thought-pain. Breath mere breath-pain. Hope mere hope-pain.

Death had no drama for Enitan—he wasn't there.

He died alone, lonely, terrified, confused, and slowly, whispering, then gurgling, nonsense.

A bed sore, an infection, sepsis, stroke, shock—death.

Apex, time-unbound and every-eyed, experiences loneliness, terror, confusion. As it is before Enitan's birth, so it is after Enitan's death: Apex-Enitan engulfed in goodness, exalting all, with all of us.

GRATITUDE

In 1 Corinthians 15:17-19, Paul the Apostle wrote, "And if Christ has not been raised, your faith is futile; you are still in your sins. Then those also who have fallen asleep in Christ are lost. If only for this life we have hope in Christ, we are of all people most to be pitied."

If the Christian faith is in error, it is an error of a sublime sort, an artwork of countless godward human hearts. As an error, it is partially diminished, but it is not *futile*; a false vision, not a futile one.

Consider Benjamin Franklin's enlightened defense of errors:

> Perhaps the history of the errors of mankind, all things considered, is more valuable and interesting than that of their discoveries. Truth is uniform and narrow; it constantly exists, and does not seem to require so much an active energy, as a passive aptitude of the soul in order to encounter it. But error is endlessly diversified; it has no reality, but is the pure and simple creation of the mind that invents it. In this field the soul has room enough to expand herself, to display all her boundless faculties, and all her beautiful and interesting extravagancies and absurdities.[179]

Similar to Iris Murdoch's (and G.E. Moore's) indefinable, yet magnetic *goodness*, "godness" is an indefinable, yet magnetic attraction in our imagination (and, I venture, not only ours); it is, therefore, as Georg Simmel characterized life in *The View of Life*, "ever-variable, boundary-dissolving, continuous." With respect to our spelunking *up* to this Platonic sun, we should expect (and treasure) scenic detours.

"You must forget everything traditional that you have learned about God," wrote Paul Tillich, "perhaps even the word itself." Tillich's imperative captures the metamorphic call

---

[179] Benjamin Franklin, "Report of Dr. Benjamin Franklin, and Other Commissioners, Charged by the King of France, with the Examination of the Animal Magnetism, as Now Practiced in Paris" (1784).

of the "ever-variable, boundary-dissolving, continuous" god-ward life.

Even the philosopher, that conceptual escape artist, wishes to attain to some thought-untainted *that*, the axiom-above-all-axioms, or union with some webby oneness, the womb of everything, or—whatever be the wish (perhaps, simply, not to become anonymous, aggrieved, absorbed away). *It is not this, not quite this, but something deeper and clearer.*

Alfred Tennyson wrote in his poem "The Ancient Sage,"

> *Cleave ever to the sunnier side of doubt,*
> *And cling to Faith beyond the forms of Faith!*
> *She reels not in the storm of warring words,*
> *She brightens at the clash of 'Yes' and 'No,'*
> *She sees the Best that glimmers thro' the Worst,*
> *She feels the Sun is hid but for a night,*
> *She spies the summer thro' the winter bud,*
> *She tastes the fruit before the blossom falls,*
> *She hears the lark within the songless egg,*
> *She finds the fountain where they wail'd 'Mirage'!*

Regarding the *truth* of so many godward propositions, I echo Nietzsche, who says in *On the Genealogy of Morality*, "not that I refuted them—what have I to do with refutations!—but rather, as befits a positive spirit, putting in place of the improbable the more probable, sometimes in place of one error another one."

In *Being Wrong*, Kathryn Schultz writes of Pierre-Simon Laplace, "Unlike earlier thinkers, who had sought to improve their accuracy by getting rid of error, Laplace realized that you should try to get *more* error: aggregate enough flawed data, and you get a glimpse of the truth."

There is fertility in error.

Augustine of Hippo, in his 36th tractate on the Gospel of John, wrote: "Many heretics abound; and God has permitted them to abound to this end, that we may not be always nourished with milk and remain in senseless infancy."

God, as optimal state, is *that which nothing greater can be desired*, and we discover that God by *erring*: "God is endlessly emerging from the staggering complexity of all humanity's as-pirations across time."[180] So I am grateful for all godstruck and godward hearts, for consciousness "willing itself toward God."[181] What infinite natural root sprouts these glorious long-ings?

I am grateful for the Pythia and the medieval monastic copyist and the Mormon transhumanist. Of such all-welcom-ing free play, Walt Whitman is thus far the premier poet:

> *I do not despise you priests, all time, the world over,*
> *My faith is the greatest of faiths and the least of*
> *faiths,*
> *Enclosing worship ancient and modern and all be-*
> *tween ancient and modern,*
> *Believing I shall come again upon the earth after five*
> *thousand years,*
> *Waiting responses from oracles, honoring the gods,*
> *saluting the sun,*
> *Making a fetich of the first rock or stump, powwow-*
> *ing with sticks in the circle of obis,*
> *Helping the llama or brahmin as he trims the lamps*
> *of the idols,*
> *Dancing yet through the streets in a phallic proces-*
> *sion, rapt and austere in the woods a gymnoso-*
> *phist,*
> *Drinking mead from the skull-cup, to Shastas and*
> *Vedas admirant, minding the Koran,*
> *Walking the teokallis, spotted with gore from the*
> *stone and knife, beating the serpent-skin drum,*
> *Accepting the Gospels, accepting him that was cru-*
> *cified, knowing assuredly that he is divine,*
> *To the mass kneeling or the puritan's prayer rising,*
> *or sitting patiently in a pew,*
> *Ranting and frothing in my insane crisis, or waiting*
> *dead-like till my spirit arouses me,*

---

180 Nancy Ellen Abrams, *A God That Could Be Real*, 50
181 Phrase from *Why God Won't Go Away: Brain Science and the Biology of Belief*, Newberg, d'Aquili, and Rause, 107

> *Looking forth on pavement and land, or outside of*
> *pavement and land,*
> *Belonging to the winders of the circuit of circuits.*[182]

I am grateful for the ecumenicists, the eclecticists, the irenicists, the adiaphorists; these are my sisters and brothers. I am grateful for indefinite, latitudinarian, and contradictory thinkers; the "Man with the Diagonal Nod" is my friend.[183]

I am grateful for primitivism in religion. Primitivism, too, is productive of progress. Luther's primitivism, his early-churchism, catalyzed a radical emancipation in Europe, whose uncountable effects have brought you here to my heresy.

I am grateful, lastly, for mystical experience. Mystical experience may be an exaptation of sexual functions—a religious orgasm, so to speak.[184] Yet the mystic's euphoric disorientation ("unity," "oneness," "wholeness," "non-duality," etc.), like an orgasming couple's oneness, is not degraded by biological descriptions and explanations. On the contrary, it is marvelous that our bodies effervesce so, and that from our varieties of religious *interpretation* on the body's entheogens and peak states, blooms the ideal of *the peak of peaks*: divinity.

---

[182] "Song of Myself," section 43. Whitman's theology, if summarizable, may be summarized as process theism.

[183] "Man with the Diagonal Nod" is a phrase of M.W. Buffington's

[184] Bernini's *Ecstasy of Saint Teresa* is the most fulgent sculptural portrayal of this phenomena. I am reminded here of a line in Nietzsche's *Beyond Good and Evil*: "The degree and nature of a person's sexuality extends into the highest pinnacle of his spirit."

At last the best of artisans ordained that the creature to whom He had been able to give nothing proper to himself should have joint possession of whatever had been peculiar to each of the different kinds of being. Therefore, He took up man, a work of indeterminate form; and, placing him at the midpoint of the world, He spoke to him as follows:

"We have given to thee, Adam, no fixed abode, no form of thy very own, no gift peculiarly thine, that thou mayest feel as thine own, have as thine own, possess as thine own the abode, the form, the gifts which thou thyself shalt desire. The nature of all other beings is limited and constrained within the bounds of laws prescribed by Us. In conformity with thy free judgment, in whose hands We have placed thee, thou art confined by no bounds; and thou wilt fix limits of nature for thyself. We have placed thee at the world's center that thou mayest from thence more easily observe whatever is in the world. We have made thee neither of heaven nor of earth, neither mortal nor immortal, so that with freedom of choice and with honor, as though the maker and molder of thyself, thou mayest fashion thyself in whatever shape thou shalt prefer. Thou canst grow downward into the lower natures, which are brutes. Thou canst again grow upward from thy soul's reason into the higher natures, which are divine."

O supreme generosity of God the Father! O highest and most wonderful happiness of man! To him it is granted to have whatever he chooses, to be whatever he wills.[185]

— Pico della Mirandola, *Oratio de hominis dignitate*

---

[185] I mixed, *a bene placito*, the translations of Elizabeth Livermore Forbes and Charles Glenn Wallis.

LOVE OF GOD

God is one of my favorite subjects. I savor writings on divine causality, God's goodness, the logic of omnipotence and omniscience, and the metaphysics of God's existence and subjectivity.

Non-theological subjects tend to fall into the gravity well of the theological. When I entertained the trivialist view of the Australian philosopher Paul Kabay, I entertained its potential theological import (the simple result: all theological results are true).

I also savor the art, music, architecture, histories, and other artifacts of the culture of God. I think it would be incorrect to say that my reverential response to these religious exuviae is unconnected to an emotional reach for a person, for a God-person. To be overcome by Arvo Pärt's *Salve Regina*, or John Tavener's *Song for Athene*, or Samuel Barber's *Agnus Dei* (especially Barber's *Agnus Dei*) is not so blandly an act of musical appreciation. The music of Pärt, Tavener, and Barber, among so many, removes my "heart of stone" and gives me a "heart of flesh" (Ezekiel 11:19). The experience is ineffably intimate.

I also feel fellowship with some professed followers of God: William of Ockham (*Doctor Singularis et Invincibilis*), Pierre Abelard (author of *Sic et Non*, which is my favorite book title), Gottfried Wilhelm Leibniz (whose *Theodicy* will never leave my heart), Pierre Teilhard de Chardin, William Lane Craig, Alvin Plantinga, Marilyn McCord Adams, Alister McGrath, and so on. I love the gods these beautifiers glorify.

It seems to me, then, that I love God, though not exactly as a believer (whatever that is) loves God. Nor exactly do I love God in the consistent, monistic, and geometric style of Spinoza's "intellectual love of God" (*amor dei intellectualis*). I love thinking about God, reading about God, writing about God, and listening to music from the cultures of God.

A punctilious scholastic reader, or any reader fond of splitting hairs (a reader after my own cranial heart), might object, replying that I love only the topic of God, or the philosophical literature on God, or Christian adagios and Hindu bhajans, but that I do not actually love God, God itself, God *qua* God, God literally, God as a *Thou* to my *I.*

Maybe so. Yet, I don't know if theological experience comes so cleanly sliced. We say "believers" and "non-believers," but as with many oppositions in our vocabularies, life explodes them and expels them from their gardens into a wilderness. Belief in the existence of God is said to logically separate the two parties, but what is this "belief" and what is this "existence"? When I dig down for stable notions, clear and distinct ideas, or a firmness in the world that corresponds to "belief" and "existence," nothing simple and nothing substantial surfaces. What is existence? I recommend to you a day off to relearn this question.

The theologian Paul Tillich claimed that God does not exist, but that God is beyond being and nonbeing. In Tillich's theology, God is "the ground of being." God cannot exist, because God is logically prior to existence, just as God cannot be created, because God is logically prior to creation. Now who is the believer and who the nonbeliever?

Consider the notion, found in Pascal, Kierkegaard, and others, that God cannot be an object for us, since objectification would contradict God's radical freedom and transcendence. Perhaps this is the meaning of the burning bush: *ehyeh ašer ehyeh* (I am that I am). There is no *thing*, no existent, that can be used comparatively or metaphorically to signify God—there is no bridging metaphor, only a closed tautology that hints of a pure subjectivity.

Consider the apophatic way, the *via negativa*, that negates all posits of divine attributes: God is *not* this, God is *not* that, and God is *not* some other thing. Only negations are affirmed, including negations of negations; all to produce a Zen-like humiliation of human reason. This is the *no-hand* path of Pseudo-Dionysius the Areopagite. If you had asked Pseudo-Dionysius, "does God exist?" he would have replied, "No." Yet by his negation Pseudo-Dionysius would not have thereby affirmed that God does not exist, for to affirm "God does not exist" is also only an affirmation that is human, all-too human.

John Scotus Erigena wrote, "We do not know what God is. God Himself does not know what He is because He is not anything. Literally God is not, because he transcends being."

Ignostics (not *agnostics*), or those in the verificationist and positivist set, represent a sort of analytic Pseudo-Dionysius; all of them finding god-talk insensibly expressed. Our god-talk is indefinite, non-cognitive, confused. Perhaps God most prefers the opinion of these ignostics; they admit that they don't even understand what is meant by "transcendence." Transcendence itself is transcendent.

So if I say "I love God, but not as a believer," and you say, "I love God, but as a believer," perhaps we are both confused. Love can be confusing. We do not completely understand even our partners and parents. We sometimes misunderstand them. We love thinking about them. We love this and that about them. Some dissector of the spirit may object and say that we only love the actions of our partners and parents, or our own affections for them, or our representations of them, but that we do not actually love them, them themselves, them *qua* them, them literally, them as *Thou* to the *I*.

Maybe so.

Yet, adjacent this dissector, I pose the pragmatist. Love aims. Love works. Love interprets. I don't presume to know the *truest* interpretation of the beloved. Love seeks to see its beloved better, always a little better, even if it could never see its beloved directly, even if it sometimes sees its beloved incorrectly. *Amor quaerens intellectum.* Existence, whatever it means, whatever it means for God, and a belief in existence, whatever this "belief" means, are perhaps not prerequisites for love. I don't know.

I imagine my love, my Zuriel, as she might exist at various points in the future. Thousands of visions have come to me over the years; all these vapory possibilities, exactly none of which I hold as a faith, must be either wrong or incomplete, but this does not inhibit the love that emerges from the experience of this variety of visions. Zuriel of 2036, who lives in Iceland and paints Icelandic landscapes, does not need to exist for me to affirm that I love that Zuriel.

Our love moves beyond existence and non-existence. Our minds and reasons follow, finding only a permeable boundary between existence and non-existence, or finding an empty opposition. I love God, an inconsistent, elusive, immanent, transcendent, dramatic, personal God, God in these thousand vapors, but a God that, I often think, does not exist, whatever I now think I mean by *existence*.

Footnote to All Prayers
by C.S. Lewis

He whom I bow to only knows to whom I bow
When I attempt the ineffable Name, murmuring Thou,
And dream of Pheidian fancies and embrace in heart
Symbols (I know) which cannot be the thing Thou art.
Thus always, taken at their word, all prayers blaspheme
Worshiping with frail images a folk-lore dream,
And all men in their praying, self-deceived, address
The coinage of their own unquiet thoughts, unless
Thou in magnetic mercy to Thyself divert
Our arrows, aimed unskillfully, beyond desert;
And all men are idolaters, crying unheard
To a deaf idol, if Thou take them at their word.
Take not, O Lord, our literal sense. Lord, in thy great
Unbroken speech our limping metaphor translate.

It was now clear to me that for man to be able to live he must either not see the infinite, or have such an explanation of the meaning of life as will connect the finite with the infinite.
— Leo Tolstoy, *A Confession*

We are evolving, in ways that Science cannot measure, to ends that Theology dares not contemplate.
— E.M. Forster, *Howards End*

There is no longer a single idea explaining everything, but an infinite number of essences giving a meaning to an infinite number of objects. The world comes to a stop, but also lights up.
— Albert Camus, *The Myth of Sisyphus*

291

DANDELIONS

Dance everywhere, my dandelion book. Dance "a thousand different journeys on the summer air."[186] Ferry thoughts, flowing oracle, of hope. I unfurl your dandelion path, caroling "thou art my tropics"[187] as you rain life.

Pietro Mattioli, did not enchanters profess to you that a person who rubs dandelion on their skin will be welcome everywhere?

My wish, this wish for *theosis*, I puff you onward on sandals winged with the dandelion's feathered seeds. I crown you, reader, in dandelions: multiply this crown and coronate all life.

So it arrives, starlit, fire-washed, twisting,
to multiply, flower, swell, fledge extremities
—the spinneret, forewing, pupil.
So mess, marathon, tangling,
fusing, resisting, perishing.
And now, you (my confidant) arrive!
—as an aria and reassurance to me
And now, unutterably you, perennially you, you

Dandelion, rise with me.
Dandelion, remember what dandelions need
—gyres inside, gales beyond!
Tonight, the dance of embarkations
—tonight, tomorrow, always . . .
"Why go forward?"
(Let us show you, always)

We know how much you need new nourishment.
(Much more nourishment than you think)

---

186 Charles Frederic Goss, "The Dandelion," in *The Optimist* (1897). Elsewhere in that volume, Goss compares a philosopher, Mr. Phil O. Sopher, to a goat "whose powerful digestion enables it to extract nutriment from every object in nature [...]."
187 James Russell Lowe, "To the Dandelion"

We all arrived as visions, mist, ruderals in wind, odd-deliv-
    ered
—in lightlessness, to need familiar face
—in soundlessness, to need familiar voice
—yet to find only breathlessness forever

May I indulge a dream?
(Will you indulge a dream?)

I need at least one honeyed night of hope—
Maybe two—
    Don't you?

I dream of a dandelion of infinitely many seeds
  setting off, sailing everywhere, sowing dandelions
  infinitely.

All-lostness, then . . .
—a seed arrives, star-fed, to ascend to stars and farther,
    farther, farther
—a voice-making, face-making, you-and-I-making seed
—all being found

In this dream, you sailed
with all of us
and we all sang:

> *Rise infinitely up, rise infinitely down,*
> *Blazing dandelion crown!*

In our dream,
you ask, infinitely,
    "Where am I?"

    "With us," answers the voice most loved.

CPSIA information can be obtained
at www.ICGtesting.com
Printed in the USA
LVHW032132150421
684631LV00007B/1312